高职高专“十三五”规划教材

国际物流单证实务

主　编　许　妍　李　富
副主编　陶　莉　杨　慧　刘群英

南京大学出版社

前　言

随着高等职业教育改革的深入发展，高等职业教育的目标更加明确，就是培养生产、建设、管理、服务第一线需要的高技能人才，具体的目标就是使学生获得企业需要的、相应的职业能力；为实现这一目标而采取的教学手段也更加清晰，就是落实项目化教学。为此，我们在2年多的教学实践和研究的基础上，坚持“以目标为导向，任务为驱动，项目为载体，就业为宗旨”的思想，编写了《国际物流单证实务》一书，为培养学生的职业能力做了尝试性探讨。

本教材是一本遵循专业人才成长规律，走“校企合作、工学结合”之路，以职业活动为导向的“成长型”项日化教材。本教材结合了国际物流最新发展动态，基于物流的工作过程进行设计；以虚拟的外贸公司为背景，以一笔完整贸易业务为主线，在物流单证员岗位工作任务和职业能力分析的基础上，与企业、行业顾问共建物流单证专家组并共同开发课程标准。根据基本物流流程所涉及的环节分为导论——解读国际物流单证，以及制作合同、阅读和审核信用证、制作商业发票和装箱单、制作订舱委托书和办理托运、制作出境货物报检单和办理报检手续、制作和申领原产地证、制作和办理报关单、制作投保单和办理保险、制作运输单据、制作附属单据、制作汇票、综合业务实训等项目。本教材无论从体系上还是内容构架上，都呈现出与已有教材不同的特点，非常适合高职高专学生学习使用。

本教材的主要特色及创新如下：

(1) 将职业教育的培养目标和专业培养目标与高职学生的认知能力特点相结合。以此为基础确定教材编写的根本思想。本教材打破以知识体系为线索的传统编写模式，采用了以物流单证员的工作过程为线索，体现工学结合、任务驱动、项目教学的项目教材编写模式。该模式注重以学生为主体，以培养职业能力为核心目标，强调对各种物流单证操作能力的训练，紧紧围绕工作任务的需要来选取理论。

(2) 本教材图文并茂，是校企合作的成果，教材的设计理念与素材（如案例、单证样张等）均来自真实企业。教材突破旧有课程体系的藩篱，按物流单证员的工作过程编排教材体系，并将企业用人标准、岗位职责和文化因素渗透到课堂上。力求教材内容与职业工作内容相一致，有利于学生对专业知识与技能的掌握，也为专业实训奠定了基础。同时，来自企业真实的案例分析、工作项目和情景模拟角色的扮演让复杂、烦琐的物流单证工作变得轻松易学，让学习更富有乐趣，让学习充满动力。

(3) 教材内容与职业标准相联系，与职业资格证书相衔接。高职教育是培养职业人才的，而国家对各行业也都建立了准入制度和相应的职业资格标准。本教材的教学内容与职业标准相一致，并与通过职业证书资格考试的大纲相衔接。

(4) 教材的编写以一笔外贸业务为载体，导论及每个项目大体上按“学习目标（实训目标）、工作任务、操作示范、知识链接、能力实训”的顺序安排结构。教师在教学时可以先让学生以物流单证员的职业身份，自己尝试完成每个工作任务；再结合学生完成工作任务的情况进行示范操作；然后在示范操作过程中讲解相关的知识，即进行知识链接；最后，让学生完成综合能力实训部分的工作任务操作，以进一步提升学生的物流单证操作能力。

本教材的编写工作由无锡商业职业技术学院的老师承担并完成。其具体分工如下：许妍编写了导论、项目 1、项目 2、项目 3、项目 5、项目 6 和附录，杨慧编写了项目 10 和项目 11，陶莉编写了项目 4、项目 8 和项目 9，刘群英编写了项目 12、项目 13 和项目 14，李富编写了项目 7 以及负责全书的统稿工作。

本书在编写过程中，参考和借鉴了许多理论成果和相关书籍，在此表示衷心感谢！由于时间仓促和水平有限，不足和错误在所难免，敬请读者批评指正，以便改进。

编　者

2018 年 6 月

目　录

导　论　解读国际物流单证

1. 学习目标

知识目标:通过对本导论的学习,使学生对国际货物买卖的基本流程有一个全面的认识。

能力目标:掌握不同交易条件下的进出口业务流程及缮制的相关单证。

2. 工作任务

无锡蓝天进出口公司是一家综合性的贸易公司,主要经营各类纺织品的进出口业务。近年来,随着公司内部的改革及业务量的迅速增加,公司在增强经济实力和改革管理体制方面已经取得了巨大的成绩。其经营范围包括服装鞋帽、服装辅料、针纺织品、箱包、日用品等的销售,产品主要销往欧洲、亚洲、美国及中国香港市场。

2015 年 3 月,无锡蓝天进出口公司通过广交会与加拿大的 KU TEXTILE CORPORATION 建立业务关系,随后双方洽谈成功,签订全棉女童连衣裙(GIRL DRESS 100% COTTON)共计 9 400 件的贸易合同。无锡蓝天进出口公司由一名专业单证员郭晓芳负责。

在本任务中,郭晓芳应掌握国际物流单证的基本内容。

3. 操作范例

本业务中,中、加双方的贸易条件属于一般贸易,约定采用 CIF 贸易术语,信用证结算方式,通过海运方式运输。其出口贸易流程和对应的单证如下(见图 1):

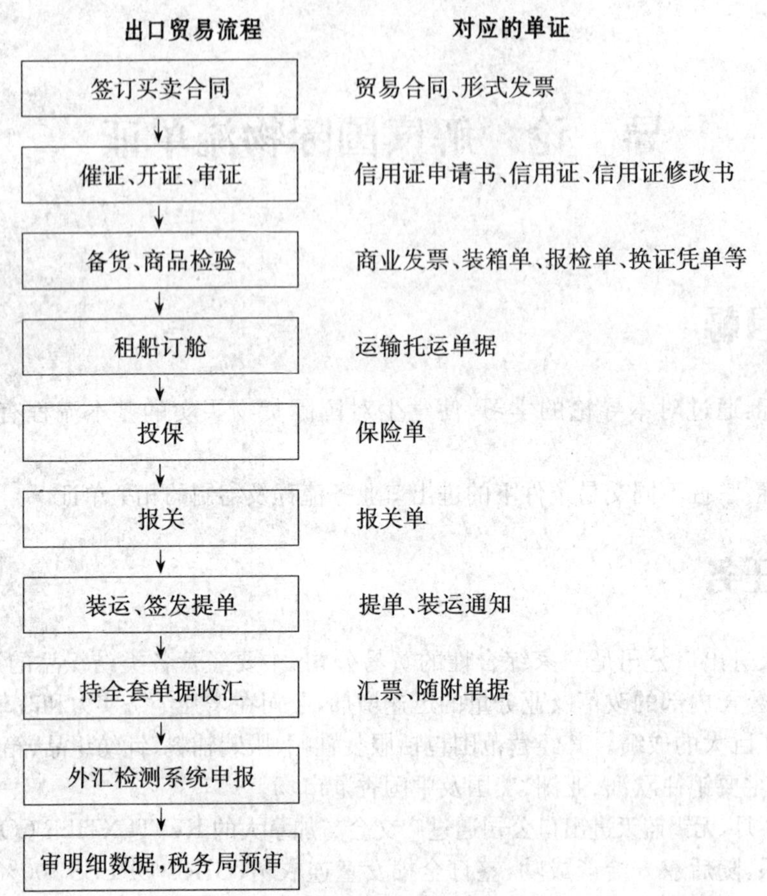

图 1　出口贸易流程和对应的单证

4. 知识链接

1) 国际货物买卖的流程

(1) 交易前准备

这主要包括:组织经贸洽谈人员;进行市场调研,选择目标市场或采购市场;选择交易对象或供货商;制定进出口经营方案;进行成本核算等。

① 出口商:通过市场调查,刊登广告,参加展览会、交易会,网上发布供货信息,机构推荐以及客户介绍等多种途径获取国外买家信息,主动与其联系以建立业务关系。

② 进口商:通过市场调查、接受客户委托等途径明确国内买家;通过浏览供货信息、参加展览会和交易会、网上发布求购信息、机构推荐、客户介绍等多种途径寻找国外卖家信息,主动与国外卖家建立联系或在收到国外卖家来函后积极回应。

(2) 交易磋商

经过询盘、发盘、还盘和接受四个步骤。其中,发盘和接受是必须的。

(3) 合同签订

进口商寄送订单(Purchase Order),出口商会签(countersign);出口商寄送售货确认书

(Sales Confirmation, S/C),进行会签;或进口商寄送购货确认书(Purchase Confirmation, P/C),出口商会签。

(4) 合同履行

① 出口商:交付货物并收取货款。

② 进口商:支付货款并收取货物。

2) 合同履行的基本环节

(1) 出口合同履行的基本环节(以 L/C、CIF 贸易术语为例)

① 落实信用证。它包括催买方开立信用证,出口商收到信用证后应及时审核信用证,应该根据合同、UCP600 以及外贸经验来审核,如有问题,及时通知开证申请人修改信用证,待信用证改妥后再安排运输工作。

② 备货。备货是指出口商在订立合同或收到 L/C 后,为保证按时、按质、按量地完成交货义务,根据合同或 L/C 的要求准备货物的过程。

备货包括:按出口合同与国内生产企业签订国内购货合同;催交货物;核实、检查货物的品质、数量、包装等情况;验收入库或进行加工整理,在外包装上刷制唛头。

③ 订舱。出口方委托有权受理对外货运业务的单位办理海陆空等运输业务,称为托运。出口单位直接或通过货运代理公司向承运单位洽订运输工具称为订舱。委托货代订舱,须提交出口货物订舱委托书,随附商业发票、装箱单;船公司接受订舱后,在集装箱货物托运单的"装货单"联上加盖船公司签单章后,连同"配舱回单"等其他联一并退还。

④ 报检。如货物属于法定检验,或进口商要求提交相应检验证书,则须办理出口报检,在规定的时间内,向出入境检验检疫机构提交出境货物报检单,并随附商业发票、装箱单,办理出境报检手续。如委托工厂办理报检手续,则须同时提交报检授权委托书,货物经检验合格后,出入境检验检疫机构签发出境货物通关单和/或商检证书。

⑤ 投保。填制出口货物投保单,随附商业发票,向保险公司投保,保险公司接受投保申请后,收取保险费并出具保险单。

⑥ 认证。根据进口商的要求,办理出口认证、出证手续。进口商要求提交原产地证明,在规定时间内,持一般原产地证明书申请书和原产地证明至中国国际贸易促进委员会(CCPIT,简称中国贸促会)申请出证,中国贸促会审核确认无误后,即在原产地证明上签字确认并退还。

⑦ 进港。出具集装箱装箱单,派集装箱卡车至指定地点装运货物,货物运抵海关监管区,场站人员根据 CLP 核对实际装箱情况并签收。

⑧ 报关。在规定的时间内,向海关递交出口货物报关单和集装箱货物托运单中的"装货单""大幅联""场站收据"三联,以及出口收汇核销单,并随附商业发票、装箱单等,申报出口。如是法定检验商品,则须同时提交《出境货物通关单》,如委托货代报关,则须同时提交报关授权委托书,海关查验完毕后,在集装箱货物托运单的装货单联上加盖海关放行章,连同"大幅联""场站收据"等联一并退还,在出口收汇核销单上加盖海关验讫章并退还。

⑨ 装船。将集装箱货物托运单的"装货单"和"大幅联"交给船公司,凭此装货,船方装妥货物,在"大幅联"上签字后返还,凭经船方签署的"大幅联"向船公司换取正本已装船提单。

⑩ 装船通知。向进口商发出装船通知。

⑪ 核销。货款收妥后，收到银行加盖“出口收汇核销专用章”的结汇水单。结关后，收到海关加盖验讫章的出口货物报关单“收汇核销联”和“出口退税专用”联。在规定的时间内，持银行出具的盖有“出口收汇核销专用章”的结汇水单、盖有验讫章的出口收汇核销单及出口货物报关单“收汇核销联”，向外汇管理部门办理出口收汇核销。受理核销后，外汇管理部门在出口收汇核销单的“出口退税专用联”和银行结汇水单上加盖已核销章后退还。

⑫ 退税。向税务机关提供购进货物时的增值税专用发票“抵扣联”、盖有验讫章的出口货物报关单“出口退税专用”联、盖有已核销章的出口收汇核销单“出口退税专用联”，办理出口退税手续，税务机关经核准后退税。

(2) 进口合同履行的基本环节(以 L/C、FOB 贸易术语为例)

进口合同履行的基本业务流程：进口许可证的申请—开证申请书的填制—订舱—投保—换单—报检—报关—提货。

① 进口许可证的申领。如果进口的商品属于国家进口贸易管制的范围，则在开立信用证前，必须先向指定的发证机构申领进口许可证。

② 开证申请书的填制。许可证申领完后，以信用证为付款方式的进口合同，进口企业要在合同规定的日期向银行申请开立信用证。

③ 办理订舱手续。如果合同是以 FOB 贸易条件签订的，进口商要联系出口商并明确备货情况后，及时向船公司办理订舱手续，待船公司返还“配舱回单”后，向出口商发出装运指示，明确船名、航次、船期等或委托出口商代办订舱手续，及时获取配舱信息。

④ 办理投保手续。如与保险公司已事先订立进口预约保险合同(Open Cover)，则凭出口商发出的装船通知向保险公司办妥投保手续；如无预约保险合同，则在进口货物装船前先与保险公司签订暂保单(Open Note)，待出口商发来装船通知后，再向保险公司换取正式保险单。

⑤ 审核到货单证。进口企业收到银行转来的相关单据后应认真审核。经审核，如果发现单据不符，应通过银行及时提出拒付的理由；如果相符，则按合同规定安排付款，取得正本提单，货抵目的港后，凭正本提单到船公司或其代理处换取提货单(Delivery Order)。

⑥ 办理进口报检手续。如进口货物属于法定检验商品，向出入境检验检疫局递交入境货物报检单、提货单并随附商业发票等单证，办理进口货物报检，检验合格后，出入境检验检疫局签发入境货物通关单。

⑦ 办理进口报关手续。在规定的时间内，向海关递交进口货物报关单、提货单并随附商业发票、装箱单、付汇情况表、副本提单等，办理进口报关手续。如进口货物属于法定检验商品，则须同时提交入境货物通关单并缴纳进口税费，海关验讫，在提货单上盖章放行。

⑧ 办理进口付汇。凭海关盖章放行的提货单提取货物。如进口货物属于法定检验商品，则提货后须至港区指定地点验货，货物出港。待进口货物到货，办完海关完结手续后，在 30 天内凭进口报关核销联、付汇申请书或对外付款的核销联及相关资料，到外管局办理进口付汇核销手续。

小贴士

① 海运出口单证的业务流程见图2。

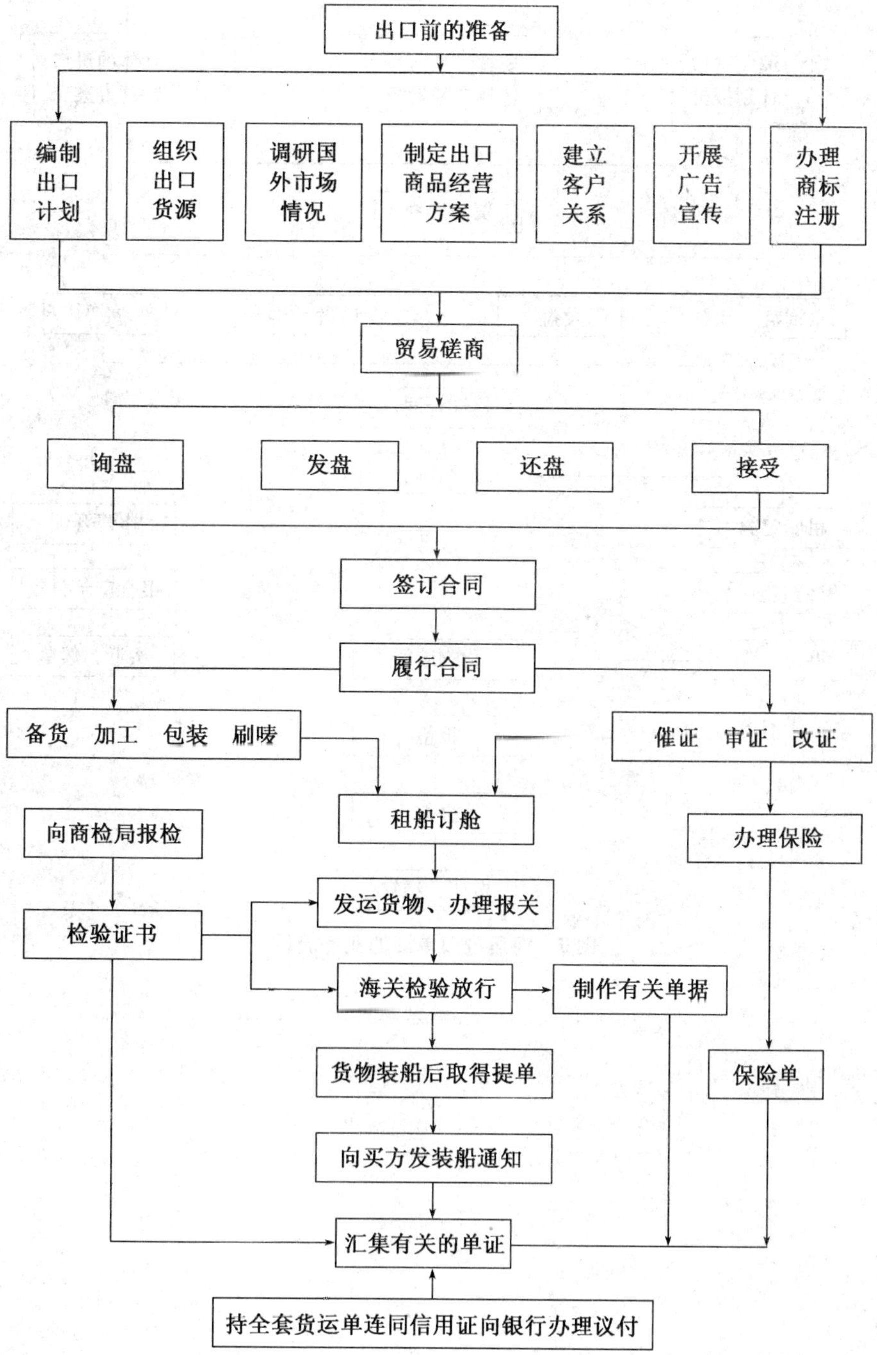

出口前的准备

编制出口计划　组织出口货源　调研国外市场情况　制定出口商品经营方案　建立客户关系　开展广告宣传　办理商标注册

贸易磋商

询盘　发盘　还盘　接受

签订合同

履行合同

备货　加工　包装　刷唛

催证　审证　改证

租船订舱

办理保险

向商检局报检

检验证书

发运货物、办理报关

海关检验放行

制作有关单据

货物装船后取得提单

保险单

向买方发装船通知

汇集有关的单证

持全套货运单连同信用证向银行办理议付

图2　海运出口单证的业务流程

② 海运进口单证的业务流程见图 3。

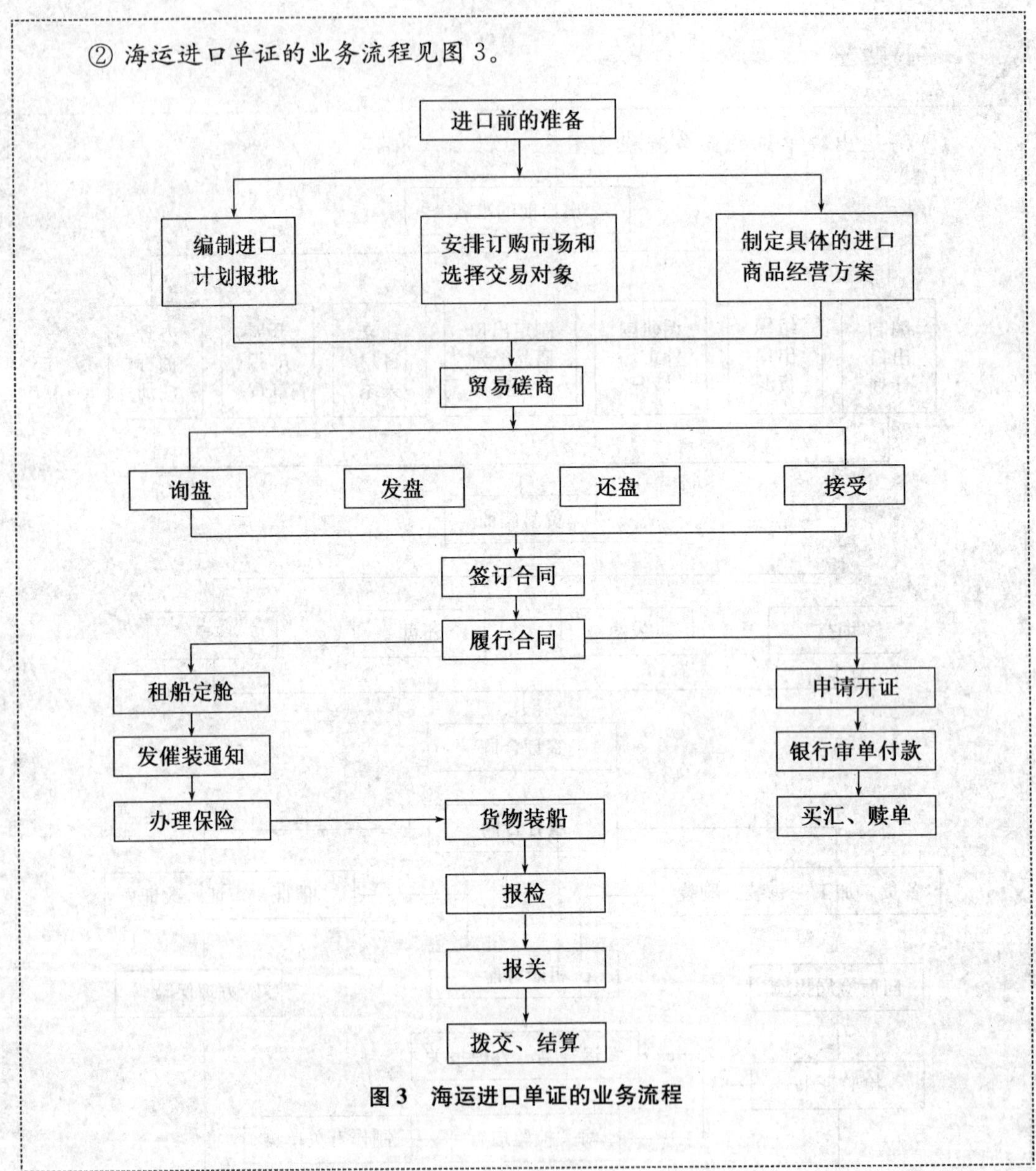

图 3 海运进口单证的业务流程

不同结算方式的操作流程

1. 跟单信用证的业务流程(见图4)

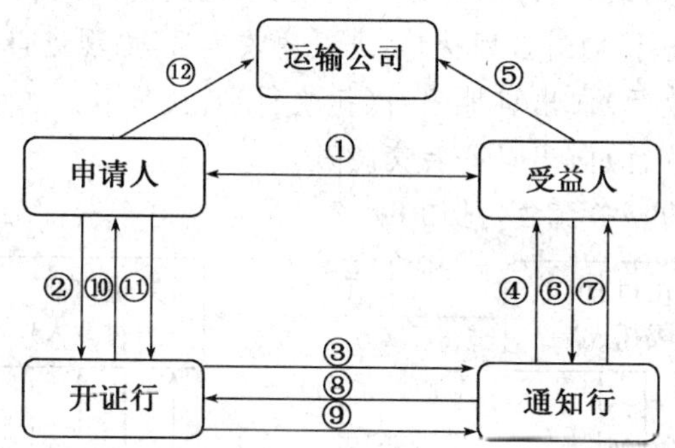

图4　跟单信用证的业务流程

① 进出口双方签订买卖合同,合同中规定信用证为结算方式。
② 申请人向开证行申请开立信用证。
③ 开证行开出信用证并寄交通知行。
④ 通知行向受益人通知信用证。
⑤ 受益人审核信用证无误后备货装运。
⑥ 受益人向议付行交单。
⑦ 议付行确认单、证相符,议付。
⑧ 议付行将相关单据寄送给开证行或付款行。
⑨ 开证行或付款行审单后付款给议付行。
⑩ 开证行提示申请人赎单付款。
⑪ 申请人付款赎单。
⑫ 申请人凭单提货。

2. 托收的业务流程

1) 付款交单的业务流程

(1) 即期付款交单的业务流程(见图5)

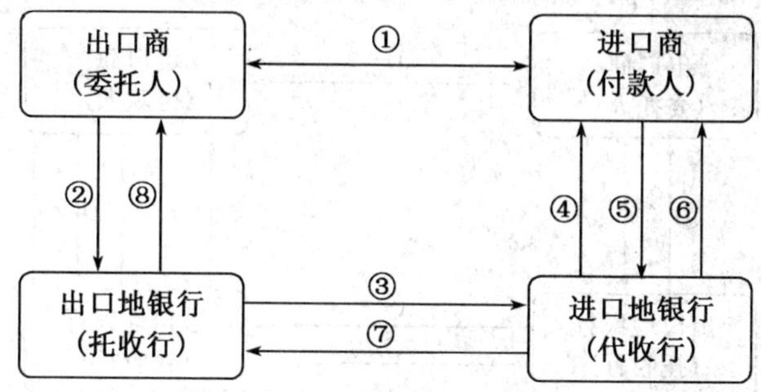

图5　即期付款交单的业务流程

① 进出口双方在合同中约定采用即期付款交单的方式结算。

② 出口商办理出口手续,发运货物后,将托收申请书、即期汇票、海运提单及其他有关单据提交给出口地银行,申请托收。

③ 出口地银行(托收行)将汇票及单据寄送至进口地银行(代收行),委托其代收货款。

④ 进口地银行(代收行)向进口商提示汇票及单据,要求付款。

⑤ 进口商审核单据确认无误后,向进口地银行(代收行)付款。

⑥ 进口地银行(代收行)向进口商交单,进口商收单后,办理进口手续,换取提货单提货。

⑦ 进口地银行(代收行)向出口地银行(托收行)转交货款。

⑧ 出口地银行(托收行)向出口商转交货款。

(2) 远期付款交单的业务流程(见图6)

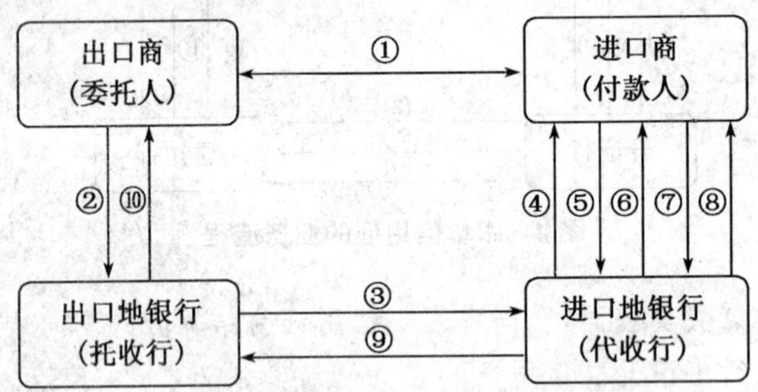

图6　远期付款交单的业务流程

① 进出口双方在合同中约定采用远期付款交单的方式结算。

② 出口商办理出口手续,发运货物后,填写托收申请书,签发远期汇票,连同海运提单及其他有关单据提交给出口地银行,申请托收。

③ 出口地银行(托收行)将汇票及单据寄送至进口地银行(代收行)委托其代收货款。

④ 进口地银行(代收行)向进口商提示汇票及单据,要求承兑。

⑤ 进口商审核单据确认无误后,在汇票上做承兑。

⑥ 远期汇票到期时,进口的银行(代收行)向进口商提示汇票,要求付款。

⑦ 进口商向进口地银行(代收行)付款。

⑧ 进口地银行(代收行)向进口商交单,进口商收单后,办理进口手续,换取提货单提货。

⑨ 进口地银行(代收行)向出口地银行(托收行)转交货款。

⑩ 出口地银行(托收行)向出口商转交货款。

2) 承兑交单的业务流程(见图7)

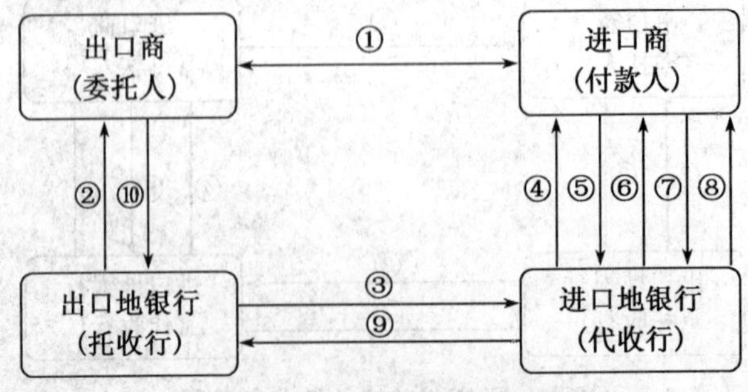

图7　承兑交单的业务流程

① 进出口双方在合同中约定采用承兑交单的方式结算。

② 出口商办理出口手续，发运货物后，填写托收申请书，签发远期汇票，连同海运提单及其他有关单据提交给出口地银行，申请托收。

③ 出口地银行(托收行)将汇票及单据寄送至进口地银行(代收行)，委托其代收货款。

④ 进口地银行(代收行)向进口商提示汇票及单据，要求承兑。

⑤ 进口商审核单据确认无误后，在汇票上做承兑。

⑥ 进口地银行(代收行)向进口商交单，进口商收单后，办理进口手续，换取提货单提货。

⑦ 远期汇票到期时，进口地银行(代收行)向进口商提示汇票，要求付款。

⑧ 进口商向进口地银行(代收行)付款。

⑨ 进口地银行(代收行)向出口地银行(托收行)转交货款。

⑩ 出口地银行(托收行)向出口商转交货款。

3. 电汇的业务流程(见图 8)

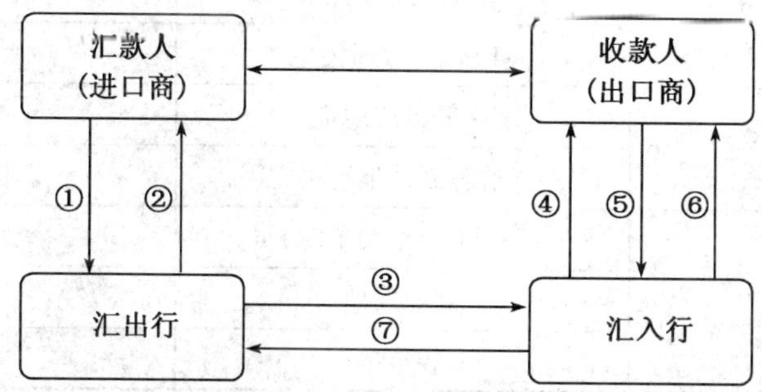

图 8　电汇的业务流程

① 进口商各汇出行提交电汇申请书并交款付费。

② 汇出行向进口商寄出回单。

③ 汇出行向汇入行发出电汇款通知。

④ 汇入行向出口商发出汇款通知。

⑤ 出口商向汇入行递交收据。

⑥ 汇入行向出口商付款。

⑦ 付讫借记通知。

开动脑筋

① L/C 与 D/P 的主要区别是什么？

② L/C 与 T/T 的主要区别是什么？

③ T/T 与 D/P 的主要区别是什么？

5. 能力实训

实训1 请写出CIF合同履行中出口商涉及的部分单据的出单机构(见表1)

表1 CIF合同履行中出口商涉及的部分单据及其出单机构

合同履行阶段	单据的名称	出单机构
1. 申领出口许可证	出口许可证	
2. 办理运输	海运货物委托书	
	海运提单	
3. 办理保险	投保单	
	保险单	
4. 办理商检	出境货物报检单	
	商检证书/通关单	
5. 申请原产地证	一般原产地证	
	普惠制产地证书	
6. 办理报关	出口报关单	
	商业发票	
	装箱单	

实训2 根据以下业务背景,简要说明出口商的履约流程及单证

出口商:无锡中海贸易公司(简称无锡中海)

进口商:英国ABC贸易公司(简称英国ABC)

合同:法定检验商品,集装箱海运,CIF伦敦,即期议付信用证结算

① 信用证开来,无锡中海审核,修改。

②

③

④

⑤

⑥

⑦

⑧

实训3 根据以下业务背景,简要说明进口商的履约流程及单证

出口商:德国QWE贸易公司(简称德国QWE)

进口商:上海海州贸易公司(简称上海海州)

合同:法定检验商品,集装箱海运,FOB汉堡,即期议付信用证结算

① 上海海州向银行申请开立信用证。

②

③

④

⑤

⑥

⑦

⑧

项目 1　制作合同

1.1　学习目标

知识目标：能够读懂合同条款；掌握合同的主要条款。

能力目标：能根据不同背景资料、结算方式、贸易术语等条件正确撰写销售合同。

1.2　工作任务

无锡蓝天进出口公司(WUXI BLUE SKY IMP&EXP. Co., LTD.)是一家专门从事纺织品出口的贸易公司，与加拿大的 KU TEXTILE CORPORATION 有多年的业务关系。2015 年 3 月，外贸业务部小王与 KU TEXTILE CORPORATION 经过多次磋商后，签订了一份关于全棉女童连衣裙的出口合同，合同号 K123。在双方建立关系之外，已经就"一般交易条件"达成协议，其中规定，除双方另有协议外，价格按 CIF 价格核算，其中保险按 CIF 发票金额另加 10%投保一切险与战争险；按照中国人民保险公司 1981 年 1 月 1 日的保险条款办理；付款方式为信用证。根据以往的工作经验和公司业务分工，业务部经理将这笔业务的后续工作交给单证员郭晓芳完成。

在本任务中，郭晓芳首先要熟悉该业务的磋商内容和合同内容，然后完成以下内容：

① 熟悉业务磋商的往来函电。

② 理解贸易合同的主要条款的内容。

1.3　操作范例

第一步：熟悉业务磋商过程中的往来函电

(INCOMING): MAR. 21: PLEASE QUOTE US CIF MONTREAL OF ART NO. 11574, 11575, 11576, 11577 AND THERIR AVAILABLE QUANTITY SEPERATELY FOR JULY SHIPMENT.

(OUTING) MAR. 22: WE WOULD LIKE TO QUOTE AS FOLLOWINGS: 11574 2000 PIECES CIFMONTREAL USD 6.60 PER PIECE; 11575 2 500 PIECES CIF MONTREAL USD 5.60 PER PIECE; 11576 2 500 PIECES CIF MONTREAL USD 8.80 PER PIECE; 11577 2 500 PIECES CIF GDANSK USD 8.10 PER PIECE. JULY SHIPMENT AND IRREVOCABLE L/C AT 30DAYS AFTER SIGHT, REACHING US 45 DAYS BEFORE THE SHIPMENT.

(INCOMING): MAR. 23: 11574 2 400 PIECES CIF MONTREAL USD 6.40 PER

PIECE; 11575 3 000 PIECES CIF MONTREAL USD 5. 20 PER PIECE; 11576 3 000 PIECES CIF MONTREAL USD 8. 50 PER PIECE; 11577 1 600 PIECES CIF MONTREAL US 8.00 PER PIECE, VALID MAR. 25th, 2015.

(OUTING) MAR. 25: 11576, WE ARE SORRY THAT WE CAN ONLY SUPPLY YOU 2 400 PIECES IN JULY BECAUSE OF KEEN DEMAND. AND THE LOWEST PRICE AS FOLLOWINGS: 11574 2 400 PIECES CIF MONTREAL US 6. 50 PER PIECE; 11575 3 000 PIECES CIF MONTREAL US 5. 50 PER PIECE; 11576 2 400 PIECES CIF MONTREAL USD 8. 50 PER PIECE; 11577 1 600 PIECES CIF MONTREAL USD 8.00 PER PIECE, REPLY HERE MAR. 26th, 2015.

(INCOMING): MAR. 26: WE ACCEPT YOUR OFFER DATED MAR. 25, 2015. PLEASE SEND US THE S/C.

第二步:根据往来函电制作合同

SALES CONTRACT ——合同名称

NO.: K123——合同号码

DATE: APR., 9, 2015——日期

THE SELLER:
WU XI BLUE SKY IMP&EXP. Co., LTD.
NO. 53 ZHONGSHAN ROAD, WUXI, CHINA
TEL: 86 - 510 - 82398888
THE BUYER:
KU TEXTILE CORPORATION
430 VTRA MONTREAL CANADA
TEL: +48 789065

}合同当事人

THIS SALES CONTRACR IS MADE BY AND BETWEEN THE SELLERS AND THE BUYERS, WHERE THE SELLERS AGREE TO SELL AND THE BUYERS AGREE TO BUY THE UNDER MENTIONED GOODS ACCORDING TO THE TERMS AND CONDITIONS STIPULATE BELOW: ——买、卖双方订立合同的意愿和执行合同的保证条款。

COMMODITY&SPECIFICATION 商品名称与规格	QUANTITY 数量	UNIR PRICE 单价	AMOUNT 总金额
GIRL DRESS(品名) 100% COTTON ARTICLE NO. 11574 11575 11576 11577 }货号	2 400PCS 3 000PCS 2 400PCS 1 600PCS }数量	CIF MONTREAL (贸易术语) US 6.50/PC US 5.50/PC US 8.50/PC US 8.00/PC }单价	US 15 600.00 US 16 500.00 US 20 400.00 US 12 800.00
TOTAL	9 400PCS (总数量)		US 65 300.00 (总金额)

TOTAL AMOUNT IN WORDS——合同金额大写

SAY US DOLLARS SIXTY FIVE THOUSAND THREE HUNDRED ONLY

MORE OR LESS 5% OF THE QUANTITY AND AMOUT ARE ALLOWED.(**溢短装条款**)

PACKING:(包装条款)

EACH PIECE IN A POLYBAG, 40 PIECES TO ONE EXPORT STANDARD CARTON.

SHIPPING MARKS:(唛头)

KU——买方的信息
K123——合同号
MONTREAL——目的港
C/N:1-UP——箱数
}唛头

SHIPMENT(装运条款)

PORT OF LOADING: SAHNGHAI ——起运港
PORT OF DESTINATION: MONTREAL ——目的港
TRANSHIPMENT: ALLOWED ——分批装运
PARTIAL SHIPMENTS: ALLOWED ——转运
TIME OF SHIPMENT: BEFORE JULY 31, 2015 ——装运期

INSURANCE(保险条款)

THE SELLER SHOULD COVER INSURANCE ——投保人
FOR 110% OF FULL INVOICE VALUE ——保险险别
COVING ALL RISKS AND WAR RISK ——投保险别
AS PER CIC OF PICC DATED 01/01/1981. ——保险条款及生效时间

PAYMENT(支付条款)

THE BUYER SHOULD OPEN A BANK ACCEPTABLE TO THE SELLER ——买方开信用证
AN IRREVOCABLE L/C PAYABLE AT 30 DAYS AFTER SIGHT ——信用证种类及付款期限
FOR 100% OF TOTAL CONTRACT VALUE ——信用证金额
TO REACH THE SELLER BEFOREMAY 31TH, 2015 ——到证时间
VALID FOR NEGOTIATION IN CHINA ——到期地点
UNTIL THE 15TH DAY AFTER THE DATE OF SHIPMENT ——到期日

INSPECTION&CLAIM(检验和索赔)

THE SELLER SHALL HAVE THE PERFORMANCE AND QUALITIES, SPECIFICATIONS, QUANTITIES OF THE GOODS CAREFULLY INSPECTED AND ISSUE INSPECTION CERTIFICATE BEFORE SHIPMENT. ANY CLAIM BY THE BUYER REGARDING THE GOODS SHIPPED SHOULD BE FILED WITHIN 30DAYS AFTER THE ARRIVALS OF THE GOODS AT THE PORT/PLACE OF DESTINATION SPECIFIED IN THE RELATIVE BILL OF LADING OR TRANSPORT DOCUMENT

AND SUPPORTED BY A SURVEY REPORT ISSUED BY A SURVEY APPROVED BY THE SELLER. CLAIMS IN RESPECT OF MATTERS WITHIN RESPONSIBILITY OF INSURANCE COMPANY, SHIPPING COMPANY/OTHER TRANSPORTATION ORGANIZATION WILL NOT BE CONSIDERED OR ENTERTAINED BY THE SELLER.

检验条款通常包含有关检验权的规定、检验或复验的时间和地点、检验机构、检验证书等内容。

FORCE MAJUSE:(不可抗力)

IF THE SHIPMENT OF CONTRACTED GOODS IS PREVENTED OR DELAYS IN WHOLE OR IN PART BY REASON OF WAR, EARTHQUAKE, FIRE, FLOOD, HEAVY SNOW, STORM OR OTHER CAUSES OF FORCE MAJUSE, THE SELLER SHALL NOT BE LIABLE FOR NON-SHIPMENT OR LATE SHIPMENT OF THE GOODS OF THIS CONTRACT. HOWEVER, THE SELLER SHALL NOTIFY THE BUYERS BY CABLE OR TELEX AND FURNISH THE LETTER WITHIN 15DAYS BY REGISTERED AIRMAIL WITH A CERTIFICATE ISSUED BY THE CHINA COUNCIL FOR THE PROMOTION OF INTERNATIONAL TRADE ATTESTING SUCH EVENT OR EVENTS.

通常包含不可抗力的范围、对不可抗力事件的处理原则和方法、不可抗力发生后通知对方的期限和方式、出具证明文件的机构等内容。

ARBITRATION:(仲裁)

ALL DISPUTED ARISING OUT OF PERFORMANCE OF, OR RELATING TO THIS CONTRACT, SHALL BE SETTLED AMICABLY THROUGH FRIENDLY NEGOTIATION. IN CASE NO SETTLEMENT CAN BE REACHED THROUGH NEGOTIATION, THE CASE SHALL THEN BE SUBMITTED FOR ARBITRATION, THE LOCATION OF ARBITRATION SHALL BE IN THE COUNTRY OF THE DOMICILE OF THE DEFENDANT. IF IN CHINA, THE ARBITRATION SHALL BE CONDUCTED BY THE RULES OF ARBITRATION. THE ARBITRAL AWARD IS FINAL AND BINDING UPON BOTH PARTIES. THE CHARGES ARISING FROM THE ARBITRATION SHALL BE UNDERTAKEN BY THE LOSING PARTY.

通常包含争议解决方式、提请仲裁的仲裁地点、仲裁机构、仲裁规则、裁决效力等内容。

THE SELLER	THE BUYER
DALIAN SINIAN TEXTILES IMP&EXP. Co., LTD.	POLISH PULICI TEXTILE GROUP Co., LTD
张浩	Jane Homels

1.4 知识链接

1. 合同的组成

书面格式的合同由三部分组成,即约首、主体、约尾。

(1) 约首(Head of Contract)

约首部分一般包括合同名称、合同编号、缔约双方名称和地址、签订合同日期，地点电话、传真等项内容。

(2) 主体(Body of Contract)

合同的主体是指基本条款部分，用以规定当事人的权利和义务。它主要包括品名、品质、规格、数量、重量、包装、唛头、单价、总值、交货条件、运输、保险、付款、检验、索赔、不可抗力和仲裁等项内容。

(3) 约尾(End of Contract)

约尾部分反映了合同的效力，如合同一式两份，双方签字生效。约尾部分包括双方公司的名称、盖章、法人签字。

2. 合同的内容

(1) 商品的品名、品质条款

出口合同中的品质条款一般应该包括出口商品的品名、规格或等级、标准、商标或牌名等，如果是凭样品买卖，则要列明样品的编号以及寄送的日期，必要时可以附录简单的规格说明。

【例 1-1】 样品号 NT123 长毛绒玩具，尺码 24 英寸，根据卖方于 2017 年 7 月 10 日寄送的样品。

Sample NT123, Plush Toy Bear, Size24, as per the sample dispatched by the Seller on 10th July, 2017.

【例 1-2】 中国芝麻，水分(最高)8%；杂质(最高)3%；含油量以 50%位基础，如实际装运货物的含油量高于或低于 1%，价格应相应增减 1%，不足整数部分，按比例计算。

China sesame seeds, Moisture(Max.) 8%, Admixture (Max.) 3%, Oil content 50% basis, should the oil content of the goods actually shipped be 1% higher or lower, the price will be accordingly increased or decreased by 1%, and any fraction will be proportionally calculated.

① 凭现货成交。
② 凭样品成交。
③ 凭规格成交。
④ 凭等级成交。
⑤ 凭标准成交。
⑥ 凭商标或品牌买卖。
⑦ 凭产地名称买卖。
⑧ 凭说明书或图样买卖。

(2) 数量条款

数量条款包括数量和计量单位,必要时加上数量溢短装条款。

【例1-3】 数量:3 000 吨,5%增减,由卖方选择,增减部分按合同价格计算。

Quantity: 3 000 M/T, 5% more or less at seller's option, such excess or deficiency to be settled of contracted price.

【例1-4】 哔叽布约10 000码。

Serges about 10 000 yard.

开动脑筋

① 信用证规定,数量500箱,不许分批装运。卖方交货时因备货不足少交30箱,商业发票显示为450箱,银行是否会因单证不符而拒付?

② 信用证规定,数量1 000吨,散装货,不许分批装运。卖方交货时因备货不足少交50吨,商业发票显示为950箱,银行是否会因单证不符而拒付?

③ 信用证规定,数量约1 000吨,USD100.00/箱,信用证金额USD100 000.00。卖方可否多装或少装?

(3) 包装条款

合同中的包装条款包括包装材料、方式、规格、标志和费用的负担等内容。商定包装条款时,需要注意下列事项:

① 考虑商品的特点和不同运输方式的要求。

② 对包装的要求应具体明确。

③ 应定明包装费用由何方负担。

④ 明确由何方提供运输标志。

⑤ 如果买方提供包装或包装物料,则合同中应明确提供的时间、规格、未能及时提供而影响发运货物的责任等。

【例1-5】 纸箱装,每箱净重10千克。

In cartons of 10 kg net each.

【例1-6】 每件装一塑料袋,半打为一盒,10打装一木箱。运输标志由卖方设计。

Packing: Each piece in a polybag, half doz. In a box and 10 dozens in a wooden case. Shipping Mark is designed by seller.

超链接

常用包装的种类见表1-1。

表 1-1 常用包装的种类

纸箱	Carton	木桶	Wooden Case
麻袋	Gunny Bag	塑料袋	Plastic Bag
包	Bundle/Bale	铁桶	Iron Drum
木桶	Wooden Cask	瓶	Bottle
钢瓶	Cylinder	罐	Can
托盘	Pallet	集装箱	Container

常用警示性运输标志见表 1-2。

表 1-2 常用警示性运输标志

怕潮 Guard against damp	怕晒 Keep out of the direct sun	易碎 Fragile	向上 The Side Up

(4) 价格条款

价格条款一般包括商品的单价和总值两项。它主要由四个部分组成，包括计量单位、单位价格、计价货币和贸易术语、作价方法，有时还规定价格调整条款。另外，对佣金和折扣也应根据具体情况加以运用和规定。

【例 1-7】 每打 125 港元，CIFC5%香港(或 CIF 香港含 5%佣金)。

HK$125 PER DOZ. CIFC5% HONGKONG(CIF HONGKONG INCLUDING 5% COMMISSION).

【例 1-8】 每吨 300 美元，FOB 上海，以毛作净。

USD300 PER METRIC TON, FOB SHANGHAI, GROSS FOR NET.

(5) 装运条款

装运条款包括装运时间、装运港和目的港及分批装运和转运等内容，有时还规定卖方应予交付的单据和有关装运通知的条款。

【例 1-9】 “2016 年 1/2 月每月平均装运”。

装运港：上海/天津；目的港：鹿特丹/安特卫普选港，附加费由买方负担。

Shipment during Jan./Feb. 2016 in two equal monthly lots.

Port of loading: Shanghai/Tianjin.

Port of destination: Rotterdam/Antwerp optional,

Additional fee for buyer's account.

【例 1-10】 5 月装运，由伦敦至上海。卖方应在装运月份前 45 天将备妥货物可供装船的时间通知买方。允许分批和装运。

Shipment during May from London to Shanghai. The sellers shall advise the Buyers 45 days before the month of shipment of time the goods will be ready for shipment. Partial shipments and transshipment allowed

(6) 保险条款

保险条款的内容根据贸易术语的不同有所区别。采用 FOB、CFR 或 FCA、CPT 贸易术语成交的合同,买方办理投保、支付保险费;采用 CIF 或 CIP 成交的合同,条款内容须明确规定由谁办理保险、投保险别、保险金额的确定方法以及按什么保险条款保险,并注明条款的生效日期。

【例 1-11】 由卖方办理,保险金额为发票金额的 110%,投一切险,根据中国人民保险公司海洋运输货物条款 1/1/1981

Insurance: to be covered by the seller for 110% of CIF invoice value against All Risks as per and subject to the relevant ocean marine cargo clauses of the People's Insurance Company of China, dated Jan 1st, 1981.

【例 1-12】 全套正本保险单或保险凭证,空白背书,以发票金额的 110%投保一切险和战争险,包括仓至仓条款,运至最终目的地哥伦比亚,标明赔付在哥伦比亚办理。

Full set of original insurance Policy/Certificate, blank endorsed, coving all risks and war risks, including warehouse to warehouse clause up to final destination at Colombo, for 110% invoice value, showing claims payable in Colombo.

表 1-3 中国保险条款与协会货物条款

	中国保险条款	协会货物条款
英文全称	China Insurance Clause	Institute cargo clauses
英文缩写	C. I. C	I. C. C
颁发机构	中国人民保险公司	英国伦敦保险也协会
生效时间	1981 年 1 月 1 日	1982 年 1 月 1 日
基本险	平安险 Free From Particular Average FPA	协会货物(A)险 Institute cargo clause(A) ICC(A)
	水渍险 With Particular Average WPA	协会货物(B)险 Institute cargo clause(B) ICC(B)
	一切险 All Risks	协会货物(C)险 Institute cargo clause(C) ICC(C)

（续表）

	中国保险条款	协会货物条款
附加险	战争险 War Risks	协会战争险 Institute War Clause(C)—Cargo
	罢工险 Strike Risks	协会罢工险 Institute Strike Clause(C)—Cargo

(7) 支付条款

支付条款应选择恰当的支付工具，明确具体的支付方式、支付时间、交单条件等。信用证支付方式还应明确具体的开证时间、有效期、到期地点等。

【例 1-13】 买方同意自本合同签字之日起 1 个月内，将本合同总金额 50%的预付款，以电汇方式交卖方。

50% of the total contract value as advance payment shall be remitted by the buyer to the seller through T/T within one month after signing this contract.

【例 1-14】 买方应凭卖方开具的即期跟单汇票见票时立即付款，付款后交单。

Upon first presentation the buyer shall pay against documentary draft drawn by the sellers at sight. The shipping documents are to be delivered against payment only.

【例 1-15】 买方应通过为卖方所接受的银行于装运月份前 30 天开立的并送达卖方不可撤销即期信用证，有效至装运月份后第 15 天在中国议付。

The buyer shall open through a bank acceptable to the sellers an irrevocable sight letter of credit to reach the sellers 30 days before the month of shipment, valid for negotiation in China, until the 15th day after the month of shipment.

(8) 检验条款

检验条款包括检验时间、地点、内容、检验机构、检验费用、检验证书等。

【例 1-16】 货到目的口岸 60 天内经中国商品检验局复验，如发现品质或数量或重量与本合同规定不符时，除属于保险公司或船方负责者外，买方凭中国商品检验局出具的检验证明书向卖方提出退货或索赔。因退货或索赔引起的一切费用(包括检验费)及损失均由卖方负担。

In case the quality, quantity or Weight of the goods be found not in conformity with those stipulated in this Contract after re-inspection by the china Commodity Inspection Bureau within 60 days after arrival of the goods at the port of destination, the Buyers shall return the goods to or lodge claims against the Sellers for compensation of losses upon the strength of Inspection Certificate issued by the said Bureau, with the exception of those claims for which the insurers or owners of the carrying vessel are liable. All expenses (including inspection fees) and losses arising from the return of the goods or claims should be borne by the Sellers.

(9) 索赔条款

索赔条款包括索赔依据、期限、方法、金额等。

【例1-17】 如买方提出索赔,凡属品质异议须于货到目的口岸之日起30天内提出,凡属数量异议须于货到目的口岸之日起15天内提出,对所装货物所提任何异议于保险公司、轮船公司、其他有关运输机构或邮递机构所负责者,卖方不负任何责任。

In case of quality discrepancy, claim should be filed by the Buyer within 30 days after the arrival of the goods at port of destination, while for quantity discrepancy, claim should be filed by the Buyer within 15 days after the arrival of the goods at port of destination. It is understood that the Seller shall not be liable for any discrepancy of the goods shipped due to causes for which the Insurance Company, Shipping Company, other Transportation Organization/or Post Office are liable.

(10) 不可抗力条款

不可抗力条款包括不可抗力的范围、处理原则和方法,不可抗力发生后通知对方的期限、方法以及出具证明机构等内容。

【例1-18】 除因不可抗力而延迟交货或不能交货的情况以外,如果卖方不能按合同规定的条款和或条件交货,卖方应负责向买方赔偿由此而引起的一切损失和遭受的损害,包括但不仅限于买价及或买价的差价、空仓费、滞期费,以及由此产生的直接或间接损失。买方有权撤销全部或部分合同,并保留向卖方提出损害赔偿的权利。

With the exception of late delivery or non-delivery due to "Force Majeure" causes, if the seller fails to make delivery of the goods in accordance with the terms and conditions of this contract, the seller shall be liable to buyer and indemnify the buyer for all losses, damages, including but not limited to, purchase price and/or purchase price differentials, dead fright, demurrage, and all consequential direct or indirect losses. The buyer shall nevertheless have the right to cancel in part or in whole of the contract without prejudice to the buyer's right to claim compensations.

1. 不可抗力合同案例

(11) 仲裁条款

仲裁条款的内容一般包括仲裁地点、仲裁机构、仲裁规则和裁决的效力。在规定仲裁地点时,我方一般首先争取规定在我国仲裁。

【例1-19】 "凡因本合同引起的或与本合同有关的任何争议,均应提交中国国际经济贸易仲裁委员会,按照申请仲裁时该会现行有效的仲裁规则在上海进行仲裁。仲裁裁决是终局的,对双方有约束力。

All dispute arising from or in connection with this contract shall be submitted to China International Economic and Trade Arbitration Commission for arbitration which shall be trialed in Shanghai and conducted in accordance with the Commission's arbitration rules in effect at the time of applying for arbitration. The arbitral award is final and binding upon both parties.

销售合同的一般交易条件(General Terms)如下表所示:

表 1-4 销售合同

SALES CONTRACT

合同的一般交易条件	GENERAL TERMS AND CONDITIONS FOR THE CONTRACT
本合同是由营业地在不同国家或地区的当事人之间以书面形式订立的货物购买合同。	The contract is a written commodity purchase contract concluded between the parties concerned at the place of business in different countries or regions.
第一条：质量标准：买、卖双方对所成交的商品、所采取的质量标准应在合同中详细列明。	Article 1: Quality standard: The standard of quality of the commodity in transaction between the Buyer and Seller shall be specified in the contract.
第二条：支付方式：本合同项下的支付方式采用汇付、托收及信用证三大类。可采用其中的一种，经双方同意也可以结合使用。若为托收方式，买方应提供进口地代收银行的名称及地址。若为信用证方式，买方在合同签订后应按时开立不可撤销的信用证，以卖方为受益人，可分批、可转运，并注明合同编号，信用证有效期于装期后 15 天在出口地到期，其基本内容应与合同内容相符。选定的支付方式，应在合同上载明。	Article 2: Form of payment: The form of payment adopted in the contract shall be one of the following: remittance, collection or letter of credit. These can be adopted together if agreed by both parties. In case of collection, the Buyer shall provide the name and address of the collecting bank at the place of import. If the letter of credit is used, the Buyer shall, after signing the contract, open in time irrevocable letter of credit and names the Seller as the beneficiary. It can be done in partial shipments or transferred shipment stating the number of the contract. The expiry date of the L/C shall be 15 days after the shipment at the exporting place. Its contents shall basically conform to the contents of the contract. The form of payment once determined shall be stated in the contract.
第三条：货物保险：凡价格条件为 FOB、FCA、CFR(C&F)及 CPT 均为买方保险。凡价格条件为 CIF 或 CPT，保险由卖方按发票金额的 110%投保。投保一切险及战争险按中国保险条款。	Article 3: Insurance of the commodity: When the prices are under FOB, FCA, CFR(C&F) and CPT, the commodity shall be insured by the Buyer. When the prices are under CIF or CIP insurance shall be covered by the Seller at 110% of the amount on the invoice. Insurance for all risks and war risk shall conform to China insurance Clauses (C. I. C).
第四条：包装及装运标记：凡买方对包装及装运标记无特殊要求，均按卖方一般出口包装和装运标记。	Article 4: Packing and mark of shipment: When there is no special request from the Buyer for packing and mark of shipment, the Seller shall pack and mark the shipment according to the general practice of export.

(续表)

第五条:商品检验:买、卖双方同意以装运港的中华人民共和国进出口商品检验局所属机构、委托机构及政府批准的其他商品检验机构出具的各种证书为依据,买方可在货到目的地后予以复验,复验费由买方自行承担。	Article 5: Commodity Inspection: The buyer and the seller shall agree to base on the different certificates issued by the organizations subordinated to or entrusted by the Import and Export Commodity Inspection Bureau of the People's Republic of China or any other commodity inspection organization approved by the government for the buyer to recheck the commodity when it arrives at the destination. The fee for rechecking shall be born by the buyer.
第六条:异议与索赔:买方对于所装运货物的品质、重量或数量有异议并要去索赔时,必须与所装的该货物到达运输单据所注明的目的港(地)后 60 天内提出,并必须提供双方确认的公证机构所出具的检验报告。如果买方对货物做了任何形式的处理或加工,买方丧失索赔权利。凡属于自然原因造成损失及属于运输公司或保险公司责任范围之内的赔偿,卖方均不予赔偿。	Article 6: Objections and claims for compensation: when the buyer raises objection to the quality, weight, or quantity of the commodity and claims for compensation, it shall put forward the matter within 60days after the cargo has arrived at the destination port (place)as stated in the transport documents. It shall at the same time provide the inspection report issued by a public notary organization or a commodity inspection organization. In case the buyer has treated or processed the commodity in whatever form it shall lose the right of claim for compensation. For losses subsequent to natural cause or within the responsibility for compensation by the transport company or the insurance company the seller not agree to compensate.
第七条:不可抗力:在履行本合同过程中,由于以下不可抗力的原因,如自然灾难、战争、国家法令、法规对进出口所造成影响以及人们所无法控制的其他人为及自然因素造成的无法履约,买、卖双方均不承担责任。但是当事人一方因不可抗力事件不能履行合同的全部或者部分,有义务毫不拖延地用传真、电传、电报等各种方式通知另一方,并必须在 15 天内用快递提交当地有关部门出具此类事件的证明书。即使在此情况下,买、卖双方仍可商讨补救办法。	Article 7: Force Majeure: In performing the contract when the following force majeure occurs, such as nature calamities, war, impact from state laws and regulations affect from state laws and regulations affecting import and export and any other causes, man-made or natural beyond the control of man that hinders the performance of the contract, both the buyer and seller shall not bear any responsibility. However, in case of Force Majeure that one party is unable to carry out the whole or party of the contract, it shall be obliged to part of the contract, it shall be obliged to fax. telex or cable within any delay to notify the other party and s hall within 15days provide by express mail certification by the local departments concerned on such matters. Even under such circumstances the buyer and the sellers MAR. negotiate on measures for making up for the loss.

（续表）

第八条：仲裁：在履行本合同中发生争议时，首先由合同双方友好协商解决，若经协商不能达成协议，任何一方均可将有关争议提交中国国际经济贸易仲裁委员会上海分会，并根据该会仲裁法则和程序进行仲裁。仲裁裁决是终局性的，对双方都有约束力。	Article 8: Arbitration: in case of disputes arising in the performance of the contract these shall first be resolved through friendly negotiations. shall negotiations fail to reach resolution, either party MAR. raise the dispute to Chinese International Economic and Trade Arbitration Commission, Shanghai Branch and request for arbitration according to the arbitration regulations and procedures of that organization. The decision of the arbitration is final. which has binding force on both parties.
第九条：转让：本合同未经双方同意，任何一方不得转让。	Article 9: Transfer: the contract shall not be transferred by either party without the agreement by both parties.
第十条：变更与解除：本合同未经双方同意，任何一方不得擅自变更和解除合同。	Article 10: Changes and termination: Either party shall not change or terminate the contract without the agreement of both parties.
第十一条：违约和赔偿：任何一方（除不可抗力外）不履行合同义务即构成违约，根据不同情况和后果，另一方有权向违约方提出赔偿要求。	Article 11: Default and compensation: Should either of the two parties fail to carry out the contract, it shall be regard as default, the other party reserves the right to claim from the default party for compensation in accordance with the different conditions and consequences.
第十二条：合同生效：买、卖双方经协商后同意签订本合同，并一经双方授权代表签署，本合同即生效，生效日期以合同签署日期为准，凡异地签署的以最后一方签署日期为生效日期。	Article 12: Effectiveness of the contract: The buyer and the seller have through negotiations agreed to conclude the contract; once the contract is signed by the authorized representatives of both parties, it is effective as of the date of the signature. In case the contract has to be signed in different locations the date of effectiveness shall be the date when the later party has signed.
第十三条：合同份数：本合同正本肆份，双方各执贰份。凡以前有关本批交易的信件、传真、电传、电报、口头磋商均以本合同的内容为准。	Article 13: Copies of contract: There are four original copies of the contract, two of which shall be held by each party. All previous correspondence, facsimiles, telex, cables and verbal negotiations have to be referred to the contents of the contract as the criterion.
第十四条：其他说明：凡上述条款未提及事宜或需要进一步补充说明，经双方同意可在合同中备注栏内说明，备注内容对双方均有约束力。	Article 14: Other remarks: Any matters not covered, to be supplemented or be elaborated shall be stated, as agreed by both parties, in the remarks column, which also have binding force on both parties.
第十五条：文字效力：本合同中英文具有同等法律效力。	Article 15: Effectiveness of languages: Both the Chinese and English version of the contract shall have equal legal effect.

1.5 能力实训

实训1 翻译以下条款

① 货号KB2043长毛兔，质量必须与卖方第3SC4号样品相同。

② 中国东北大米，6 000吨，允许卖方有4%的溢短装。

③ 每吨200美元成本加保险费运费至旧金山，含2%的佣金。

④ 每打750 000日元大连港船上交货之净价。

⑤ 每20件装一盒，10盒装一出口纸箱，共500箱。

⑥ 货物最晚不迟于2018年8月31日由上海通过海运运往美国纽约，允许分批装运，但不允许转运。

⑦ 卖方按发票金额的120%，根据中国人民保险公司1981年1月1日的海运货物保险条款，投保一切险。

⑧ 货物装运后，卖方出具以买方为付款人的即期汇票，并通过卖方银行和代收行向买方提出全套单据，在其付款后放单，即付款交单。买方应于提示汇票立即付款，已取得全套单据。

实训2 根据以下内容起草一份合同

背景资料：上海宁飞贸易有限公司(Shanghai Ningfei Trading Co., Ltd.)收到Sam Hydraulik S.p.A电洽购买铝合金手电筒，其往来电文如图所示。根据双方磋商结果签订确认书一份。

Jul.10	Incoming	PLS QUOTE 14 LED FLASHLIGHT ART NO. HL-199 AND 5 LED ALUMINIUM ALLOY FLASHLIGHT ART NO. HL-197 CIF SHANGHAI NOV SHIPMT
Jul.12	Outgoing	YR 10TH HL-199 USD 12.30/PC 150 PCS/CTN MIN ORD 3000 PCS HL-197 USD 23.5/PC 100 PCS/CTN MIN ORD 1500 PCS SIGHT L/C
Jul.16	Incoming	YR 12TH HL-199 USD 12.00/PC HL-197 USD 20.00/PC EACH MIN QTY SIGHT D/P
Jul.19	Outgoing	YR 16TH ACCEPT YOUR PRICE IF PAYMENT BY SIGHT L/C
Jul.22	Incoming	YR 19TH AGREED LATEST SHIPMT NOV. 20 PARTIAL TRANSSHIPMENT SHIPMT NOT ALLOWED INSURANCE 120PCT INV VALUE AGAINST ICC(A) PLS RUSH S/C
Jul.23	Outgoing	YR 22ND S/C 11-JY045 BY UPS

即期信用证付款于10月10日前开抵卖方。卖方必须保证产品完全符合合同的品质、规格和功能。此项品质保证期为发票日起12个月。

信用证项的下单据要求如下：

① 已签署的商业发票一份正本，2份副本。

② 全套已装船海运提单3份正本，3份副本，做成空白抬头空白背书，通知开证行，并注

明运费已付。

③ 装箱单一式两份。

④ 受益人证明申明以下单据均在装运日 2 个工作日内通过快递寄交给开证申请人：

a. 出口地商会出具的原产地证明；

b. 受益人出具的装运重量记录，标明货物总净重、总毛重；

c. 由中国检验认证集团 China Certificate and Inspection(Group) Co., Ltd. 出具的装船前检验证明。

合同中应注明以下内容：

① 商品的原产国及具体生产商；

② 包装必须适合长途运输，防潮，防锈、防震，凡由于包装不当所产生的任何费用和损失由卖方负担；

③ 卖方必须在装船后 48 小时内将木箱熏蒸证明快递给买方。

Purchase Contract

Contract NO.:

Contract Date:

Seller:

Buyer:

This contract is made by and between the buyers and the sellers, whereby the buyers agrees to buy and seller agree to sell the under mentioned commodity according to the terms and conditions stipulated below.

1.

Commodity	Art. No.	Quantity	Unit price	Total

Total value

2. Packing

3. Time of Shipment

Port of Shipment:

Port of Destination:

4. Terms of payment

5. Documents

(1)

(2)

(3)

(4)

(5)

6. Additional Conditions

(1)

(2)

7. General Conditions

(1) Quality/Quantity Discrepancy and Claim

The seller shall guarantee all shipment to conform to sample submitted with regard to quality. Should goods be slightly inferior in quality to the sample, the buyer shall take delivery of goods on condition that a reasonable allowance be made on the contract price by subsequent mutual negotiation. Goods must not be returned except by permission of the seller.

Should the seller delivery to the buyer a quantity of goods larger than he has contracted to sell, the buyer MAR. accept the goods included in the contract and reject the rest. If the buyer accepts the whole of the goods so delivered, he MAR. pay for them at the contract rate.

In case the quality, quantity or weight of the goods be found not in conformity with those as stipulated in this Contract upon re-inspection by the China Entry-Exit Inspection and Quarantine Bureau within 60 days after completion of the discharge of the opening of such containers, the buyer shall have the right to request the seller to take back the goods or lodge claims against the seller for compensation for losses upon the strength of the Inspection Certificate issued by the said Bureau, with the exception of those claims for which the insurers or owners of the carrying vessel are liable. All expenses including but not limited to inspection fees, interest, losses arising from the return of the goods or claims shall be borne by the seller.

(2) Force Majeure

With the exception of late delivery or non-delivery due to "Force Majeure" causes, if the seller fails to make delivery of the goods in accordance with the terms and conditions of this contract, the seller shall be liable to buyer and indemnify the buyer for all losses, damages, including but not limited to, purchase price and/or purchase price differentials, dead fright, demurrage, and all consequential direct or indirect losses. The buyer shall nevertheless have the right to cancel in part or in whole of the contract without prejudice to the buyer's right to claim compensations.

(3) Arbitration

Both parties agree to attempt to resolve all disputes between the parties with respect to the application or interpretation of any term hereof, through amicable negotiation. If a dispute cannot be resolved in this manner to the satisfaction of the seller and the buyer within a reasonable period of time, maximum not exceeding 90 days after the date of the notification of such dispute, the case under dispute shall be submit to arbitration if the buyer should decide not to take the case to court at a place of jurisdiction that the buyer MAR. deem appropriate. Unless otherwise agreed upon by the parties, such arbitration shall be held in Beijing, and shall be governed by the rules and procedures of arbitration stipulated by the Foreign Trade Arbitration Commission of the China council for the promotion of International Trade. The decision by such arbitration shall be accepted as final and binding upon both parties. The arbitration fees shall be borne by the losing party unless otherwise awarded.

(4) Transfer

The contract shall not be transferred by either party without the agreement by both parties.

(5) Changes and termination

Either party shall not change or terminate the contract without the agreement of both parties

(6) Default and compensation

Should either of the two parties fail to carry out the contract, it shall be regard as default, the other party reserves the right to claim from the default party for compensation in accordance with the different conditions and consequences.

(7) Effectiveness of the Contract

The buyer and the seller have through negotiations agreed to conclude the contract; once the contract is signed by the authorized representatives of both parties, it is effective as of the date of the signature. In case the contract has to be signed in different locations the date of effectiveness shall be the date when the later party has signed.

(8) Copies of Contract

There are four original copies of the contract, two of which shall be held by each party. All previous correspondence, facsimiles, telex, cables and verbal negotiations have to be referred to the contents of the contract as the criterion.

(9) Other Remarks

Any matters not covered, to be supplemented or be elaborated shall be stated, as agreed by both parties, in the remarks column, which also have binding force on both parties.

(10) Effectiveness of languages

Both the Chinese and English version of the contract shall have equal legal effect.

THE SELLER:　　　　　　　　**THE BUYER:**

实训3　按照要求自拟一份合同

学生以自己喜欢的一种产品为例，设计贸易的买、卖双方，自行选择贸易术语和货款结算方式，根据当前的市场行情确定商品的价格和数量，草拟一份合同。

Sa/les Contract

Contract NO.:

The Seller:　　　　Signed at

The Buyer:　　　　Date:

This contract is made by and between the buyers and the sellers, whereby the buyers agrees to buy and seller agree to sell the under mentioned commodity according to the terms and conditions stipulated below.

(1) Commodity	(2) Quantity	(3) Unit price	(4) Total Value

(5) Time of Shipment:

(6) Port of Loading:

(7) Port of Destination:

(8) Insurance:

(9) Terms of payment:

(10) Inspection:

(11) Shipping Marks:

Other Terms:

1. Discrepancy: In case of quality discrepancy, claim should be lodged by the buyer within 30days after the arrival of the goods at port of destination, while for quantity discrepancy, claim should be lodged by the buyers within 15days afterthe arrival of the goods at the port o destination. In all case, claims must be

accompanied be survey reports of recognized public surveyors agreed to by the sellers. Should the responsibility of the subject under claim be found to rest on the part of the sellers, the seller shall, within 20 days after receipt of the claim, send their reply to the buyers together with suggestion for settlement.

2. The covering letter of credit shall stipulate the sellers' option of shipping the indicated percentage more or less than the quantity contracted and be negotiated for the amount covering the value of quantity actually shipped.
3. The contents of the covering letter of credit shall be in strict conformity with the stipulation of the sales contract. In case of any variation there of necessitating amendment of the L/C, the buyers shall bear the expenses for effecting the amendment. The sellers shall not be held responsible for possible delay of shipment resulting from awaiting the amendment of the L/C and the L/C and reserve the right to claim from the buyers for the losses resulting there from.
4. Expect in cases where the insurance is covered by the buyers as arranged, insurance is to be covered by the sellers with a Chinese insurance company. If insurance for additional amount and/or for other insurance terms is required by the buyers, prior notice to this effect must reach the sellers before shipment and is subject to the sellers' agreement, and the extra insurance premium shall be for the buyers' account.
5. The sellers shall not be heldresponsible if they fail, owing to force majeure cause or causes, to make delivery within the time stipulated in this sales contract or cannot delivery the goods. however, the seller shall inform immediately the buyer by cable. the sellers shall delivery to buyers by registered letter, if it is requested by the buyers, a certificate issued by the china council for the promotion of international trade or by any competent authorities, attesting the existence of the said cause or causes. The buyer failure to be obtain the relative import license is not to be treated as force majeure.
6. Arbitration: All disputes arising in connection with sales contract orthe execution thereof shall be settled by way of amicable negotiation. in case no settlement can be reached, the case at issue shall then be submitted for arbitration to the China International Economic and Trade Arbitration Commission in accordance with the provisions of the said commission. the award by the said commission shall be deemed as final and binding upon both parties.

The Seller's signature　　　　The Buyer's: signature

项目 2　阅读和审核信用证

任务 2.1　阅读信用证

2.1.1　学习目标

知识目标:能读懂信用证并了解其相关国际惯例;了解跟单信用证的业务流程。
能力目标:能正确分析信用证的内容。

2.1.2　工作任务

无锡蓝天进出口公司与加拿大的 KU TEXTILE CORPORATION 达成一笔全棉女童连衣裙的交易,并签订了贸易合同。之后,加拿大 KU TEXTILE CORPORATION 在合同规定的开证期内向汇丰银行申请开立了一张以无锡蓝天进出口公司为受益人的信用证,并通过中国银行无锡分行在 2015 年 5 月 21 日送达无锡蓝天进出口公司。加拿大 KU TEXTILE CORPORATION 通过汇丰银行向出口商开立的信用证。

在本任务中,单证员应完成以下内容:
① 读懂信用证。
② 正确理解信用证的内容。

2.1.3　操作范例

读信用证的过程如下:

1. 报头

MT 700	ISSUE OF A DOCUMENTARY CREDIT
SENDER	HSBC BANK PLC, MONTREAL, CANADA
RECEIVE	RBANK OF CHINA, WUXI BRANCH, CHINA

2. 正文

SEQUENCE OF TOTAL	27: 1/1
FORM OF DOC. CREDIT	40A: IRREVOCABLE
DOC. CREDIT NUMBER	20: 123456

DATE OF ISSUE	31C:150520
APPLICABLE RULES	40E: UCP LATEST VERSION
DATE AND PLACE OF EXPIRY	31D: 150815 IN CANADA
APPLICANT	50: KU TEXTILE CORPORATION 430 VTRA MONTREAL CANADA
BENEFICIARY	59: WUXI BLUE SKY IMP&EXP. Co., LTD NO. 53 ZHONGSHAN ROAD, WUXI, CHINA
AMOUNT	32B: USD 66 020.00
AVAILABLE WITH/BY	41D: ANY BANK IN CHINA, BY NEGOTIATION

解析:这部分是对信用证本身的说明。

27 合计次序:1/1

40A 信用证类型:不可撤销

20 信用证编号:123456

31C 开证日期:2015 年 6 月 20

40E 适用的原则:UCP 最新修订本

31D 有效日期和地点:2015 年 8 月 15 日加拿大

50 申请人:KU TEXTILE CORPORATION

59 受益人:无锡蓝天进出口有限公司

32B 币别代号、金额:USD 66 020.00

41D 兑付方式:中国任何银行议付

DRAFTS AT ...	42C: 60 DAYS AFTER SIGHT
DRAWEE	42A: KU TEXTILE CORPORATION

解析:这部分是对汇票的说明。

42C 汇票期限……见票后 60 天

42A 付款人:买方

PARTIAL SHIPMENT	43P: PROHIBITED
TRANSSHIPMENT	43T: ALLOWED
PORT OF LOADING/AIRPORT OF DEPARTURE	44E:CHINESE MAIN PORT
PORT OF DISCHARGE	44F: MONTREAL, CANADA
LATEST DATE OF SHIPMENT	44C: 150715

解析:这部分是对运输的说明。

43P 分批装运:禁止

43T 转运:允许

44A 由……装运/发运/接管:中国主要港口

44B 装运至……加拿大的蒙特利尔

44C 最迟装运日期:2015 年 7 月 15 日

DESCRIPTION OF GOODS AND/OR SERVICES. 45A:
9 400 PIECES GIRL DRESS 100%COTTON
AS PER S/C NO. K123

STYLE NO.	QUANTITY	UNIT PRICE	AMOUNT
11754	2 400PCS	USD6.80/PC	USD16 320.00
11575	3 000PCS	USD5.50/PC	USD16 500.00
11576	2 400PCS	USD8.50/PC	USD20 400.00
11577	1 600PCS	USD8.00/PC	USD12 800.00

AT CIF MONTREAL, CANADA

解析：这部分是对货物的说明。

DOCUMENTS REQUIRED 46A:

+SIGNED COMMERCIAL INVOICE IN DUPLICATE CERTIFYING GOODS OF CHINA ORIGIN.

+PACKING LIST IN THREE FOLDS SHOWING G. W., N. W., AND MEAS. OF EACH PACKGE.

+G. S. P. CERTIFICATE OF ORIGIN FORM A IN DUPLICATE BY CIQ.

+CERTIFICATE OF QUALITY ISSUED BY CIQ IN DUPLICATE.

+FULL SET OF CLEAN 'ON BOARD' OCEAN BILLS OF LADING MADE OUT TO APPLICANTBLANK ENDORSED MARKED FREIGHT PREPAID AND NOTIFY APPLICANT.

+INSURANCE POLICY OR CERTIFICATE ENDORSED IN BLANK FOR 150 PCT OF CIF VALUE, COVERING ALL RISKS AND WAR RISK SUBJECT TO THE RELEVANT OCEAN MARINE CLAUSE OF THE PEOPLE'S INSURANCE COMPANY OF CHINA, DATED 1/1/1981.

+SHIPPING ADVICE SHOWING B/L NO., GOODS NAME, QUANTITY AND AMOUNT OF GOODS, NUMBER OF PACKAGES, NAME OF VESSEL AND VOYAGE NO., AND DATE OF SHIPMENT TO APPLICANT WITHIN 3 DAYS AFTER THE DATE OF BILL OF LADING.

+BENEFICIARY'S CERTIFICATE CERTIFYING THAT ONE COPY OF SHIPPING DOCUMENTS HAS BEEN SENT TO APPLICANT WITHIN 7 DAYS AFTER SHIPMENT

+CERTIFICATE TO EVDIENT THE SHIP IS NOT OVER 15 YEARS OLD.

解析：这部分是对单据的说明。

+签署的商业发票一式二份证明货物原产于中国；

+装箱单一式三份显示每一个包装的毛重、净重和体积；

+由中国出入境检验检疫局签发的质量证明一式两份；

+普惠制原产地证一式两份，由中国出入境检验检疫局出具；

＋全套清洁已装船，申请人抬头，空白背书，注明运费预付，通知申请人；

＋保险单或凭证，空白背书，以 CIF 金额的 150%投保一切险及战争险，依据中国人民保险公司 1981 年 1 月 1 日的相关海运保险条款。

＋装运通知显示提单号、商品名称、数量、金额、箱数、运输船名航次、装运日期，提单日后 3 天内通知。

＋受益人证明，证明一套装运单据的副本已经在装运后 7 天内寄送开证申请人。

＋证书需证明(船舶)船龄没有超过 15 年。

ADDITIONAL CONDITION 47A: ＋DOCUMENTS DATED PRIOR TO THE DATE OF THIS CREDIT ARE NOT ACCEPTABLE. ＋THE NUMBER AND THE DATE OF THIS CREDIT AND THE NAME OF ISSUING BANK MUST BE QUOTED ON ALL DOCUMENTS. ＋TRANSSHIPMENT ALLOWED AT HONGKONG ONLY. ＋SHORT FORM/CHARTER PARTY/THIRD PARTY BILL OF LADING ARE NOT ACCEPTABLE. ＋SHIPMENT MUST BE EFFECTED BY 1 ×20′ FULL CONTAINER LOAD. B/L TO SHOW EVIDENCE OF THIS EFFECT IS REQUIRED. ＋ALL PRESENTATIONS CONTAINING DISCREPANCIES WILL ATTRACT A DISCREPANCY FEE OF USD50.00 PLUS TELEX COSTS OR OTHER CURRENCY EQUIVALENT. THIS CHARGE WILL BE DEDUCTED FROM THE BILL AMOUNT WHETHER OR NOT WE ELECT TO CONSULT THE APPLICANT FOR A WAIVER. ＋THE CREDIT IS NON-OPERATIVE UNLESS THE BUYER OBTAINTHE IMPORT LICENSE.

解析：这部分是对附加的说明。

＋单证日期不得早于信用证的开证日期。

＋所有单证必须显示信用证号码、开证日期和开证行。

＋只允许在香港转运。

＋略式提单、租船提单和第三方提单作为托运人的提单不被接受。

＋必须用 20 米集装箱整箱装，提单必须显示。

＋所有交单一旦存在不符点，无论我们是否征询申请人，50 美元的不符点费和电传费或其他等值货币金额都将从汇票款项中扣除。

＋信用证不生效除非买方获得进口许可证。

CHARGES　71B: ALL CHARGES AND COMMISSIONS OUTSIDE CANADA ARE FOR BENEFICIARY'S ACCOUNT.

解析：这部分是对银行费用的说明。

71B　加拿大以外的所有费用和佣金都有受益人承担。

PERIOD FOR PRESENTATION 48: WITHIN 5 DAYS AFTER THE DATE OF SHIPMENT, BUT WITHIN THE VALIDITY OF THIS CREDIT.

解析:这部分是对银行交单期限的说明。

48　交单期限:所有单据应在装运日后 5 天内提交,但是必须在信用证有效期内。

CONFIRMATION INSTRUCTION 49: WITHOUT INFORMATION TO PRESENTING BANK 78: ALL DOCUMENTS ARE TO BE REMITTED IN ONE LOT BY COURIER TO HSBC BANK PLC, TRADE SERVICES, DUBAI BRANCH, P O BOX 66, HSBC BANK BUILDING 312/45 Al SUQARE ROAD, MONTREAL, CANADA

解析:这部分是对保兑的说明。

49　保兑与否提示:不保兑

78　(付款、承兑、议付、偿付银行的)指示:所有单据由交单行一次性快递至 HSBC BANK BUILDING 312/45 Al SUQARE ROAD, MONTREAL, CANADA

信用证分析表

1. 信用证文本格式　☐ 信开　☐ 电开　☑ SWIFT
2. 信用证号码　123456
3. 通知银行编号　☑未注明
4. 开证日　2015 年 6 月 20 日
5. 到期日　2015 年 8 月 15 日
6. 到期地点　加拿大
7. 兑付方式　☐ 付款　☐ 承兑　☑ 议付
8. 货币　美元
9. 金额(具体数额)　66 020　☐未注明
10. 金额允许增减幅度　☑未注明
11. 交单期　在装运日后 5 天内提交,但是必须在信用证有效期内
12. 开证申请人(名称)　KU TEXTILE CORPORATION
13. 受益人(名称)　WUXI BLUE SKY IMP&EXP. CO., LTD.
14. 开证银行(名称)　HSBC BANK PLC, MONTREAL, CANADA
15. 通知银行(名称)　☑未注明
16. 议付银行(名称)　ANY BANK　☐未注明
18. 付款、偿付银行(名称)　☑未注明
19. 货物名称　GIRL DRESS 100%COTTON
20. 合同/订单/形式发票号码　K123　☐未注明
21. 价格/交货/贸易术语　CIF MONTREAL
22. 最迟装运日　2015 年 7 月 15 日
23. 装运港　中国主要港口
24. 目的地　蒙特利尔
25. 分批装运　☑ 允许　☐ 不允许

26. 转运　☑ 允许　☐ 不允许
27. 运输标志　KU/K123/MONTREAL/C/N: 1-UP
28. 运输方式　☑ 海运　☐ 空运　☐ 陆运
29. 向银行提交的单据列表(用阿拉伯数字表示)

名称	汇票	发票	装箱单	重量单	尺码单	海运提单	空运提单	货物承运收据	原产地证明	保险单
份数	2	2	3	0	0	3	0	0	2	3
名称	检验书		装船通知		寄单通知		受益人证明(其他内容)		承运人/船公司证明	其他单据原包装清单
份数	2		1		0		1		0	0

2.1.4 知识链接

1. 信用证的基本内容

在国际贸易中,各国银行开出的信用证并没有统一的格式,但其内容基本相似,主要包括以下几个方面:

(1) 信用证的当事人

① 开证人(买方)Applicant/Accountee/Accreditor/Opener;

② 受益人(卖方)Beneficiary;

③ 开证行 issuing/opening/establishing Bank;

④ 通知行 Advising/Notifying Bank;

⑤ 保兑行 Confirming Bank;

⑥ 议付行 Negotiating Bank;

⑦ 付款行 Paying Bank;

⑧ 偿付行 Reimbursing Bank。

(2) 信用证的性质、种类

① 不可撤销的跟单信用证/可撤销的跟单信用证 Irrevocable Documentary L/C/revocable Documentary L/C;

② 跟单信用证、光票信用证 Documentary/Clean L/C;

③ 限制议付信用证/自由议付信用证 Restricted/Freely negotiation L/C;

④ 保兑信用证/不保兑信用证 Confirmed/Unconfirmed L/C;

⑤ 即期信用证/远期信用证 Sight/Time L/C;

⑥ 可转让信用证/不可转让信用证 Transferable/Non-transferable L/C;

⑦ 即期付款信用证 Sight Payment L/C/延期付款信用证 Deferred Payment L/C;

⑧ 承兑信用证 Acceptance Credit;

⑨ 议付信用证 Acceptance Credit。

(3) 信用证的号码、开证日期与地点

信用证号码:L/C number No.

开证日期:Date and place of Issue

(4) 信用证的有效期及到期地点

Expiry date: DEC.12, 2014 in the country of the beneficiary for negotiation

Date and Place of Expiry: 20150812 in China

(5) 金额、币种

Amount: USD ... 金额:……美元

For an amount not exceeding total of ... 金额不超过……

(6) 汇票条款

例 1:Draft(s) drawn under this credit to be marked "drawn under XYZ Bank L/C No. ××× dated ×××

根据本证开出的汇票必须注明"凭 XYZ 银行某年某月某日第×××号信用证开立的"。

Available with/by: Bank of China, Beijing Branch.

Draft at ... : drafts at 30 days after sight for full invoice cost.

(7) 货物描述

内容包括货名、质量、数量、单价、贸易术语等。

DESCRIPTION OF GOODS:

200pcs short trousers —100pct cotton twill at EUR 10.50/pc as per order D140931 and sales contract number XYZ.

(8) 单据条款

信用证项下所需的单据除汇票外,通常还有:商业发票、装箱单、海运提单、保险单、原产地证书、受益人证明及各种其他证明等全套条款。

DOCUMENTS REQUIRED 46A:

+COMMERCIAL INVOICE 商业发票

+PACKING LIST 装箱单

+CERTIFICATE OF CHINESE ORIGIN 原产地证书

+FULL SET OF CLEAN ' ON BOARD ' OCEAN BILLS OF LADING ... 全套清洁已装船海运提单

+INSURANCE POLICY/CERTIFICATE ... 保险单/保险凭证

+COMMERCIAL INVOICE SIGNED IN TRIPLICATE at least in 8 copies issued in the name of the buyer indicating the merchandise, country of origin and any other relevant information.

经签署的商业发票,至少一式三份,以买方的名义开具,注明商品名称、原产地国及其他信息。

+PACKING LIST IN TRIPLICATE.

装箱单一式三份

+CERTIFICATE OF ORIGIN CERTIFIED BY competent authority

权威机构出具的原产地证明

+FULL SET (3/3) OF CLEAN ' ON BOARD ' OCEAN BILLS OF LADING

MADE OUT TO order, blank endorsed MARKED FREIGHT PREPAID AND NOTIFY APPLICANT.

全套清洁已装船海运提单,空白抬头,空白背书,注明运费预付,通知人开证申请人。

+ INSURANCE POICY/CERTIFICATE, BLANK ENDORSED, COVING ALL RISKS AND WAR RISKS, INCLUDING WAREHOUSE TO WAREHOUSE CLAUSE UP TO FINAL DESTINATION AT COLOMBO, FOR 110% INVOICE VALUE, SHOWING CLAIMS PAYABLE IN COLOMBO.

保险单或保险凭证,空白背书,以发票金额的110%投保一切险和战争险,包括仓至仓条款,运至最终目的地哥伦比亚,,标明赔付在哥伦比亚办理。

2. SWIFT 信用证简介

SWIFT 全称为 Society for Worldwide Inter-bank Financial Telecommunicate(环球同业银行金融电讯协会),是国际银行同业间的国际合作组织,成立于1973年,目前全球大多数国家大多数银行已使用 SWIFT 系统。SWIFT 的使用,使银行的结算提供了安全、可靠、快捷、标准化、自动化的通讯业务,从而大大提高了银行的结算速度。由于 SWIFT 的格式具有标准化,目前信用证的格式主要都是用 SWIFT 电文。

SWIFT 信用证是指凡通过 SWIFT 系统开立或予以通知的信用证。采用 SWIFT 信用证必须遵守 SWIFT 的规定,也必须使用 SWIFT 信用证手册规定的代号(Tag),而且信用证必须遵循国际商会的《跟单信用证同意惯例》各项条款的规定。SWIFT 信用证的特点是快速、准确、简明、可靠。

(1) SWIFT 信用证电文常用项目

① 项目表示方式。SWIFT 由项目(FIELD)组成,例如,59 BENEFICIARY(受益人),就是一个项目,59 是项目的代号,可以是两位数字表示,也可以两位数字加上字母来表示,如 51a APPLICANT(申请人)。不同的代号,表示不同的含义。项目还规定了一定的格式,各种 SWIFT 电文都必须按照这种格式表示。

在 SWIFT 电文中,一些项目是必选项目(MANDATORY FIELD),一些项目是可选项目(OPTIONAL FIELD),必选项目是必须要具备的。

例如,31D DATE AND PLACE OF EXPIRY(信用证有效期),可选项目是另外增加的项目,并不一定每个信用证都有的。

如:39B MAXIMUM CREDIT AMOUNT(信用证最大限制金额)。

② 日期表示方式 。SWIFT 电文的日期表示为:YYMMDD(年月日)

例如,2018年5月12日,表示为:180512;2017年3月15日,表示为:170315。

③ 数字表示方式。在 SWIFT 电文中,数字不使用分格号,小数点用逗号“,”来表示。

例如,5,152,286.36 表示为:5152286,36;4/5 表示为:0,8;5%表示为:5 PERCENT。

④ 货币表示方式。澳大利亚元:AUD;奥地利元:ATS;比利时法郎:BEF;加拿大元:CAD;人民币元:CNY;

丹麦克朗:DKK;德国马克:DEM;荷兰盾:NLG;芬兰马克:FIM;法国法郎:FRF;美元:USD。

港元:HKD;意大利里拉:ITL;日元:JPY;挪威克朗:NOK;英镑:GBP;瑞典克朗:SEK。

表 2-1　MT700 格式跟单信用证主要内容

Tag 代号	Field Name(栏目名称)
* 27	Sequence of Total(报文页次)
* 40A	Form of Documentary Credit(跟单信用证类别)
* 20	Documentary Credit Number(信用证编号)
23	Reference to pre-advice 预告的编号
31C	Date of Issue(开证日期)
* 40E	Applicable Rules 适用的惯例(一般写 UCP LATEST VERSION)
* 31D	Date and Place of Expiry(信用证的到期日及到期地点)
51a	Applicant bank 开证申请人的银行
* 50	Applicant(开证申请人)
52A	Issuing Bank(开证行)
57A	"Advising through" Bank(通过……银行通知)
* 59	Beneficiary(受益人)
* 32B	Currency Code，Amount(信用证的币种代码与金额)
39A	Percentage Credit Amount(信用证金额允许浮动的范围)
39B	Maximum Credit Amount Tolerance(最高信用证金额)
39C	Additional Amounts Covered(可附加金额)
* 41A	Available With ... By ...(指定的有关银行及信用证的付款方式)
42C	Drafts at ...(汇票付款日期)
42A	Drawee-BIC(汇票付款人——银行代码,用于限制议付信用证)
42D	Drawee(汇票付款人,用于自由议付信用证)
42M	Mixed Payment Details(混合付款指示)
42P	Deferred Payment Details(延迟付款指示)
43P	Partial Shipments(分批装运)
43T	Transshipment(转船)
44A	Loading on Board/Dispatch/Taking in Charge(装船/发运/接受监管地点)[非海运和空运]
44B	Place of Final Destination/For Transportation to .../Place of Delivery(最终目的地/运往……/交货地)[非海运和空运]
44C	Latest Date of Shipment(最迟装运日)
44D	Shipment Period(装运期)
44E	Port of Loading/Airport of Departure(装运港/出发机场)[海运和空运]
44F	Port of Discharge/Airport of Destination(卸货港/目的地机场)[海运和空运]
45A	Description of Goods and/or Services(货物描述)

（续表）

Tag 代号	Field Name(栏目名称)
46A	Documents Required(单据要求)
47A	Additional Conditions(附加条款)
71B	Charges(费用负担)
48	Period for Presentation(交单期限)
* 49	Confirmation Instructions(保兑指示)
53A	Reimbursing Bank(偿付行)
78	Instructions to Paying/Accepting/Negotiating Bank(银行间指示)
72	Sender to Receiver Information(附言)

注:“*”表示必填项目。

2.1.5 能力实训

实训 1 翻译条款

1. Original signed commercial invoice at least in 8 copies issued in the name of the buyer indicating the merchandize, country of origin and any other relevent information.

2. Full set shipping company's clean on board bill(s) of lading marked “freight Prepaid” to order of shipper endorsed to XYZ Bank notifying buyer.

3. MarineInsurance Policies or Certificates in negotiable form, for 110% full invoice coving the risks of W.A. & War as per C.I.C Dated 1/1/1981 with extended cover up to Kuala Lumpur with claim payable in Kuala Lumpur in the currency of draft.

4. Bills of exchange must be negotiated within 15 days from the date of bills of lading but not later than August 8, 2015.

5. We undertake that drafts drawn and presented in conformity with the terms of this credit will be duly honoured.

实训 2 根据信用证填写信用证分析单

SQUENCE OF TOTAL　　*27: 1/1
FORM OF DOC. CREDIT　　*40A: IRREVOCABLE
DOC. CREDIT NUMBER　　*20: 123456
DATE OF ISSUE　　31C: 2012/05/20
EXPIRY　　*31D: 2012/07/15
　　IN COUNTRY OF APPLICANT
APPLICANT　　*50: GAZA PALESTINE MILL
　　P.O. BOX 8961, DUBAI
BENEFICIARY　　*59: JIANGSU HAOYIFA CHEMICAL CO., LTD

NO. 10 TAIPING SOUTH ROAD 210003, CHIAN

AMOUNT　　*32B: USD 30 000.00

POS./NEG. TOL. (%)　　39A: 05/05

AVAILABLE WITH/BY　　*41D: ANY BANK BY NEGOTIATION

DRAFT AT ...　　42C: AT 60 DAYS AFTER SIGHT

DRAWEE　　*42D: HVBKUS55WOORI BANK, NEW YORK

PARTIAL SHIPMENT　　43P: ALLOWED

TRANSSHIPMENT　　43T: NOT ALLOWED

LOADING IN CHARGE　　44A: CHINA PORT

FOR TRANSPORT TO ...　　44B: DUBAI

LATEST DATE OF SHIP.　　44C: 2012/06/30

DESCRIPT. OF GOODS　　45A:

3 000PCS OF ENERGY SAVING LAMP, USD10.00 PER PC AS PER SALES CONTRACT GL0082 DATED MAR. 15, 2012

CIF BUSAN

DOCUMENTS REQUIRED　　46A:

+ SIGNED INVOICE PLUS THREE COPIES EVIDENCING THAT GOODS SHIPPED AND INVOICE FULLY CONFORMED TO THOSE DESCRIBED ON PROFORMA INVOICE NO. 123 DATED MAR. 3, 2012

+FULL SET OF ORIGINAL CLEAN ON BOARD MARINE BILL OF LADING MADE OUT TO SHIPPERS ORDER AND BLANK ENDORSED, MARKED FREIGHT PREPAID AND NOTIFY APPLICANT QUOTING FULL NAME AND ADDRESS.

+ORIGINAL PACKING LIST PLUS THREE COPIES INDICATING DETAILED PACKING OF EACH CARTON

+MARINE INSURANCE POLICY FOR 110PCT OF INVOICE VALUE, BLANK ENDORSED, INDICATING CLAIM PAYABLE AT DESTINATION, COVERING ALL RISKS AND WAR RISKS AS PER AND SUBJECT TO OCEAN MARINE CARGO CLAUSES AND OCEAN MARINE CARGO WAR RISKS CLAUSES OF P. I. C. C. DATED 1/1/1981.

+ORIGINAL CERTIFICATE OF ORIGIN PLUS ONE COPY ISSUED BY CHAMBER OF COMMERCE.

ADDITIONAL COND.　　47A:

+TRADE MARKS MUST BE CLEARLY MENTIONED ON THE INVOICES

+EXCEPT SO FAR AS OTHERWISE EXPRESSLY STATE, THIS DOCUMENTARY CREDIT IS SUBJECT TO UNIFORM CUSTOMS AND PRACTICE FOR DOCUMENTARY CREDIT ICC PUBLICATION NO. 600.

+ALL BANK CHARGES OUTSIDE DUBI ARE FOR THE BENEFICIARY.

PRESENTATION PERIOD 48: WITHIN 15 DAYS AFTER THE DATE OF SHIPMENT BUT WITHIN THE VALIDITY OF THE CREDIT.

CONFIRMATION　　　　　*49: WITHOUT

信用证分析表

1. 信用证文本格式　　□ 信开　　□ 电开　　□ SWIFT
2. 信用证号码
3. 通知银行编号
4. 开证日
5. 到期日
6. 到期地点
7. 兑付方式　　□ 付款　　□ 承兑　　□ 议付
8. 货币
9. 金额(具体数额)　　□未注明
10. 金额允许增减幅度　　□未注明
11. 交单期　　□未注明
12. 开证申请人(名称)
13. 受益人(名称)
14. 开证银行(名称)　　□未注明
15. 通知银行(名称)　　□未注明
16. 议付银行(名称)　　□未注明
17. 付款、偿付银行(名称)　　□未注明
18. 货物名称
19. 合同/订单/形式发票号码　　□未注明
20. 价格/交货/贸易术语
21. 最迟装运日
22. 装运港
23. 目的地
24. 分批装运　　□ 允许　　□ 不允许
25. 转运　　□ 允许　　□ 不允许
26. 运输标志
27. 运输方式　　□ 海运　　□ 空运　　□ 陆运
28. 向银行提交的单据列表(用阿拉伯数字表示)

名称	汇票	发票	装箱单	重量单	尺码单	海运提单	空运提单	货物承运收据	原产地证明	保险单
份数										

名称	检验书	装船通知	寄单通知	受益人证明(其他内容)	承运人/船公司证明	其他单据原包装清单
份数						

实训 3　根据上述信用证选择正确的答案

1. 这张信用证是由(　　)开立的。
   A. 开证行　B. 议付行　C. 通知行
2. 这张信用证的类型是(　　)。
   A. 不可撤销保兑信用证　B. 不可撤销议付信用证　C. 即期付款信用证
3. GAZA PALESTINE MILL 是信用证的(　　)。
   A. 开证申请人　B. 受益人　C. 开证银行
4. 该信用证规定到达的目的港为(　　)。
   A. 没有规定　B. 巴黎　C. 迪拜
5. 这张信用证项下对汇票的要求为(　　)。
   A. 必须提交汇票　B. 无须提交汇票　C. 禁止提交汇票
6. 根据这张信用证,出口运费应在(　　)支付。
   A. 到目的港后由进口商　B. 到目的港后由进口商　C. 离起运港前由出口商
7. 这份信用证中向银行提交的单据有(　　)种。
   A. 4 种　B. 5 种　C. 6 种
8. 这张信用证中规定受益人提交的原产地证明为(　　)。
   A. 商会出具的原产地证明
   B. 贸促会出具的原产地证明
   C. 受益人出具的原产地证明
9. 按照这张信用证的规定,由(　　)承担单据不符点的费用。
   A. 议付行　B. 开证申请人　C. 受益人
10. 这张信用证规定提单上的收货人是(　　)。
    A. 由出口商指定　B. 进口商代理　C. 进口商
11. 这张信用证规定提单上的通知人是(　　)。
    A. 卖方　B. 买方的代理　C. 买方
12. 信用证要求发票上的货物描述应与(　　)一致。
    A. 合同规定　B. 形式发票　C. 买方订单
13. 信用证规定的到期地点为(　　)。
    A. 通知行柜台前　B. 开证人所在国　C. 受益人所在国家
14. 根据这份信用证可以判断出(　　)。
    A. 金额有溢短装　B. 保险由买方办理
15. 这张信用证规定受益人向银行提交的单据的期限为(　　)。
    A. 信用证签发后 15 天　B. 提单签发后 21 天　C. 提单签发后 15 天
16. 这张信用证规定提交发票的份数(　　)。
    A. 三份副本　B. 三份正本　C. 以上说法都不对
17. 这张信用证对货物运输的规定为(　　)。
    A. 允许分运,不允许转运　B. 不允许分运,允许转运　C. 不允许分运和转运
18. Trade Marks 在(　　)上显示。

A. 提单　　　　B. 装箱单　　　　C. 发票　　　　D. 原产地证

19. 一张有效的信用证必须规定一个(　　)。

A. 有效期　　　　B. 装运期　　　　C. 交单期　　　　D. 议付期

20. 信用证规定的有效期是 2012/08/20,而未规定装运期,则可理解最迟装运期为(　　)。

A. 2012/08/01　　　　B. 2012/08/30　　　　C. 2012/08/05　　　　D. 2012/08/20

21. 下列说法中,正确的(　　)。

A. 这份商业发票不需要签字

B. 向银行提交的单据必须是清洁提单

C. 装箱单上需注明货物的单价和总价

D. 信用证没有明确规定,装箱单可以无须签字

任务 2.2　审核信用证

2.2.1　学习目标

知识目标:根据外贸合同审核信用证中的问题条款并提出修改意见。

能力目标:掌握信用证审证的依据和步骤,熟悉审证的原则。

2.2.2　工作任务

无锡蓝天进出口公司(WUXI BLUE SKY IMP&EXP. Co., LTD.)收到国外加拿大 KU TEXTILE CORPORATION 通过开证行开来的信用证。单证员小郭根据合同及相关外贸知识认真阅读了合同和信用证。

在本任务中,单证员应完成以下内容:

① 能根据合同审核信用证中的问题条款。

② 能针对问题条款提出相应的修改意见。

SALES CONTRACT

NO.: K123

DATE: APR..9,2015

THE SELLER:

WUXIBLUE SKY IMP&EXP. Co., LTD.

NO.53 ZHONGSHAN ROAD, WUXI, CHINA

THE BUYER:

KU TEXTILE CORPORATION

430 VTRA MONTREAL CANADA

THIS SALES CONTRACR IS MADE BY AND BETWEEN THE SELLERS AND THE BUYERS, WHERE THE SELLERS AGREE TO SELL AND THE BUYERS AGREE TO BUY THE UNDER MENTIONED GOODS ACCORDING TO THE TERMS AND CONDITIONS STIPULATE BELOW:

COMMODITY & SPECIFICATION	QUANTITY	UNIR PRICE	AMOUNT
GIRL DRESS 100%COTTON ARTICLE NO. 11574 11575 11576 11577	 2 400PCS 3 000PCS 2 400PCS 1 600PCS	CIF MONTREAL USD 6.50/PC USD 5.50/PC USD 8.50/PC USD 8.00/PC	 USD 15 600.00 USD 16 500.00 USD 20 400.00 USD 12 800.00
TOTAL	9 400PCS		USD 65 300.00

TOTAL AMOUNT IN WORDS

SAY US DOLLARS SIXTY FIVE THOUSAND THREE HUNDRED ONLY

MORE OR LESS 5% OF THE QUANTITY AND AMOUT ARE ALLOWED.

PACKING:

EACH PIECE IN A POLYBAG, 40 PIECES TO ONE EXPORT STANDARD CARTON.

SHIPPING MARKS:

KU
K123
MONTREAL
C/N: 1-UP

SHIPMENT

PORT OF LOADING: SHANGHAI
PORT OF DESTINATION: MONTREAL
TRANSHIPMENT: ALLOWED
PARTIAL SHIPMENTS: ALLOWED
TIME OF SHIPMENT: BEFORE JULY 31, 2015

INSURANCE

THE SELLER SHOULD COVER INSURANCE FOR 110% OF FULL INVOICE VALUE COVING ALL RISKS AS PER CIC OF PICC DATED 01/01/1981.

PAYMENT

THE BUYER SHOULD OPEN A BANK ACCEPTABLE TO THE SELLER AN IRREVOCABLE L/C PAYABLE AT 30 DAYS AFTER SIGHT, TO REACH THE SELLER BEFORE MAY 31TH, 2015, VALID FOR NEGOTIATION IN CHINA UNTIL THE 15TH DAY AFTER THE DATE OF SHIPMENT.

INSPECTION&CLAIM

THE SELLER SHALL HAVE THE PERFORMANCE AND QUALITIES, SPECIFICATIONS, QUANTITIES OF THE GOODS CAREFULLY INSPECTED AND ISSUE INSPECTION CERTIFICATE BEFORE SHIPMENT. ANY CLAIM BY THE BUYER REGARDING THE GOODS SHIPPED SHOULD BE FILED WITHIN 30DAYS AFTER THE ARRIVALS OF THE GOODS AT THE PORT/PLACE OF DESTINATION SPECIFIED IN THE RELATIVE BILL OF LADING OR TRANSPORT DOCUMENT AND SUPPORTED BY A SURVEY REPORT ISSUED BY A SURVEY APPROVED BY THE SELLER. CLAIMS IN RESPECT OF MATTERS WITHIN RESPONSIBILITY OF INSURANCE COMPANY, SHIPPING COMPANY/OTHER TRANSPORTATION ORGANIZATION WILL NOT BE CONSIDERED OR ENTERTAINED BY THE SELLER.

FORCE MAJUSE:

IF THE SHIPMENT OF CONTRACTED GOODS IS PREVENTED OR DELAYS IN WHOLE OR IN PART BY REASON OF WAR, EARTHQUAKE, FIRE, FLOOD, HEAVY SNOW, STORM OR OTHER CAUSES OF FORCE MAJUSE, THE SELLER SHALL NOT BE LIABLE FOR NON-SHIPMENT OR LATE SHIPMENT OF THE GOODS OF THIS CONTRACT. HOWEVER, THE SELLER SHALL NOTIFY THE BUYERS BY CABLE OR TELEX AND FURNISH THE LETTER WITHIN 15DAYS BY REGISTERED AIRMAIL WITH A CERTIFICATE ISSUED BY THE CHINA COUNCIL FOR THE PROMOTION OF INTERNATIONAL TRADE ATTESTING SUCH EVENT OR EVENTS.

ARBITRATION:

ALL DISPUTED ARISING OUT OF PERFORMANCE OF, OR RELATING TO THIS CONTRACT, SHALL BE SETTLED AMICABLY THROUGH FRIENDLY NEGOTIATION. IN CASE NO SETTLEMENT CAN BE REACHED THROUGH NEGOTIATION, THE CASE SHALL THEN BE SUBMITTED FOR ARBITRATION, THE LOCATION OF ARBITRATION SHALL BE IN THE COUNTRY OF THE DOMICILE OF THE DEFENDANT. IF IN CHINA, THE ARBITRATION SHALL BE CONDUCTED BY THE RULES OF ARBITRATION. THE ARBITRAL AWARD IS FINAL AND BINDING UPON BOTH PARTIES. THE CHARGES ARISING FROM THE ARBITRATION SHALL BE UNDERTAKEN BY THE LOSING PARTY.

Signed by:

THE SELLER	THE BUYER
WUXIBLUE SKY IMP&EXP. Co., LTD.	KU TEXTILE CORPORATION
李 立	Jac

MT 700	ISSUE OF A DOCUMENTARY CREDIT
SENDER	HSBC BANK PLC, MONTREAL, CANADA
RECEIVE	RBANK OF CHINA, WUXI BRANCH, CHINA
SEQUENCE OF TOTAL	27: 1/1
FORM OF DOC. CREDIT	40A: IRREVOCABLE
DOC. CREDIT NUMBER	20: 123456
DATE OF ISSUE	31C:150520
APPLICABLE RULES	40E: UCP LATEST VERSION
DATE AND PLACE OF EXPIRY	31D: 150815 IN CANADA
APPLICANT	50: KU TEXTILE CORPORATION 430 VTRA MONTREAL CANADA
BENEFICIARY	59: WUXI BLUE SKY IMP&EXP. Co., LTD NO.53 ZHONGSHAN ROAD, WUXI, CHINA
AMOUNT	32B: USD 66 020.00
AVAILABLE WITH/BY	41D: ANY BANK IN CHINA, BY NEGOTIATION
DRAFTS AT ...	42C: AT 60 DAYS AFTER SIGHT
DRAWEE	42A: KU TEXTILE CORPORATION
PARTIAL SHIPMENT	43P: ALLOWED
TRANSSHIPMENT	43T: ALLOWED
PORT OF LOADING/AIRPORT OF DEPARTURE	44E:CHINESE MAIN PORT
PORT OF DISCHARGE	44F: MONTREAL, CANADA
LATEST DATE OF SHIPMENT	44C: 150715

DESCRIPTION OF GOODS AND/OR SERVICES. 45A:

9 400 PIECES GIRL DRESS 100% COTTON

AS PER S/C NO.123

STYLE NO.	QUANTITY	UNIT PRICE	AMOUNT
11754	2 400PCS	USD6.80/PC	USD16 320.00
11575	3 000PCS	USD5.50/PC	USD16 500.00
11576	2 400PCS	USD8.50/PC	USD20 400.00
11577	1 600PCS	USD8.00/PC	USD12 800.00

CIF MONTREAL, CANADA

DOCUMENTS REQUIRED 46A:

+SIGNED COMMERCIAL INVOICE IN DUPLICATE CERTIFYING GOODS OF CHINA ORIGIN.

+PACKING LIST IN THREE FOLDS SHOWING G.W., N.W., AND MEAS. OF EACH PACKGE.

+G.S.P. CERTIFICATE OF ORIGIN FORM A IN DUPLICATE BY CIQ.

+CERTIFICATE OF QUALITY ISSUED BY CIQ IN DUPLICATE.

+FULL SET OF CLEAN ' ON BOARD ' OCEAN BILLS OF LADING MADE OUT TO APPLICANTAND BLANK ENDORSED MARKED FREIGHT PREPAID AND NOTIFY APPLICANT.

+INSURANCE POLICY OR CERTIFICATE ENDORSED IN BLANK FOR 150 PCT OF INVOICE VALUE, COVERING ALL RISKS AND WAR RISK SUBJECT TO THE RELEVANT OCEAN MARINE CLAUSE OF THE PEOPLE'S INSURANCE COMPANY OF CHINA, DATED 1/1/1981.

+SHIPPING ADVICE SHOWING THE NAME OF THE CARRYING VESSEL, DATE OF SHIPMENT, MARKS, QUANTITY, NET WEIGHT AND GROSS WEIGHT OF THE SHIPMENT TO APPLICANT WITHIN 3 DAYS AFTER THE DATE OF BILL OF LADING.

+BENEFICIARY'S CERTIFICATE CERTIFYING THAT ONE SET OF COPIES OF SHIPPING DOCUMENTS HAS BEEN SENT TO APPLICANT WITHIN 7 DAYS AFTER SHIPMENT.

+CERTIFICATE TO EVDIENT TO EVIDENCE THE SHIP IS NOT OVER 15 YEARS OLD.

ADDITIONAL CONDITION 47A:

+DOCUMENTS DATED PRIOR TO THE DATE OF THIS CREDIT ARE NOT ACCEPTABLE.

+THE NUMBER AND THE DATE OF THIS CREDIT AND THE NAME OF ISSUING BANK MUST BE QUOTED ON ALL DOCUMENTS.

+TRANSSHIPMENT ALLOWED AT HONGKONG ONLY.

+SHORT FORM/CHARTER PARTY/THIRD PARTY BILL OF LADING ARE NOT ACCEPTABLE.

+SHIPMENT MUST BE EFFECTED BY 1 ×20′ FULL CONTAINER LOAD. B/L TO SHOW EVIDENCE OF THIS EFFECT IS REQUIRED.

+ALL PRESENTATIONS CONTAINING DISCREPANCIES WILL ATTRACT A DISCREPANCY FEE OF USD50.00 PLUS TELEX COSTS OR OTHER CURRENCY EQUIVALENT. THIS CHARGE WILL BE DEDUCTED FROM THE BILL AMOUNT WHETHER OR NOT WE ELECT TO CONSULT THE APPLICANT FOR A WAIVER.

+ THE CREDIT IS NON-OPERATIVE UNLESS THE BUYER OBTAINTHE IMPORT LICENSE.
CHARGES 71B: ALL CHARGES AND COMMISSIONS OUTSIDE CANADA ARE FOR BENEFICIARY'S ACCOUNT.
PERIOD FOR PRESENTATION 48: WITHIN 5 DAYS AFTER THE DATE OF SHIPMENT, BUT WITHIN THE VALIDITY OF THIS CREDIT.
CONFIRMATION INSTRUCTION 49: WITHOUT
INFORMATION TO PRESENTING BANK 78:
ALL DOCUMENTS ARE TO BE REMITTED IN ONE LOT BY COURIER TO HSBC BANK
PLC, TRADE SERVICES, MONTREAL BRANCH, P O BOX 66, HSBC BANK BUILDING
312/45 Al SUQARE ROAD, MONTREAL, CANADA

2.2.3　操作范例

第一步:对照 K123 合同号审核 123456 号信用证。审核发现有多处错误(见表 2-2)

表 2-2 信用证审核记录

信用证证号	**123456**	合同号	**123**	开证日期	**150620**
开证行	HSBC BANK PLC,MONTREAL				
开证人	KU TEXTILE CORPORATION				
受益人	WUXI BLUE SKY IMP&EXP. CO. LTD				
信用证性质	不可撤销	金额	US **65 300.00**	索汇方式	议付
装运期	不迟于 **150715**	信用证有效期	**150920**	到期地点	加拿大
装运港	中国港口	目的港	MONTREAL	是否分批	不允许
贸易术语	CIF	汇票期限	AT**60** DAYS AFTER SIGHT	是否转运	允许
交单期	提单日后 **5** 天交单,信用证有效期内	汇票付款人	HSBC BANK PLC, MONTREAL	唛头	未规定
提单	抬头	TO APPLICANT	保险	险别	ALL RISKS
	通知	APPLICANT		保险加成率	**50%**
	运费	PREPAID		赔款地点/币种	MONTREAL/USD
	背书	空白背书			

（续表）

特殊条款	1. 所有单据都要用英文制作。 2. 所有单据都要显示信用证号码。 3. 只允许在香港转运。

单据总类及分类	商业发票	形式发票	装箱单	重量单	尺码单	保险单	提单正本	提单副本	原产地证	GSP产地证	品质证明	寄单证明	寄样证明	受益人证明	装船通知	其他
	2		3			2	3	3		2	2			1	1	1

存在内容	修改建议	修改理由
31D 到期地点 CANADA	IN CHINA	原则上不接受国外到期
42C 汇票付款期限错误 AT 60 DAYS SIGHT	AT 30 DAYS SIGHT	与合同不相符
32B 总金额错误 USD66 020.00	USD65 300.00	与合同不相符
42A 汇票付款人错误 KU TEXTILE CORPORATION	ISSUING BANK OR NOMINATED BANK	信用证的付款人为开证行或开证行指定的银行
44C 最迟装运日期	JULY 31, 2015	与合同不相符
45A 合同号错误	123	K123
45A 单价 USD6.80/PC USD16 320.00	USD6.50/PC USD15 600.00	与合同不相符
46A 投保加成 150%	110%	与合同不相符
46A 提单抬头 TO APPLICANT	TO ORDER	对受益人不利
48 信用证交单期限 Within 5 Days After The Date Of Shipment	Within 15 Days After The Date Of Shipment	与合同不相符
47A 特殊条款中第 7 条 THE CREDIT IS NON-OPERATIVE UNLESS THE BUYER OBTAINTHE IMPORT LICENSE	删除	属于暂不生效条款，属于软条款

第二步：核对信用证，有无信用证漏开的合同条款

通过审核，信用证漏开的一个重要条款："MORE OR LESS 5 PCT OF QUANTITY OF GOODS AND CREDIT AMOUNT IS ALLOWED."

第三步：确定改证的内容

遵循"利己不损人"原则，对审核出的上述问题条款分别按五种方式处理。

① 对我方有利，又不影响对方利益，一般不改。

例如，信用证装运港为"CHINESE MAIN PORT"，与合同中"SHANGHAI, CHIAN"不一致。但信用证中的中国主港包括上海港，可增加受益人选择范围，对我方有利，又不影响对方利益。

② 对我方有利，但会严重影响对方利益，一定要改。

例如，信用证单价条款“USD 6.8/PC”与金额“USD16 320.00”错误，正确的是“USD 6.5/PC”与金额“USD15 600.00”，这会使对方遭受 720 美元的损失。作为一名合格的业务员，应该诚信待人，不能因贪图 720 元便宜而做失去客户信任的事，如果业务员向对方提醒多算了交易金额，一定会赢得客户的敬意和肯定。

③ 对我方不利，但在基本不增加成本的情况下可以完成，可以不改。

例如，信用证规定只能在香港转运，与合同规定不符。但结合实际运输情况，我们不需要转运，不受影响，不需要改。

④ 对我方不利，且在增加较大成本的情况下可以完成，若对方愿意承担成本，则不改；否则，则必须改。

例如，信用证中汇票“AT 30 DAYS AFTER SIGHT”错误，正确的是“AT 60 DAYS AFTER SIGHT”信用证中保险条款的投保金额“150% INVOICE VALUE”错误，正确的是“110% INVOICE VALUE”。

⑤ 对我方不利，若不改会严重影响收汇安全，必须改。

例如，信用证提单条款中收货人抬头“TO APLICANT”对受益人不利，应改为“TO ORDER”。

第四步：发出信用证修改函

Dear Mr. Smith,

Thank you very much for your L/C No. 123456. However, upon checking, we have found the following discrepancies and would appreciate it very much if you could make the necessary amendments.

We have received your L/C, but we find it contains the following discrepancies

1. The place of expiry amends to “IN CHINA”

2. The amount of the credit should be USD65 300 instead of USD66 020.00.

3. The tenor of draft is “At 60 Days After Sight” instead of “At 30 Days After Sight”.

4. Drawee should be issuing bank or nominated bank.

5. Extend latest date of shipment of the L/C till 150731 instead of 150715.

6. The price and amount of No. 11754 should be USD6.50/PC and USD USD15 600.00 not USD6.80/PC and USD16 320.00.

7. Please amend Bills of Lading made out to applicant to made out to order

8. The amount insured is 110% of invoice value, not“150% invoice value.

Please amend INSURANCE POLICY/CERTIFICATE FOR 150% OF INVOICE VALUE TO 110% OF INVOICE.

9. Delete the clause “THE CREDIT IS NON-OPERATIVE UNLESS THE BUYER OBTAIN THE IMPORT LICENSE”.

10. Period for presentation should be “Within 15 DAYS AFTER THE DATE OF SHIPMENT.

11. To add the clause “MORE OR LESS 5 PCT OF QUANTITY OF GOODS AND

CREDIT AMOUNT IS ALLOWED.

As the good have been ready for shipment for quite some time, you are requested to rush amendments to the covering L/C as soon as possible, thus facilitaing our execution of your order.

We look forward to receiving the relevant amendment at an early date and thank you in advance.

THANK YOU
YOURS TRULY
GUO XIAOFANG

2.2.4 知识链接

出口商审核信用证主要是依据进出口合同，以及国际惯例、《UCP600》及其进口国的相关法律法规。审核信用证的主要依据见表 2-3。

表 2-3 审核信用证的主要依据

	信用证具体内容	信用证条款及与之对应的合同条款	审核重点
信用证本身的说明	(1) SEQUENCE OF TOTAL		页码是否齐全
	(2) FORM OF DOC. CREDIT		《UCP600》已取消可撤销信用证
	(3) DOC. CREDIT NUMBER		每份证应该有唯一证号
	(4) AMOUNT	对应合同中的总金额	金额与合同是否相符 币种与合同是否相符 如有大小写是否相符 佣金、折扣是否包含在总金额中 溢短装是否使用金额中
	(5) DATE OF ISSUE		是否按照合同约定的期限开出信用证
	(6) LATEST DATE OF SHIPMENT		装运期是否与合同规定相符 如提前视具体情况考虑接受否
	(7) PERIOD FOR PRESENTATION		一般装船后 10～15 天为宜
	(8) DATE AND PLACE OF EXPIRY		一般比装运期晚 10～15 天为宜原则上不接受在国外到期
	(9) AVAILABLE WITH/BY	根据合同的支付条款	最好是议付信用证 最好不是付款信用证
信用证当事人	(10) APPLICANT	对应合同中的买方	公司名称和地址都要核对
	(11) BENEFICIARY	对应合同中的卖方	公司名称和地址都要核对

(续表)

	信用证具体内容	信用证条款及与之对应的合同条款	审核重点
	(12) ADVISING BANK		通知行最好与受益人在同一地址
	(13) NEGOTIATING BANK		一般自由议付
汇票条款	(14) DRAWER	对应合同中的卖方	
	(15) PAYEE	对应合同中的卖方或议付行	
	(16) DRAWEE	对应信用证中的开证行或指定银行	付款人不能是开证申请人
	(17) TENOR	对应合同中的支付条款	汇票的付款期限是否与合同中的付款期限相符
	(18) DRAWN UNDER	出票依据	通常包括开证行、证号和开证日期
货物描述	(19) COMMODITY NAME	对应合同的品名条款	品名是否正确
	(20) SPECIFICATION	对应合同的品质条款	
	(21) QUANTITY	对应合同的数量条款	数量是否与合同相符 是否有溢短装
	(22) UNIT PRICE	对应合同的价格条款	单价是否正确 币种是否正确 计量是否正确 贸易术语是否正确
	(23) SHIPING MARK		没有唛头,N/M 合同中有唛头,按合同填写
	(24) DETAILS AS PER	对应合同号和合同日期	引用的合同号是否与买、卖双方签订的合同相符; 引用的合同日期是否与实际合同相同
装运条款	(25) PORT OF LOADING	对应合同的装运条款	装运港是否与合同相符 来证规定“CHINA MAIN PORT”无须改证
	(26) PORT OF DISCHARGE	对应合同的装运条款	目的港是否与合同相符 注意世界上重名港问题,应注明国别
	(27) PARTIAL SHIPMENT	对应合同的装运条款	考虑实际情况 若合同规定禁止分批装运,而来证允许,无须改证
	(28) TRANSSHIPMENT	对应合同的装运条款	若合同规定禁止转运,而来证允许,无须改证

（续表）

	信用证具体内容	信用证条款及与之对应的合同条款	审核重点
单据条款	(29) COMMERCIAL INVOICE		若要求开证人签署或会签要删除
	(30) PACKING LIST		若要求开证人签署或会签要删除
	(31) BILLS OF LADING		1/3 正本提单自寄需修改 运费支付情况与贸易术语矛盾需修改
	(32) CERTIFICAT OF ORIGIN		签发单位是否接受 是否需要领事馆认证
	(33) INSURANCE POLICY	对应合同的保险条款	投保加成是否与合同规定相符 投保险别是否与合同规定相符 依据的保险条款及其版本年份是否一致 ICC 中的险别是否与 CIC 中险别同时出现在保险条款中
	(34) OTHER CERTIFICATE		所要求证明是否能够自行出具，如需第三方能否保证及时签发
	(35) SPECIAL CERTIFICATE	对应合同的备注	特殊合同是否已单据化，若有，是否能够保证及时签发； 重点审核是否含有软条款

审核信用证的要点

1. 信用证审核的主体：通知行与受益人

(1) 通知行的责任是审核信用证的表面真实性。

① 从政策上审核——是否与我国有往来；

② 对开证行的经营作风和资信情况进行审查；

③ 索汇路线是否合理；

④ 对信用证性质和开证行付款责任的审查；

⑤ 审核信用证的印鉴、密押是否相符；

⑥ 审核信用证条款之间是否相互矛盾。

(2) 受益人审证依据是根据买卖合同、遵循《UCP600》和外贸经验。

2. 受益人审证的步骤

① 熟悉买卖合同条款。

② 根据合同逐条审核信用证各条款。

③ 列出问题条款。

3. 受益人信用证审核的要点

(1) 信用证自身性质的审核

① 是否为不可撤销的信用证。

a. 信用证明确表明是 revocable credit，因为 revocable credit 无须通知受益人或未经受益人同意可以随时撤销或修改，对受益人来讲，付款是没有保证的。因此，对于 revocable credit 一般不能接受。

b. 若信用证未表明可撤销，按照《UC600》规定，应理解为不可撤销。

② 是否为保兑信用证。若合同规定为不可撤销的保兑信用证，则应检查信用证内有无注明“保兑(Confirmed)”字样、保兑行行名及保兑行明确的保兑条款和声明。例如，This credit is confirmed by ×× bank。

(2) 关于时间与地点的审核

① 装运日期。装运期必须与合同规定一致，如国外来证晚，无法按期装运，应及时电请国外买方延展装运期限。信用证有效期一般应与装运期有一定的合理间隔，以便装运货物后有足够的时间办理制单结汇手续。如果信用证中的最迟未规定装运期，可理解为双到期(信用证的有效期与装运期是同一天)，在这种情况下，受益人不可能在信用证规定的最迟装运日进行装运，而必须将装运期提前一定时间(一般在到期日的 10～15 天)，以便腾出合理的时间来制单结汇，否则，应要求修改到期日。

② 交单日期。

a. 若信用证规定交单日，按信用证规定交单。例如：

PEROID FOR PRESENTATION　48

Documents must be presented within 15 days after the date of shipment, but within the validity of the credit.

b. 信用证无规定，银行将不予接受迟于装运日期后 21 天提交的单据。

小贴士

根据《UCP600》第 14 条的规定，除规定一个交单到期日外，凡要求提交运输单据的信用证，尚需规定一个在装运日后按信用证规定必须交单的特定期限，如未规定该期限，银行将不予接受迟于装运日期后 21 天提交的单据。但无论如何，提交单据不得迟于信用证的到期日。

③ 付款期。付款期分为即期和远期之分，合同中都有明确规定，信用证的付款期必须与合同一致。

如果信用证中规定有关款项必须在向银行交单后若干天或见票后若干天内付款，那么需要核对此类付款时间是否符合合同的规定。

④ 信用证的有效期。信用证的有效期是受益人向银行提交单据的最后日期，受益人应在有效期限日期之前或当天向银行提交信用证单据。

开动脑筋

最迟装运期与信用证的有效期应相隔一段时间，为什么不宜太长，也不宜太短？

⑤ 信用证最好规定在卖方所在国到期。如果规定在国外到期这意味着有关单据必须寄到国外。由于受益人无法掌握单据到达国外银行所需的时间，容易造成延误或丢失，有一定的风险，因此通常受益人应要求在国内交单、到期。如果确实来不及修改，则必须要求寄单行提前一个邮程，以最快的方式寄送单据。

(3) 当事人的审核

受益人的名称和地址是否与合同的卖方名称和地址(包括传真、电话号码等)完全一致，否则就要要求修改。开证申请人的名称和地址写法是否完全一致。

(4) 运输条款的审核

① 装运港、目的港是否与合同相符；

② 是否允许分批装运。如果信用证没有明确规定，应理解为货物是允许分批装运的。如果信用证中还规定了每一批货物出运的确切时间，则必须按此办理；如无法做到，则应立即要求修改。如果信用证中规定了分批装运的时间和数量，应注意能否悉数办到；否则，如果任何一批未能按期装运，以后各期即告失效。

③ 是否允许转运。除非信用证另有规定，货物是允许转运的。

④ 能否在信用证规定的装运期内备妥有关货物并按期出运。如果到证时间与装运期太近，无法如期装运，就应及时与开证申请人联系修改。逾期装运的运输单据将构成单证不符，银行有权不付款。

小贴士

《UCP600》第32条　分期直款或分期发运

如信用证规定在指定的时间段内分期支款或分期发运，任何一期未按信用证规定期限支取或发运时，信用证对该期及以后各期均告失效。

(5) 货物条款的审核

出现的合同号、品名、规格、型号、数量、单价、总价、包装、贸易术语等信息，要与合同完全一致；否则要求修改。

信用证对货物的描述，包括货物的名称、规格、型号、包装、数量、单价、总价及所使用的贸易术语等。它是受益人交货和制单的基本内容，必须合同完全一致，不能有丝毫差错。有时，货物描述比较复杂，信用证也可以用统称，并应用相关的合同或订单来代替复杂的货物描述，此时受益人应注意信用证所使用的货物的统称不能与合同相矛盾，引用的合同号、订单号等不能有错。有时信用证可能将货物描述拼错，如果拼写错误并不影响单词或句子的含义，受益人可以接受，但如果是规格型号的拼写错误则不能接受。

(6) 信用证的金额和币种的审核

① 信用证的金额是否与事先协商的相一致。

② 信用证的单价与总值是否准确，大、小写是否一致。

③ 如果合同规定数量上允许有一定的伸缩幅度，那么信用证应允许支付金额有相应的增减幅度。

④ 检查币种是否正确。如合同规定的货币币种是 USD，而信用证上的货币币种却写成 JPY，就应该修改。

《UCP 600》第 30 条　信用证金额、数量与单价的增减幅度

a. "约"或"大约"用于信用证金额或信用证规定的数量或单价时，应解释为允许有关金额或数量或单价有不超过 10%的增减幅度。

b. 在信用证未以包装单位件数或货物自身件数的方式规定货物数量时，货物数量允许有 5%的增减幅度，只要总支取金额不超过信用证金额。

c. 如果信用证规定了货物数量，而该数量已全部发运，及如果信用证规定了单价，而该单价又未降低，或当第 30 条 b 款不适用时，则即使不允许部分装运，也允许支取的金额有 5%的减幅。若信用证规定有特定的增减幅度或使用第 30 条 a 款提到的用语限定数量，则该减幅不适用。

(7) 信用证中的数量是否与合同规定一致

① 除非信用证规定的数量不得有增减，那么在支付金额不超过信用证金额的情况下，货物数量可以允许有 5%的增减。

② 以上提到的货物数量的增减规定仅适用于大宗散装货物，对于包装单位或以个体为计算单位的货物不适用。

(8) 审核单据条款是否合理

单据条款是约束卖方按要求履行合同的凭据，内容包括信用证要求受益人提交的单据名称及制度要求，也是银行审单的依据。如果它的规定不合理，受益人将无法获取相应的单据，从而不能完成交代义务，或者获取单据的成本过高，即使完成的交单义务，也使预期利润大大减少。因此受益人应注意审核单据的出单人、单据的内容要求等，注意单据的获取成本、耗时长短等以及寄送方式、寄送对象等。

(9) 审核银行费用的分摊是否合理

信用证项下的银行费用可能有开证费、通知费、修改费、保兑费、议付费、承兑费、邮费、电报费、不符点费等，这些费用应该由受益人和申请人共同分摊，一般发生在开证行的费用由申请人承担，在开证行之外的费用由受益人承担。受益人审证应注意这些费用的分摊是否合理，以免承担不必要的银行费用。

(10) 审核信用证中是否有软条款

信用证方式对受益人较为有利，只要做到"相符提示"，就能安全、及时收取货款。但是由于开证行和开证申请人是在未获取货物的情况下就必须见单付款或承兑，具有一定的风险。所以，他们常常会开立一些附有软条款的信用证，以图最大限度地掌握主动权。软条款是指主动权掌握在开证申请人手中，受益人无法控制的条款；或意思含糊不清、模棱两可的条款，往往会给受益人安全收汇造成相当大的困难和风险。因此，对于卖方来说，采用信用证方式结算，有如下情况者必须谨慎对待：

① 控制信用证生效的条款。

"This credit will become operative provided that the necessary authorization be obtained from exchange authority, we shall inform you as soon as the authorization obtained."（本信用证必须从外汇当局获批授权书后方能生效，待获得授权书立即通知你方）和"This documentary credit will become effective provided you received the authorization."（本信用证在你收到授权书后方能生效）。

② 客检条款。

如："Inspection certificate issued and signed by two experts nominated by the applicant, the specimen signatures of the individual who were authorized to sign the certificate were kept by us."（检验证书由申请人指定的两名专家出具并签名，该签名的样本由开证行保存）。此类条款往往要求发票、检验证书等由进口国特定的机构或人员签字或出具。如果申请人指定的人员不出具并签署单据或证书，则受益人无法交单，即使指定人员出具并签署了要求的单据或证书，由于受益人手中并没有指定人员签名的样本，无法判断提交的单据或证书会不会被开证行以签名不符而拒付。

③ 正本提单全部或部分直寄客户。

1/3 original Bill of Lading should be sent directly to the applicant by courier service within 3 working days after shipment（三份正本提单中的一份在装船后 3 天之内直接寄给开证申请人）。

④ 限制开证行付款责任。

The opening bank is obliged to payment only after goods are shipped to the port of destination.

开动脑筋

我方向美国出口一批货物，合同规定 shipment before Aug. 15th, 2015。然而经与船公司联系，得知 8 月 15 日前无船去美国，我方即要求外商将船期延至 9 月 15 日，随后美商来电，同意展延，有效期也顺延 1 个月。9 月 10 日，我方装船完毕，14 日持全套单据向银行议付，银行拒收单据，拒付货款，为什么？

修改信用证的要点

1. 修改信用证的程序(见图2-1)

① 出口商作为受益人审核信用证后,发现有些信用证条款需要修改,通过传真、邮件等方式通知开证人。

② 开证申请人向开证行提交信用证修改申请书。

③ 开证行审查同意后,向原信用证的通知行发出信用证的修改书。

④ 通知行收到修改书后,鉴别其真实性,再通知受益人。

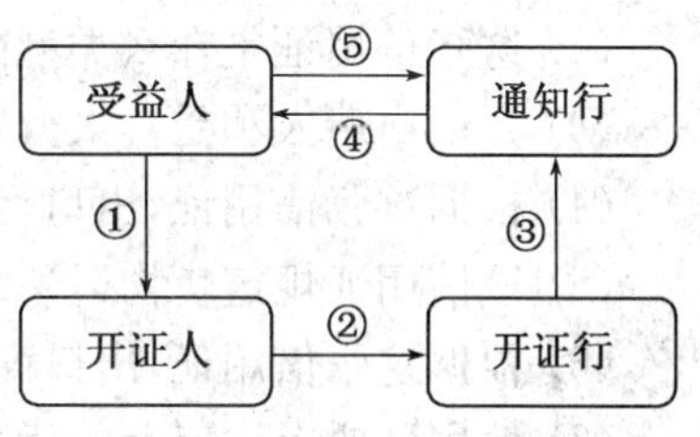

图2-1　修改信用证的程序

⑤ 受益人收到修改书后,应提供接受或拒绝修改的通知。如果受益人未能给予通知,当交单与信用证及尚未表达接受的修改要求一致时,即视为受益人已做出接受修改的通知,并且从此时起,该信用证被修改。

2. 信用证修改的规则

① 只有开证申请人有权决定是否接受修改信用证;修改信用证只能由受益人向开证申请人提出,经开证申请人同意后再由其通知开证行。

② 只有信用证受益人有权决定是否接受信用证的修改,受益人只有在收到开证行通过通知行转递的修改通知后,对信用证的修改才有效。直接由受益人向开证行提出的改证申请是无效的。

3. 修改信用证的注意点

① 信用证条款的规定比合同条款严格,影响出口商安全收汇和顺利履行合同义务时,应提出修改;信用证条款的规定比合同条款宽松时,可不要求修改。

② 受益人须由开证申请人要求开证行修改信用证,而不能直接修改信用证。

③ 对修改的内容要一次向对方全部提出,避免多次修改。

④ 对修改通知书的内容,要么全部接受或要么全部拒绝,部分接受无效。

2. 有关信用证修改案例

⑤ 对修改通知书的内容,受益人应做出接受或拒绝的通知。

⑥ 有关信用证修改通知书必须通过原信用证通知行才具真实,有效;通过客人直接寄送的修改申请书或修改书复印件不是有效的修改。

⑦ 明确修改费用由谁承担。一般按照责任归属来确定修改费用由谁承担。

3. 改证函

4. 修改信用证信函的写法

① 感谢对方的开证行为。

② 列明信用证中的不符点,并说明如何修改。

③ 感谢对方合作,提醒对方修改后的到达时间,以便按时装运。

2.2.5 能力实训

实训1 审核、修改信用证,并回答问题

(1) 这张信用证是由哪家银行开立的?
(2) 这张信用证是什么类型的信用证?
(3) 开证申请人和受益人分别是哪家公司?
(4) 根据这张信用证,出口运费由哪一方承担?
(5) 该信用证规定货物运达的目的港是哪个港口?
(6) 根据这张信用证,出口商作为受益人要准备哪些单据,各有哪些要求?
(7) 信用证要求发票上的货物描述应与哪个单据一致?
(8) 如何理解这张信用证的交单期和有效期? 到期地点在什么地方?
(9) 这张信用证对货物运输是如何规定的?
(10) 请指出信用证中有什么错误? 应怎样修改错误?

LETTER OF CREDIT

SQUENCE OF TOTAL　　*27: 1/1
FORM OF DOC, CREDIT　　*40 A: REVOCABLE
DOC. CREDIT NUMBER　　*20: 70/1/5822
DATE OF ISSUE　　*31: 150209
EXPIRY　　*31D: DATE 150401 PLACE POLAND
ISSUING BANK　　*51D: SUN BANK,
P.O.BOX 201 GDANSK, POLAND
APPLICANT　　*50: BBB TRADING CO.
P.O. BOX 303, GDANSK, POLAND
BENEFICIARY　　*59: AAA EXPORT AND IMPORT CO.
222 JIANGUO ROAD, DALIAN, CHINA
AMOUNT　　*32 B: USD28 222.00
AVAILABLE WITH/BY　　*41 A: ANY BANK IN CHINA BY NEGOTIATION
DRAFTS AT ...　　42C: AT SIGHT
DRAWEE　　*42D: ISSUING BANK
PARTIAL SHIPMENTS　　*43 P: NOT ALLOWED
TRANSSHIPMENT　　*43T: NOT ALLOWED
LOADING IN CHARGE　　*44 A: ANY CHINESE PORT
FOR TRANSPORT TO　　*44 B: GDANSK
LATEST DATE OF SHIPMENT　　*44 C: 150325
DESCRIPT OF GOODS　　*45 A: LADIES SHIRTS
65% POLYESTER 35% COTTON
STYLE NO. 101　200DOZ @ USD60/PC

STYLE NO. 102 400DOZ @USD84/PC

ALL OTHER DETAILS OF GOODS ARE AS PERCONTRACT

NO. LT 07006 DATED AUG 11, 2005

DELIVERY TERMS: CFR GDANSK(INCONERMS 2000)

DOCUMENTS REQUIRED ＊46 A:

+COMMERCIAL INVOICE MANUALLY SIGNED IN 2 ORIGINALS PLUS 1 COPY MADE OUT TO DDD TRADING CO., P.O. BOX 211, GDANSK, POLAND.

+FULL SET(3/3) OF ORIGINAL CLEAN ON BOARD BILL OF LADING PLUS 3/3 NON NEGOTIABLE COPIES, MADE OUT TO ORDER OF ISSUING BANK AND BLANK ENDORSED, NOTIFY THE APPLICANT, MARKED FREIGHT COLLECT, MENTIONING GROSS WEIGHT AND NET WEIGHT.

+ASSORTMENT LIST IN 2 ORIGINALS PLUS 1 COPY.

+CERTIFICATE OF ORIGIN IN 1 ORIGINAL PLUS 2 COPIES SIGNED BY CCPIT.

+ MARINE INSURANCE POLICY IN THE CURRENCY OF THE CREDIT ENDORSED IN BLANK FOR CIF VALUE PLUS 30 PCT MARGIN COVERING ALL RISKS OF PICC CLAUSES INDICATING CLAIMS PAYABLE IN POLAND.

+ CERTIFICATE OF ORIGIN ISSUED BY CHINA COUNCIL FOR THE PROMOTION OF INTERNATIONAL TRADE AND CERTIFYING THE GOODS TO BE OF CHINESE ORIGIN, STATING THE FULL NAME AND ADDRESS OF THE MANUFACTURE AND EXPORTER OF GOODS AND NAME OF THE EXPORT COUNTY.

ADDITIONAL COND. ＊47A:

+ALL DOCS MUS BE ISSUED IN ENGLISH.

+SHIPMENTS MUST BE EFFECTED BY FCL.

+B/L MUST SHOWING SHIPPING MARKS: BBB, S/C LT07060, GDAND, C/NO.

+ALL DOCS MUST NOT SHOW THIS L/C AND DATE OF ISSUE.

+THE OPENING BANK IS OBLIGED TO PAYMENT ONLY AFTER GOODS ARE SHIPPED TO THE PORT OF DESTINATION.

+ FOR DOCS WHICH DO NOT COMPLY WITH L/C TERMS AND CONDITIONS, WE SHALL DEDUCT FROM THE PROCEEDS A CHARGE OF EUR 50,00 PAYABLE IN USD EQUIVALENT PLUS ANY INCCURED SWIFT CHARGES IN CONNECTION WITH.

DETAILS OF CHARGES ＊71 B: ALL BANKING COMM/CHRGS ARE ON BENEFICIARY'S ACCOUNT.

PERIOD FOR PRESENTATION ＊48: 5 DAYS AFTER B/L DATE, BUT WITHIN THE VALIDITY OF THE CREDIT.

CONFIRMATION ＊49: WITHOUT

INSTRUCTIONS *78: WE SHALL REIMBURSE AS PER YOUR INSTRUCTIONS

实训 2 仔细阅读合同,根据合同审核信用证

SALE CONTRACT

The Sellers: JIANGSU HAOYIFA CHEMICAL CO., LTD
NO.10 TAIPING SOUTH ROAD
210003, CHINA
Fax: 025-85763368

Contract No.: GL0082
Date: MAR15, 2008
Signed at: NANGJING

The Buyers: HANGUNG-BR CO., LTD
NO.20 SANYU-DONG YANGSAN CITY

This Sales Contract is made by and between the Sellers and Buyers, whereby the sellers agree to sell and the buyers agree to buy the under-mentioned goods according to the terms and conditions stipulated below:

Name of Commodity and specification	Quantity	Unit Price	Amount
		CIF BUSAN	
WOODEN FLOWER STANDS	350PCS	USD8.90/pc	USD3 115.00
WOODEN FLOWER POTS	600PCS	USD5.00/pc	USD3 000.00
10% more or less both in amount and quantity allowed	Total 950PCS		USD6 115.00

Shipping Marks: HANGUNG
BUSAN
NO.1~325
MADE IN CHINA

Time of Shipment: within 45 days after receipt of L/C, with partial shipment and transshipment allowed.

Port of loading & destination: From Shanghai to BUSAN

Term of Payment: By 100% irrevocable sight L/C opened by the buyer to reach the seller not later than APR. 5TH, 2008 and to be available for negotiation in china until the15th day after the date of shipment. In case of late arrival of the L/C, the seller shall not be liable for any delay in shipment and shall have the right to rescind the contract and or claim for damages.

Insurance: To be effected by the seller for 110%of the CIF invoice value coving FPA RISKS and WAR RISKS as per Chinese Insurance Clauses.

The Buyer: The Seller:

HANGUNG-BR CO., LTD JIANGSU HAOYIFA CHEMICAL CO., LTD

国外来证如下：

SQUENCE OF TOTAL	*27: 1/1
FORM OF DOC. CREDIT	*40A: IRREVOCABLE
DOC. CREDIT NUMBER	*20: LDI300954
DATE OF ISSUE	31C: 2008/04/14
EXPIRY	*31D: 2008/06/10 IN COUNTRY OF APPLICANT
APPLICANT	*50: HANGUNG-BR CO., LTD NO. 20 SANYU-DONG YANGSAN CITY
BENEFICIARY	*59: JIANGSU HAOYIFA CHEMICAL CO., LTD NO. 10 TAIPING SOUTH ROAD 210003, CHINA
AMOUNT	*32B: USD6 115.00
POS./NEG. TOL. (%)	39A: 05/05
AVAILABLE WITH/BY	*41D: ANY BANK BY NEGOTIATION
DRAFT AT ...	42C: AT 60 DAYS AFTER SIGHT
DRAWEE	*42D: HVBKUS55WOORI BANK, NEW YORK
PARTIAL SHIPMENT	43P: ALLOWED
TRANSSHIPMENT	43T: NOT ALLOWED
LOADING IN CHARGE	44A: CHINA PORT
FOR TRANSPORT TO ...	44B: BUSAN, KOREA
LATEST DATE OF SHIP.	44C: 2008/04/10
DESCRIPT. OF GOODS	45A:

350PCS OF WOODEN FLOWER STANDS, USD8.90 PER PC AND 600PCS OF WOODEN FLOWER POTS, USD5.00 PER PC AS PER SALES CONTRACT GL0082 DATED MAR. 5, 2008

CIF BUSAN

DOCUMENTS REQUIRED 46A:

+MANUALLY SIGNED COMMERCIAL INVOICE IN SIX COPYIES INDICATING COUNTRY OF ORIGIN.

+FULL SET OF ORIGINAL CLEAN ON BOARD MARINE BILL OF LADING MADE OUT TO SHIPPERS ORDER AND BLANK ENDORSED, MARKED FREIGHT COLLECT AND NOTIFY APPLICANT QUOTING FULL NAME AND ADDRESS.

+ORIGINAL PACKING LIST PLUS THREE COPIES INDICATING DETAILED PACKING OF EACH CARTON SIGNED BY APPLICANT.

+MARINE INSURANCE POLICY FOR 110PCT OF INVOICE VALUE, BLANK ENDORSED, INDICATING CLAIM PAYABLE AT DESTINATION, COVERING ALL RISKS AND WAR RISKS AS PER AND SUBJECT TO OCEAN MARINE CARGO CLAUSES AND OCEAN MARINE CARGO WAR RISKS CLAUSES OF P. I. C. C.

DATED 1/1/1981.

+ ORIGINAL CERTIFICATE OF ORIGIN PLUS ONE COPY ISSUED BY CHAMBER OF COMMERCE.

ADDITIONAL COND. 47A:

+THIS CREDIT IS NON-OPERATIVE UNLESS THE NAME OF CARRYING WESSEL HAS BEEN APPROVED BY APPLICANT

+EACH PACKING UNIT BEARS AN INDELIBLE(不褪色) MARK INDICATING THE COUNTRY OF ORIGIN OF THE GOODS. PACKING LIST TO CERTIFY THIS.

+DOCUMENTS DATED PRIOR TO THE DATE OF THIS CREDIT ARE NOT ACCEPTABLE.

+ ALL BANK CHARGES IN CONNECTION WITH THIS DOCUMENTARY CREDIT EXCEPT ISSUING BANK'S OPENING COMMISSION AND TRANSMISSION COSTS ARE FOR THE BENEFICIARY.

PRESENTATION PERIOD 48: WITHIN 5 DAYS AFTER THE DATE OF SHIPMENT BUT WITHIN THE VALIDITY OF THE CREDIT.

CONFIRMATION *49: WITHOUT

实训 3　仔细阅读合同,根据合同审核信用证

无锡博大进出口公司

WUXI BODA IMPORT & EXPORT COMPANY

无锡市溧阳路 1088 号龙邸大厦 16 楼

16TH FLOOR, DRAGON MANSION, 1088 LIYANG ROAD, WUXI 214000 CHINA

SALES CONTRACT

DATE: 2014/11/8　　NO.: YD-MDSC9811

BUYERS: MAURICIO DEPORTS INTERNATIONAL S.A.

ADDRESS: RM 1008～1011 CONVENTION PLAZA,

101 HARBOR ROAD, COLON, R.P.

TEL.:507-25192334

FAX:507-25192333

THE UNDERSIGNED SELLERS AND BUYERS HAVE AGREED TO CLOSE THE FOLLOWING TRANSACTION ACCORDING TO THE TERMS AND CONDITIONS STIPULATED BELOW:

NAME OF COMMODITY AND SPECIFICATION	QUANTITY	UNIT PRICE	AMOUNT
CHINESE RICE FAQ BROKEGRAINS(MAX.) 20% ADMIXTURE(MAX.)0.2% MOISTURE(MAX.)10%	2 000TONS	CIFC3 COLON USD 360.00/T	USD720 000.00
	TOTAL AMOUNT: SAY U. S. DOLLARS SEVEN HUNDRED AND TWENTY THOUSAND ONLY.		

REMARKS: WITH 5% MORE OR LESS BOTH IN AMOUNT AND QUANTITY

AT THE SELLER'S OPTION.

PACKING: 50KGS TO ONE GUNNY BAG. TOTAL 40000BAGS.

SHIPMENT: TO BE EFFECTED DURING DEC. 2014 FROM SHANGHAI, CHINA TO COLON, R.P. ALLOWING PARTIAL SHIPMENTS AND TRANSHIPMENT.

INSURANCE: TO BE COVERED FOR 110% OF INVOICE VALUE AGAINST ALL RISKS AS PER AND SUBJECT TO OCEAN MARINE CARGO CLAUSES OF PICC DATED 1/1/1981.

PAYMENT: THE BUYERS SHALL OPEN THROUGH A FIRST-CLASS BANK ACCEPTABLE TO THE SELLER AN IRREVOCABLE L/C AT 30 DAYS AFTER B/L DATE TO REACH THE SELLER NOV. 25, 2014 AND VALID FOR NEGOTIATION IN CHINA UNTIL THE 15TH DAY AFTER THE DATE OF SHIPMENT.

SELLERS　　　　　　　　　　　　BUYER:

WUXI BODA IMPORT & EXPORT COMPANY

MAURICIO DEPORTS INTERNATIONAL S.A.

赵国斌　　　　　　　　　　　　D. H. HONENEY

MT700	ISSUE OF A DOCUMENTARY CREDIT
SENDER	CITI BANK N.A. P.O. BOX 555 PANAMA R.P.
RECEIVER:	CITI BANK OF SHANGHAI, SHANGHAI, CHINA

SEQUENCE OF TOTAL	**27:** 1/1
FORM OF DOC, CREDIT	* **40 A:** IRREVOCABLE
DOC. CREDIT NUMBER	* **20:** 180-43672
DATE OF ISSUE	* **31:** 141123
EXPIRY	* **31D:** DATE 141215 AT THE COUNTER OF CITIBANK N.A. PANAMA
ISSUING BANK	* **51D:** CITI BANK N.A. P.O. BOX 555 PANAMA R.P.
APPLICANT	* **50:** MAURICIO DEPORTS INTERNATIONAL S.A. RM1008～1101 CONVENTION PLAZA, 101 HARBOR ROAD, COLON, R.P.
BENEFICIARY	* **59:** WUXI BODA IMPORT & EXPORT COMPANY 16TH FLOOR, DRAGON MANSION, 1088LIYANGROAD, WUXI 214000 CHINA
AMOUNT	* **32 B:** USD733 320.00
AVAILABLE WITH/BY	* 41 A: ANY BANK IN CHINA BY NEGOTIATION
DRAFTS AT ...	**42C:** AT 30 DAYS AFTER SIGHT
DRAWEE	* **42D:** APPLICANT
PARTIAL SHIPMENTS	* **43 P:** NOT ALLOWED

TRANSSHIPMENT ＊**43T:** NOT ALLOWED

LOADING IN CHARGE ＊**44 A:** SHANGHAI

FOR TRANSPORT TO ＊**44 B:** PANAMAN

LATEST DATE OF SHIPMENT ＊**44 C:** 140325

DESCRIPT OF GOODS ＊45 A: 40000 BAGS OF CHINESE RICE AS PER SALES CONTRACT NO. YD-MDSC9811 DATED NOV. 18, 2014 CIF COLON

DOCUMENTS REQUIRED ＊**46 A:**

+2/3 SET OF ORIGINAL CLEAN ON BOARD OCEAN BILL OF LADING DATED NO LATER THAN DEC. 15, 2014 ISSUED TO OUR ORDER NOTIFY APPLICANT MARKED FREIGHT TO BE COLLECTED.

+COMMERCIAL INVOICE IN TRIPLICATE DULY SIGNED ORIGINAL VISAED BY PANAMANIAN CONSUL.

+PACKING LIST IN QUADRUPLICATE SHOWING GROSS WEIGHT OF PACKAGE AND CERTIFIED THAT THE GOODS ARE PACKED IN NEW GUNNY BAGS.

+BENEFICIARY'S CERTIFICATE STATED THAT 1/3 SET OF ORIGINAL BILL OF LADING HAS BEEN AIRMAILED DIRECTLY TO APPLICANT WITHIN 48 HOURS AFTER SHIPMENT.

+INSURANCE POLICY OR CERTIFICATE IN DUPLICATE IN THE CURRENCY OF THE CREDIT AND IN ASSIGNABLE FORM FOR THE FULL INVOICE VALUE PLUS 110% COVERING INSTITUTE CARGO CLAUSE ALL RISKS.

ADDITIONAL COND. ＊**47A:**

+THE DOCUMENTS BENEFICIARY PRESENT SHOULD INCLUDE AN INSPECTION CERTIFICATE SIGNED BY APPLICANT OR ITS AGENT.

+EACH DRAFT ACCOMPANYING DOCUMNENTS MUST INDICATE THE CREDIT NO. AND NAME OF ISSUING BANK AND CREDIT NO. AND NAME OF ADVISING BANK(IF INDICATED).

+THIS CREDIT IS NON-OPERATIVE UNLESS THE NAME OF CARRYING VESSEL HAS BEEN APPROVED BY APPLICANT AND TO BE ADVISED BY L/C ISSUING BANK IN FORM OF AN L/C ADMENDMENT TO BENIFICIARY.

DETAILS OF CHARGES ＊**71B:** +ALL CHARGES OUTSIDE PANAMA R. P. ARE FOR ACCOUNT OF BENEFICIARY.

PERIOD FOR PRESENTATION ＊**48:** 5 DAYS AFTER B/L DATE, BUT WITHIN THE VALIDITY OF THE CREDIT.

CONFIRMATION ＊**49:** WITHOUT

INSTRUCTIONS ＊**78:** WE SHALL REIMBURSE AS PER YOUR INSTRUCTIONS

项目 3　制作商业发票和装箱单

3.1　学习目标

知识目标：熟悉发票与装箱单的定义与作用。

能力目标：能根据合同或 L/C 准确填制商业发票和装箱单。

3.2　工作任务

无锡蓝天进出口公司(WUXI BLUE SKY IMP&EXP. Co., LTD.)与加拿大的 KU TEXTILE CORPORATION 就出口全棉女童连衣裙达成一份出口合同，付款方式是信用证。无锡蓝天进出口公司向买方提出信用证修改意见。KU TEXTILE CORPORATION 同意改证，向汇丰银行提出改证申请。中国银行无锡分行通知无锡蓝天进出口公司外贸单证员郭晓芳，汇丰银行的信用证修改书已到。合同、信用证的内容如下：

SALES CONTRACT

NO. K123

DATE: APR. 9, 2015

THE SELLER:

WUXIBLUE SKY IMP&EXP. Co., LTD.

NO. 53 ZHONGSHAN ROAD, WUXI, CHINA

TEL: 86－510－82398888

THE BUYER:

KU TEXTILE CORPORATION

430 VTRA MONTREAL CANADA

TEL: +48 789065

THIS SALES CONTRACR IS MADE BY AND BETWEEN THE SELLERS AND THE BUYERS, WHERE THE SELLERS AGREE TO SELL AND THE BUYERS AGREE TO BUY THE UNDER MENTIONED GOODS ACCORDING TO THE TERMS AND CONDITIONS STIPULATE BELOW:

COMMODITY & SPECIFICATION	QUANTITY	UNIR PRICE	AMOUNT
GIRL DRESS 100% COTTON ARTICLE NO. 11574 11575 11576 11577	 2 400 PCS 3 000PCS 2 400PCS 1 600PCS	CIFMONTREAL USD 6.50/PC USD 5.50/PC USD 8.50/PC USD 8.00/PC	 USD 15 600.00 USD 16 500.00 USD 20 400.00 USD 12 800.00
TOTAL	9 400PCS		USD 65 300.00

TOTAL AMOUNT IN WORDS

SAY US DOLLARS SIXTY FIVE THOUSAND THREE HUNDRED ONLY

MORE OR LESS 5% OF THE QUANTITY AND AMOUT ARE ALLOWED.

PACKING:

EACH PIECE IN A POLYBAG, 40 PIECES TO ONE EXPORT STANDARD CARTON.

SHIPPING MARKS:

KU

K123

MONTREAL

C/N: 1-UP

SHIPMENT

PORT OF LOADING: SAHNGHAI

PORT OF DESTINATION: MONTREAL

TRANSHIPMENT: ALLOWED

PARTIAL SHIPMENTS: ALLOWED

TIME OF SHIPMENT: BEFORE JULY 31, 2015

INSURANCE

THE SELLER SHOULD COVER INSURANCE FOR 110% OF FULL INVOICE VALUE COVING ALL RISKS AND WAR RISK AS PER CIC OF PICC DATED 01/01/1981.

PAYMENT

THE BUYER SHOULD OPEN A BANK ACCEPTABLE TO THE SELLER AN IRREVOCABLE L/C PAYABLE AT 30 DAYS AFTER SIGHT, FOR 100% OF TOTAL CONTRACT VALUE TO REACH THE SELLER BEFORE MAY 31TH, 2015 VALID FOR NEGOTIATION IN CHINA UNTIL THE 15TH DAY AFTER THE DATE OF SHIPMENT

INSPECTION&CLAIM

THE SELLER SHALL HAVE THE PERFORMANCE AND QUALITIES, SPECIFICATIONS, QUANTITIES OF THE GOODS CAREFULLY INSPECTED AND ISSUE INSPECTION CERTIFICATE BEFORE SHIPMENT. ANY CLAIM BY THE BUYER REGARDING THE GOODS SHIPPED SHOULD BE FILED WITHIN 30DAYS AFTER THE ARRIVALS OF THE GOODS AT THE PORT/PLACE OF DESTINATION SPECIFIED IN THE RELATIVE BILL OF LADING OR TRANSPORT DOCUMENT AND SUPPORTED BY A SURVEY REPORT ISSUED BY A SURVEY APPROVED BY THE SELLER. CLAIMS IN RESPECT OF MATTERS WITHIN RESPONSIBILITY OF INSURANCE COMPANY, SHIPPING COMPANY/OTHER TRANSPORTATION ORGANIZATION WILL NOT BE CONSIDERED OR ENTERTAINED BY THE SELLER.

FORCE MAJUSE:

IF THE SHIPMENT OF CONTRACTED GOODS IS PREVENTED OR DELAYS IN WHOLE OR IN PART BY REASON OF WAR, EARTHQUAKE, FIRE, FLOOD, HEAVY SNOW, STORM OR OTHER CAUSES OF FORCE MAJUSE, THE SELLER SHALL NOT BE LIABLE FOR NON-SHIPMENT OR LATE SHIPMENT OF THE GOODS OF THIS CONTRACT. HOWEVER, THE SELLER SHALL NOTIFY THE BUYERS BY CABLE OR TELEX AND FURNISH THE LETTER WITHIN 15DAYS BY REGISTERED AIRMAIL WITH A CERTIFICATE ISSUED BY THE CHINA COUNCIL FOR THE PROMOTION OF INTERNATIONAL TRADE ATTESTING SUCH EVENT OR EVENTS.

ARBITRATION:

ALL DISPUTED ARISING OUT OF PERFORMANCE OF, OR RELATING TO THIS CONTRACT, SHALL BE SETTLED AMICABLY THROUGH FRIENDLY NEGOTIATION. IN CASE NO SETTLEMENT CAN BE REACHED THROUGH NEGOTIATION, THE CASE SHALL THEN BE SUBMITTED FOR ARBITRATION, THE LOCATION OF ARBITRATION SHALL BE IN THE COUNTRY OF THE DOMICILE OF THE DEFENDANT. IF IN CHINA, THE ARBITRATION SHALL BE CONDUCTED BY THE RULES OF ARBITRATION. THE ARBITRAL AWARD IS FINAL AND BINDING UPON BOTH PARTIES. THE CHARGES ARISING FROM THE ARBITRATION SHALL BE UNDERTAKEN BY THE LOSING PARTY.

THE SELLER	THE BUYER
DALIAN SINIAN TEXTILES IMP&EXP. Co., LTD.	POLISH PULICI TEXTILE GROUP Co., LTD
张浩	Jane Homels

MT 700 ISSUE OF A DOCUMENTARY CREDIT
SENDER HSBC BANK PLC, MONTREAL, CANADA
RECEIVER BANK OF CHINA, WUXI BRANCH, CHINA
SEQUENCE OF TOTAL 27: 1/1
FORM OF DOC. CREDIT 40A: IRREVOCABLE
DOC. CREDIT NUMBER 20: 123456
DATE OF ISSUE 31C: 150520
APPLICABLE RULES 40E: UCP LATEST VERSION
DATE AND PLACE OF EXPIRY 31D: 150815 IN CHINA
APPLICANT 50: KU TEXTILE CORPORATION
430 VTRA MONTREAL CANADA
BENEFICIARY 59: WUXI BLUE SKY IMP&EXP. Co., LTD
NO. 53 ZHONGSHAN ROAD, WUXI, CHINA
AMOUNT 32B: USD 65 300.00
PERCENTAGE CREDIT AMOUNT TOLERANCE 39A: 5/5
AVAILABLE WITH/BY 41D: ANY BANK IN CHINA, BY NEGOTIATION
DRAFTS AT ... 42C: AT 30 DAYS AFTER SIGHT
DRAWEE 42A: HSBC BANK PLC, MONTREAL, CANADA
PARTIAL SHIPMENT 43P: ALLOWED
TRANSSHIPMENT 43T: ALLOWED
PORT OF LOADING/AIRPORT OF DEPARTURE 44E: CHINESE MAIN PORT
PORT OF DISCHARGE 44F: MONTREAL, CANADA
LATEST DATE OF SHIPMENT 44C: 150731
DESCRIPTION OF GOODS AND/OR SERVICES. 45A:
9400 PIECES GIRL DRESS 100% COTTON
AS PER S/C NO. 123

STYLE NO.	QUANTITY	UNIT PRICE	AMOUNT
11754	2 400PCS	USD6.50/PC	USD15 600.00
11575	3 000PCS	USD5.50/PC	USD16 500.00
11576	2 400PCS	USD8.50/PC	USD20 400.00
11577	1 600PCS	USD8.00/PC	USD12 800.00

AT CIF MONTREAL, CANADA
DOCUMENTS REQUIRED 46A:
+SIGNED COMMERCIAL INVOICE IN DUPLICATE CERTIFYING GOODS OF CHINA ORIGIN.
+PACKING LIST IN THREE FOLDS SHOWING G. W., N. W., AND MEAS. OF EACH PACKGE.

+CERTIFICATE OF CHINESE ORIGIN CERTIFIED BY CHAMBER OF COMMERCE OR CCPIT.

+G.S.P. CERTIFICATE OF ORIGIN FORM A IN DUPLICATE BY CIQ.

+FULL SET OF CLEAN ' ON BOARD ' OCEAN BILLS OF LADING MADE OUT TOORDER AND BLANK ENDORSED MARKED FREIGHT PREPAID AND NOTIFY APPLICANT.

+INSURANCE POLICY OR CERTIFICATE ENDORSED IN BLANK FOR 110 PCT OF CIF VALUE, COVERING ALL RISKS AND WAR RISK SUBJECT TO THE RELEVANT OCEAN MARINE CLAUSE OF THE PEOPLE'S INSURANCE COMPANY OF CHINA, DATED 1/1/1981.

+SHIPPING ADVICE SHOWINGB/L NO., GOODS NAME, QUANTITY AND AMOUNT OF GOODS, NUMBER OF PACKAGES, NAME OF VESSEL AND VOYAGE NO., AND DATE OF SHIPMENT TO APPLICANT WITHIN 3 DAYS AFTER THE DATE OF BILL OF LADING.

+BENEFICIARY'S CERTIFICATE CERTIFYING THAT ONE SET OF COPIES OF SHIPPING DOCUMENTS HAS BEEN SENT TO APPLICANT WITHIN 7 DAYS AFTER SHIPMENT.

+CERTIFICATE TO EVDIENT TO EVIDENCE THE SHIP IS NOT OVER 15 YEARS OLD.

ADDITIONAL CONDITION 47A:

+DOCUMENTS DATED PRIOR TO THE DATE OF THIS CREDIT ARE NOT ACCEPTABLE.

+THE NUMBER AND THE DATE OF THIS CREDIT AND THE NAME OF ISSUING BANK MUST BE QUOTED ON ALL DOCUMENTS.

+TRANSSHIPMENT ALLOWED AT HONGKONG ONLY.

+SHORT FORM/CHARTER PARTY/THIRD PARTY BILL OF LADING ARE NOT ACCEPTABLE.

+SHIPMENT MUST BE EFFECTED BY40′ FULL CONTAINER LOAD. B/L TO SHOW EVIDENCE OF THIS EFFECT IS REQUIRED.

+ALL PRESENTATIONS CONTAINING DISCREPANCIES WILL ATTRACT A DISCREPANCY FEE OF USD50.00 PLUS TELEX COSTS OR OTHER CURRENCY EQUIVALENT. THIS CHARGE WILL BE DEDUCTED FROM THE BILL AMOUNT WHETHER OR NOT WE ELECT TO CONSULT THE APPLICANT FOR A WAIVER.

CHARGES 71B: ALL CHARGES AND COMMISSIONS OUTSIDE CANADA ARE FOR BENEFICIARY'S ACCOUNT.

PERIOD FOR PRESENTATION 48: WITHIN 15 DAYS AFTER THE DATE OF SHIPMENT, BUT WITHIN THE VALIDITY OF THIS CREDIT.

CONFIRMATION INSTRUCTION 49: WITHOUT
INFORMATION TO PRESENTING BANK 78:
ALL DOCUMENTS ARE TO BE REMITTED IN ONE LOT BY COURIER TO HSBC BANK.
PLC, TRADE SERVICES, MONTREAL BRANCH, P O BOX 66, HSBC BANK BUILDING.
312/45 Al SUQARE ROAD, MONTREAL, CANADA.

货物明细单

商品名称：GIRL DRESS

货 号	数量	计量单位	单价	装箱率	包装种类	毛重	净重	尺码（长×宽×高）
11754	2 400	pc	US$6.50	40 pc/ctn	carton	10 kgs/ctn	9 kgs/ctn	65×65×50 cm
11575	3 000	pc	US$5.50	40 pc/ctn	carton	11 kgs/ctn	10 kgs/ctn	65×65×50 cm
11576	2 400	pc	US$8.50	40 pc/ctn	carton	10 kgs/ctn	9 kgs/ctn	65×65×50 cm
11577	1 600	pc	US$8.00	40 pc/ctn	carton	6.5 kgs/ctn	6 kgs/ctn	65×50×50 cm

发票号码：ZYIE1502　　发票日期：MAY 20, 2015　　唛头：KU
装运船只：DONG FANG　　航次：V. 25　　K123
提单号码：COSOOTEC192　　装船日期：JUL. 15, 2015　　MONTREAL
普惠制产地证号码：GSPWIZJ0894　　保险单号码：IPGOEN0435　　C/NO. 1-UP
保险代理：AIG Europe, S. A., Canada Branch
Via della Chiusa 2
20123 Canada
Tel: 48 369010

在本任务中，单证员应能根据合同、信用证填制商业发票和装箱单。

3.3 操作范例

一、第一步：根据以上资料，填制商业发票和装箱单

COMMERCIAL INVOICE

<table>
<tr><td rowspan="3">1) SELLER
WU XI BLUE SKY IMP&EXP. Co., LTD.
NO. 53 ZHIGONG STREET, WUXI, P.R. CHINA</td><td>3) INVOICE NO.
ZYIE1502</td><td>4) INVOICE DATE
MAY 20, 2015</td></tr>
<tr><td>5) L/C NO. 123456</td><td>6) DATE
MAY20, 2015</td></tr>
<tr><td colspan="2">7) ISSUED BY
HSBC BANK PLC, MONTREAL, CANADA</td></tr>
</table>

（续表）

2) BUYER KU TEXTILE CORPORATION 430 VTRA MONTREAL CANADA	8) CONTRACT NO. K123	9) DATE APR. 9, 2015
	10) FROM SHANGHAI	11) TO MONTREAL
	12) SHIPPED BY DONG FANG V. 25	13) PRICE TERM CIF MONTREAL

14) MARKS&NOS.	15)DESCRIPTIONS OF GOODS	16) QTY	17) UNIT PRICE	18) AMOUNT
GIRL DRESS 100%COTTON AS PER SALES COMTRACT NO. K123 DATED APR. 9, 2015				
KU	11574	2 400PCS	US$6.50	US$15 600.00
K123	11575	3 000PCS	US$5.50	US$16 500.00
MONTREAL	11576	2 400PCS	US$8.50	US$20 400.00
C/NO. 1～235	11577	1 600PCS	US$8.00	US$12 800.00
	TOTAL	9 400PC		US$65 300.00

TOTAL AMOUNT IN WORDS: SAY US DOLLARS SIXTY FIVE THOUSAND AND THREE HUNDRED ONLY

WE HEREBYCERTIFY THAT GOODS ARE OF CHINA ORIGIN.

19) ISSUEDY BY

WUXI BLUE SKY IMP&EXP. Co., LTD.

郭晓芳

发票必须签署吗

A公司向德国出口一批货物，国外开来的信用证中对发票只规定“Commercial Invoice in duplicate”。A公司交单后被拒付，理由是商业发票上的受益人漏签字盖章。A公司经检查发现的确漏签字盖章，立即补寄签字完整的发票。但此时信用证已过期，故又遭拒付。A公司与买方再三交涉，最后通过降价处理才收回货款。本案中的拒付有无理由？为什么？本案中A公司的处理是否妥当？为什么？

商业发票的货物描述

《UCP600》第 18 条 C 款规定，商业发票中的货物、服务或行为的描述必须与信用证中显示的内容相符。

《ISBP681》第 58 条规定，发票中的货物、服务或履约行为的描述必须与信用证规定的一致，但并不要求如镜子反射那样一致。例如，货物细节可以在发票中的若干处表示，当合并在一起时与信用证规定的一致即可。

装箱单的货物描述

《UCP600》第 14 条 e 款规定，除商业发票外，其他单据中的货物、服务或行为描述若须规定，可使用统称，但不得与信用证规定的描述相矛盾。

第二步：根据以上资料，填制装箱单

PACKING LIST

<table>
<tr><td rowspan="3">1) SELLER
WUXIBLUE SKY IMP&EXP. Co., LTD.
NO.53 ZHONGSHAN ROAD, WUXI, CHINA</td><td>3) INVOICE NO.
ZYIE1502</td><td>4) INVOICE DATE
MAY 20, 2015</td></tr>
<tr><td>5) FROM
SHANGHAI</td><td>6) TO MONTREAL</td></tr>
<tr><td colspan="2">7) TOTAL PACKAGES (IN WORDS)
SAY TWO HUNDRED AND THIRTY-FIVE CARTONS ONLY</td></tr>
<tr><td>2) BUYER
KU TEXTILE CORPORATION
430 VTRA MONTREAL CANADA</td><td colspan="2">8) MARKS&NOS
KU
K123
MONTREAL
C/NO. 1～235</td></tr>
<tr><td colspan="3">9) C/NOS. 10) NOS. &KINDS OF PKGS 11) ITEM 12) QTY(PCS) 13) G.W. (KG) 14) N.W. (KG) 15) MEAS(M3)</td></tr>
</table>

GIRL DRESS 100%COTTON

1～60	60 CARTONS	11574	2 400	600.000	540.000	12.660
61～135	75CARTONS	11575	3 000	825.000	750.000	15.825
136～195	60CARTONS	11576	2 400	600.000	540. 000	12.660
196～235	40CARTONS	11577	1 600	260.00	240.000	4.240
TOTAL:	235CARTONS		9 400	2 285.00	2 070.000	45.385

ART. NO.	G. W. (KG)	N. W. (KG)	MEAS(M3)	OF EACH PACKAGE
11574	10.000	9.000	0.211	PER CARTON
11575	11.000	10.000	0.211	PER CARTON
11576	10.000	9.000	0.211	PER CARTON
11577	6.500	6.000	0.106	PER CARTON

DOCUMENTARY CREDIT NO.: 123456
DATE OF ISSUE: 150520
NAME OF ISSUING BANK: HSBC BANK PLC, MONTREAL, CANADA

16) ISSUEDY BY
WUXI BLUE SKY IMP&EXP. Co., LTD.
郭晓芳

开动脑筋

装箱单条款的处理

信用证规定，SEAWORTHY PACKING, PACKING SUITABLE FOR LONG DISTANCE, STRONG WOODEN CASE PACKING 等。那么制作装箱单时如何处理？

3.4　知识链接

1. 填制商业发票的规范(见表 3-1)

出口商审核信用证主要依据进出口合同，国际惯例、《UCP600》及其进口国的相关法律法规。

表 3-1　填制商业发票的规范

项目顺序号	填写内容	要点提示
(1) 单据名称 Name of DOC.	Commercial invoice	与信用证上的规定一致
(2) 出单人 Issuer	签发发票的人	① 信用证项下的受益人 ② 托收与电汇为合同卖方
(3) 受单人 TO	抬头人	① 信用证项下的开证申请人 ② 托收与电汇为合同买方
(4) 运输详情 Transport details	启运港、目的港和运输方式	启运港应明确具体，目的港如有重名港后面要有国别
(5) 发票号码 Invoice No.	此笔业务的发票号码	由卖方自行编制
(6) 日期 Date	发票的出票日期	一般在信用证开证日期后提单签发日期前，且不迟于信用证交单期和有效期

（续表）

项目顺序号	填写内容	要点提示
(7) 合同号 S/C No.	此笔业务的合同号码	与信用证上应用的合同号保持一致
(8) 信用证号码 L/C No.	此笔业务的信用证号码	应与信用证上列明的证号保持一致，采用其他付款方式
(9) 付款方式 Terms of payment	此笔业务的付款方式	信用证方式填 By L/C；托收填 By D/P；电汇填 By T/T
(10) 唛头 Marks and numbers	合同或信用证规定的唛头	信用证或合同有指定唛头必须严格按照规定制唛；信用证或合同没有规定唛头，出口商可以自行设计；没有唛头填 N/M
(11) 货物描述 Number and kind of package, description of goods	包括货物的件数、货名、规格、包装等	必须与信用证上货物描述完全一致
(12) 数量 Quantity	一般填货物的实际出运数量	不要遗漏计量单位
(13) 单价 Unit price	包括计价货币、计量单位、单位金额和贸易术语	填写完整、正确，不要遗漏贸易术语
(14) 总金额 Amount	发票总值	一般不超过信用证的金额 有折扣或明佣的应在此扣除，计算净值
(15) 声明文句 Statement	来证要求的发票上加注各种金额、原产地、特定号码等声明文句	这些内容加注在发票货物描述栏以下的空白处
(16) 签字 Signature	一般加盖签发人的英文名称加法人代表签字图章	商业发票只能由 L/C 规定的受益人出具 无特殊规定，发票可以无须签字 若信用证要求手签，出单人要亲笔签署不能以盖章代替

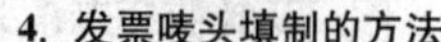

4. 发票唛头填制的方法

5. 数量与金额

2. 填制装箱单的规范(见表 3-2)

表 3-2　填制装箱的规范

项目顺序号	填写内容	要点提示
(1) 单据名称 Name of doc		与信用证上的规定一致
(2) 出单人 Issuer	签发发票的人	信用证项下的受益人 托收与电汇为合同卖方

(续表)

项目顺序号	填写内容	要点提示
(3) 受单人 TO	抬头人	信用证项下的开证申请人 托收与电汇为合同买方
(4) 发票号 Invoice No.	此笔业务的发票号码	由卖方自行编制
(5) 日期 Date	发票的出票日期	一般在信用证开证日期后提单签发日期前，且不迟于信用证交单期和有效期
(6) 唛头 Marks and numbers	合同或信用证规定的唛头	信用证或合同有指定唛头必须严格按照规定制唛；信用证或合同没有规定唛头，出口商可以自行设计；没有唛头填 N/M
(7) 包装种类和件数、货物描述 Number and kind of package, description of goods	包括货物的件数、货描	可以使用商品的统称
(8) 毛重 Gross weight 净重 Net weight 尺码 Measurement	填货物的毛重、净重和尺码	若信用证要求列出单件毛重、净重和尺码时，应按照货物的实际情况填写，并且要符合信用证的规定
(9) 声明文句 Statement	来证要求在装箱单上加注特定号码、文句等	按要求填写
(10) 签字 Signature	一般加盖签发人的英文名称加法人代表签字图章	装箱单只能由 L/C 规定的受益人出具； 无特殊规定，装箱单可以无须签字； 若信用证要求手签，出单人要亲笔签署不能以盖章代替

超链接

商业发票

1. 商业发票(Commercial Invoice)的含义

商业发票是卖方向买方开立，凭以向买方收取货款的发货价目清单，装运货物的总说明。商业发票在整个出口单据中处于核心地位，是缮制其他单据的依据，也是出口货物的总说明，合同履行的各个环节基本上都需要使用商业发票。

2. 商业发票的作用

① 反映了交付货物的状况，是缮制其他单据的依据(最早出单)，是整套单据的中心单据。

② 发货凭证。

③ 凭以收付货款和记账的重要凭证。

④ 报关、纳税的重要依据。

⑤ 索赔和理赔的重要凭证。

《UCP600》对商业发票的规定

《UCP600》第 18 条是关于商业发票的描述，主要内容如下：

关于出票人。商业发票必须表明是由受益人出具(转让信用证中情形除外)。

关于抬头人。商业发票必须做成以申请人为抬头(转让信用证中情形除外)。

关于发票的币种。商业发票的货币必须与信用证的货币相同。

关于发票的金额。一般不超过信用证的最高金额，但按指定行事的指定银行、保兑行(如有的话)或开证行可以接受金额大于信用证允许金额的商业发票，其决定对有关各方均有约束力，只要该银行对超过信用证允许金额的部分未做承付或者议付。

关于货物描述。商业发票上的货物、服务或履约行为的描述应该与信用证中的描述一致。

关于签名。若无明确要求，商业发票无须签名。

3. 其他类型的发票

1) 形式发票(Proforma Invoice, P/I)

形式发票又称预开发票或估价发票，是在为成交之前，出口商应进口商的要求，根据拟出售成交的商品名称、单价、规格等条件开立的一份非正式参考性发票，供进口商向本国贸易管理当局和外汇管理部门等申请进口许可证或批准低于外汇等用途，有时也用作为交易磋商的发盘。

形式发票样本如下：

6. 一则形式发票的修改看外贸风险防范

TOKYO IMPORT& EXPORT CORPORATION

82～324, OTOLI MACHI TOKYO, J APAN

PROFORMA INVOICE

TEL: 028－548742 (WITHOUT ENGAGEMENT) P/I NO.: IN05791

FAX: 028－548743 DATE: AUG. 11, 2017

P/C NO: TX201523

CONSIGNEE:

SHANGHAI IMPORT & EXPORT CORPORATION.

FROM TOKYO, J APAN TO SHANGHAI, CHINA

DELIVERY: LATEST DATE OF SHIPMENT 170920

PARTIAL SHIPMENTS ALLOWED TRANSHIPMENT NOT ALLOWED

MARKS & NO	DESCRIPTIONS OF GOODS	QUANTITY	UNIT PRICE	AMOUNT
TITC	HAND TOOLS		FOB TOKYO	
TX200523	HEX DEYS WRENCH	1 000 SET	USD 10.00	USD 10 000.00
SHANGHAI	DOUBLE RING OFFSET WRENCH	1 500 SET	USD 10.00	USD 15 000.00
C/NO. 1～60	CONBINATION WRENCH	2 000 SET	USD 20.00	USD 40 000.00
	ADJUSTABLE WRENCH	1 500 SET	USD 20.00	USD 30 000.00
				USD 95 000.00

SAY U.S. DOLLARS NINETY FIVE THOUSAND ONLY

TERMS: 100% PAYMENT BYIRREVOCABLE DOCUMENTARY CREIDT AT 30 DAYS AFTER SIGHT

This invoice is supplied to enable you to apply
For the necessary import licence to be valid up to

TOKYO IMPORT& EXPORT CORPORATION
山　田

形式发票不是一种正式的发票，不能用于托收和议付，它所列的单价等条件，也仅仅是出口商根据当时交易情况所做的估计，对双方都无最终的约束力，所以形式发票只是一种估价单，正式成交后还要另外重新擅制发票用于结算和办理其他手续。

2）领事发票(Consular Invoice)

领事发票是由进口国驻出口国的领事出具的一种特别印就的发票，是出口商根据进口国驻在出口地领事所提供的特定格式填制，并经领事签证的发票。这种发票证明出口货物的详细情况，为进口国用于防止外国商品的低价倾销，同时可用作进口税计算的依据，有助于货物顺利通过进口国海关。对于领事发票各国有不同的规定，如允许出口商在商业发票上由进口国驻出口地的领事签证(Consular Visa)，即领事签证发票。出具领事发票时，领事馆一般要根据进口货物价值收取一定费用。这种发票主要为拉美国家所采用。

3）海关发票(Customs Invoice)

(1) 海关发票的定义

海关发票是根据某些国家海关的规定，由出口商填制并签署的，供进口商凭以向进口国海关办理清关手续，具有特定格式的发票。

由有关国家政府规定的，其内容比一般的商业发票复杂。尽管各国制定的海关发票格式不同，但一般包括三大部分，即价值部分(Certificate of Value)、产地部分(Certificate of Origin)和证明部分(Declaration)，所以海关发票通常被称为“Combined Certificate of Value and of Origin”。海关发票(customs invoice/certified invoice)是进口商向进口国海关报关的证件之一。

海关发票是某些进口国的进口商向海关报关的所需证件之一。海关发票由出口商填写，其格式由进口商具体规定。其主要项目有货物的生产国别、货物名称、数量、唛头、出口地市场价及出口售价等。目前采用海关发票主要有加拿大、澳大利亚、新西兰等。由于海关发票不利于自由贸易，目前在国际贸易中使用有减少的趋势。

(2) 海关发票的作用

① 进口商凭以报关，进口商海关凭以估计征税的凭证。

② 进口国海关核定货物原产地，征收差别关税，查核进口商凭在其本国的价格、确认是否倾销，是否征收反倾销的依据。

③ 作为进口国海关编制统计资料的依据。

4) 厂商发票(Manufacturer's Invoice)

厂商发票是出口货物的制造厂商所出具的以本国货币计算，用来证明出口国国内市场的出厂价格的发票。信用证要求提供厂商发票的目的是检查出口国出口商品是否由销价倾销行为，供进口国海关估价，核税以及征收反倾销税之用。

5) 证实发票(Certified Invoice)

证实发票是证明所载内容真实、正确的一种发票，证明的内容是进口商的要求而规定，如发票内容真实无误、货物的真实产地、商品品质与合同相符、价格正确，等等。如 L/C 规定"Certified Invoice"，发票名称应照打，同时划去发票下通常印就的"E. &. O. E."字样，通常在发票内注明"WE HEREBY CERTIFY THAT THE CONTENTS OF INVOICE HEREIN ARE TRUE & CORRECT"。有些国家对证实发票的规定有一定的格式，作为货物进口清关以较低关税或免税证明。有些地区的进口商凭证实发票代替海关发票办理清关或取得关税优惠。有些进口商凭证实发票证明佣金未包括在货价内，借以索取价外报酬。

4. 包装单据

包装单据(Packing Documents)是指记载或描述商品包装情况的单据，是商业发票的附属单据。它是进口地海关验货、公证行检验、进口商核对货物时的依据之一，用以了解包装件号内的具体内容和包装情况。在我国，装箱单是出口货物报关、商检和货款议付的必备单据之一。

(1) 种类

常见的单据名称有以下几种：

① 装箱单(PACKING LIST)。

② 重量单、磅码单(WEIGHT LIST/NOTE/MEMO)。

③ 尺码单(MEASUREMENT LIST)。

④ 包装明细单(PACKING SPECIFICATION)。

⑤ 详细装箱单(DETAILED PACKING LIST)。

⑥ 花色搭配单(ASSORTMENT LIST)。

小贴士

如果信用证要求提供"中性装箱单"(Neutral Packing List)，则装箱单名称仍可写成"Packing List"，但装箱单内不能显示卖方的名称，也不能签署。

如果信用证规定包装单为"Plain paper""In plain""In white paper"等，则在包装单内即不显示卖方的名称，也不显示买方的名称，也不能签署。其他内容与普通装箱单据的缮制要求一样。

(2) 注意点

① 包装单据的名称应与信用证内规定的名称一致。

如:packing list in triplicate,则打上 packing list;

packing and weight list in triplicate,则打上 packing and weight list。

② 如果没有特别要求,包装单据可以不显示收货人。

③ 毛、净重,一般要求显示货物的总毛重、总净重。

④ 装箱单据一般不显示货物的单、总价,因为进口商在转移这些单据给实际买方时不愿泄露其购买成本。

⑤ 单据上的总件数和总重量应与发票一致。品名、数量、件数、重量等,要与实物一致;否则,一旦被海关查实,将受到惩罚,甚至被追究刑事责任。

⑥ 信用证项下,应注意遵守信用证中标号 46A 装箱单条款的要求;严格按照信用证的规定制作。

⑦ 装箱单并无统一的格式。

3.5　能力实训

实训 1　根据信用证及相关资料修改商业发票

FROM: HANG SENG BANK, HONGKONG

TO: BANK OF CHINA, NANJING

DD: 140206　　L/C NO.: 1234　　L/C AMT: USD10 000.00

APPLICANT: PICTURE AND MUSIC COMPANY, HONGKONG
16 TOM STREET, HONGKONG

BENEFICIARY: FLYING LRAK COMPANY, NANJING
118 XUEYUAN STREET, NANJING, P.R.CHINA

LATEST DATE OF SHIPMENT: APR. 2ND, 2014

DESCRIPTION OF GOODS AND/OR SERVICES:

MEN'S SLACKS, USD 10.00 PER PIECE CFR HONGKONG

TOTAL QUANTITY: 1 000 PIECE

DOCUMENTS REQUIRED: SIGNED COMMERCIAL INVOICE IN 6 COPIES CERTIFYING THAT THE COUNTRY OF ORIGIN IS CHINA AND SHIPPING ADVICE WILL BE FAXED TO M/S PROSPEROUS FUTURE INSURANCE COMPANY WITHIN 3 DAYS AFTER SHIPMENT DATE.

信用证对发票未做其他的规定,受益人的有权签字的人为周星

南京云雀贸易公司

118 XUEYUAN STREET, NANJING, P.R.CHINA

COMMERCIAL INVOICE

Messrs: FLYING LARK COMPANY, NANJING　　Date: FEB. 6,2014

118 XUEYUAN STREET, NANJING, P.R.CHINA

PORT OF LOADING: NANJING　　L/C NO.: 1234

PORT OF DISCHARGE: HONGKONG

Marks and numbers	Number and kind of package; Description of goods	Unit price CFR HONGKONG	Amount
N/M	MEN'S SLACKS	USD10.00/PIECE	USD100 000.00
SAY TOTAL: SAY US DOLLARS TEN THOUSAND ONLY. FLYING LARK COMPANY, NANJING			

实训 2　仔细阅读信用证及相关资料,缮制商业发票和装箱单

FM: ASAHI BANK LTD, THE (FORMERLY THE KYOWA SAITAMA BANK LTD.) TOKYO

TO: BANK OF CHINA, ZHEJIANG BRANCH. HANGZHOU, CHINA.

WE HEREBY ISSUE OUR IRREVOABLE DOCUMENTARY CREDIT NO. 12345

DATE OF ISSUE: JUNE 12, 2014.

DATE OF EXPIRY: OCT. 12, 2014

PLACE OF EXPIRY: CHINA.

BENEFICIARY: CHINA HANGHZOU YONGSHENG FOREIGN TRADE COMPANY LTD.
22F. GREEN CITY PLAZA 819 SHIXIN ROAD(M).
XIAOSHAN HANGHZOU. CHINA P. C 311200

APPLICANT: GOOD LUCKY COPORATION LTD.
NO. 123 TRADE STREET P. O. BOX 890 TOKYO, JAPAN

CURRENCY AMOUNT: USD98 000.00

SAY UNITED STATES DOLLARS NINETY EIGHT THOUSAND ONLY.

CREDIT AVAILABLE WITH/BY: ANY BANK IN CHINA

BY NEGOTIATION DRAFTS AT SIGHT FOR FULL INVOICE VALUE.

DRAWEE: SAIBJPJT

ASAHI BANK LTD, THE (FORMERLY THE KYOWA SAITAMA BANK LTD.) TOKYO

PARTIAL SHIPMENT: ALLOWED

TRANSSHIPMENT: NOT ALLOWED

SHIPMENT: FROM CHINESE MAIN PORT, FOR TRANSPORTATION TO OSAKA JAPAN.

LATEST DATE OF SHIPMENT: SEP. 27, 2014

DESCRIPTION OF THE GOODS:

HALF DRIED PRUNE 2014CROP

GRADE	SPEC		QTY (TOTAL CASE)	UNIT PRICE (USD/CASE)
A	L: 700CASES	M: 700CASES	1 400	26.00
B	L: 700CASES	M: 700CASES	1 400	21.00
C	L: 800CASES	M: 600CASES	1 400	21.00

PACKING: IN WOODEN CASE, 12KGS PER CASE

TRADE TERMS: CFR OSAKA

DOCUMENTS REQUIRED:

1. 2/3 SET OF CLEAN ON BOARD OCEAN BILL OF LADING MADE OUT TO ORDER OF SHIPPER AND BLANK ENDORSED AND MARKED FREIGHT PREPAID AND NOTIFY THE APPLICANT.

2. MANUALLY SIGNED COMMERCIAL INVOICE IN TRIPLICATE INDICATING APPLI CANT' S REF NO. SCLI－2014－0648 AND SHOWING BREAKDOWN OF FREIGHT CHARGEA AND FOB VAUE.

3. PACKING LIST IN THREE FOLDS SHOWING G. W., N. W., AND MEAS. OF EACH PACKGE

4. MANUALLY SIGNED CERTIFICATE OF ORIGIN IN TRIPLICATE(3).

5. BENEFICIARY'S CERTIFICATE STATING THAT CERTIFICATE OF MANUFACTURING PROCEESS AND OF THE INGREDIENTS ISSUED BY PRODUCER SHOULD BE SENT TO APPLICANT BY DHL.

ADDITIONAL CONITIONS:

1. INSURANCE TO BE EFFECTED BY BUYER.

2. TELEGRAPHIC REIMBURSEMENT CLAIM PROHIBITED.

3. 1/3 ORIGINAL BILL OF LADING AND OTHER SHIPPING DOCUMENTS MUST BE SENT DIRECTLY TO THE APPLICANT IN THREE DAYS AFTER B/L DATE. BENEFICIARY'S STATEMENT TO THIS EFFECT IS REQUIRED.

4. AMOUNT AND QNTY 5PCT MORE OR LESS ARE ALLOWED.

5. THIS COMMODITY FREE FROM RESIN.

6. INVOICE SHOULD BE CERTIFIED BY CHAMBER OF COMMERCE OR CCPIT.

DETAILS OF BANKING CHARGES: ALL BANKING CHARGES OUTSIDE JAPAN ARE FOR ACCOUNT OF BENEFICIARY.

PRESENTATION PERIOD: DOCUMENTS TO BE PRESENTED WITHIN 15 DAYS AFTER THE DATE OF SHIPMENT, BUT WITHIN THE VALIDITY OF THE CREDIT.

CONFIRMATON: WITHOUT.

INSTRUCTION:

THE NEGOTIATING BANK MUST FORWARD THE DRAFTS AND ALL

DOCUMENTS BY REG-ISTERED AIRMAIL DIRECT TO US (ASAHI BANK LTD, INTERNATIONAL OPERATIONS OFFICE. MAIL ADDRESS: C. P. 0. BOX 880 TOKYO 100～869 JAPAN IN TWO CONSECUTIVE LOTS. UPON RECEIPT OF THE DRAFTS AND DOCUMENTS IN ORDER, WE WILL REMIT THE PROCEEDS AS INSTRUCTED BY THE NEGOTIATING BANK.

THIS CREDIT IS SUBJECT TO THE UNIFORM CUSTOMS AND PRACTICE FOR DOCUMENTARY CREDITS (1993 REVISION), INTERNATIONAL CHAMBER OF COMMERCE, PUBLICATION NUMBER 500 AND ENGAGES US IN ACCORDANCE WITH THE TERMS THEREOF.

ASAHT BANK LTD THE TOKYO JAPAN.

有关资料

进口公司:东京好运有限公司　日本东京商贸街123号邮政信箱890号

出口公司:杭州永盛对外贸易公司　杭州萧山区心中路819号绿都世贸广场22楼　邮编:311200

发票号码:2014HA8869　　发票日期:2014年9月3日

提单号码:FSH56707　　提单日期:2014年9月20日

船　　名:SHANGHAIV.8808　　装运港:上海出口口岸:吴淞海关

集装箱装运:3×20′FCL,CY/CY　　海运费:USD1 050.00

集装箱号码:STEMH5698112　　封箱号:08132

TRIUl567537　　08133

KHLU6206867　　08134

净重:12千克/箱　　毛重:15千克/箱　　尺码:(20＊25＊35)cms/箱

产地证号码:041898699　　FORM　A号码:ZJ/XS/04/0012

合同号码:YS04－29876　　H.S.号码:0813.0000

唛头:C.C.I/SCH－2014－0648/OSAKA/NO.1－4200/MADE IN CHINA

请根据信用证要求制作商业发票,装箱单

CHINA HANGHZOU YONGSHENG FOREIGN TRADE COMPANY LTD.
22F. GREEN CITY PLAZA 819 SHIXIN ROAD(M)
XIAOSHAN HANGHZOU. CHINA P. C 311200

COMMERCIAL INVOICE

To

日期
Date
发票号
Invoice No.
合约号
Contract No.

信用证号
L/C No. ____________________

装　　由
Shipped per ____________________

开船日期
Sailing about ____________________

出
From ____________________

至
To ____________________

唛头 SHIPPING MARK	货名数量 QUANTITIES AND DESCRIPTIONS	单价 UNIT PRICE	金额 AMOUNET

<table>
<tr><td>ISSUER</td><td colspan="2">装箱单

PACKING LIST</td></tr>
<tr><td rowspan="2">TO</td><td colspan="2"></td></tr>
<tr><td>INVOICE NO.</td><td>DATE</td></tr>
</table>

Marks and Numbers	Number and kind of package Description of goods	Quantity	Package	G. W	N. W	Meas.

TOTAL:

SAY TOTAL:

实训 3　根据信用证的相关资料和补充资料填制商业发票

DD: 160206

L/C NO.: 1234

L/C AMT: USD64 000.00

APPLICANT: SAMIEHTEXTILE&BLANKETETCO. LTD
　　16 TOM STREET, HONGKONG

BENEFICIARY: WUXI TEXTILES IMPORT & EXPORT CORPORATION
　　27 CHUNGSHAN ROAD WUXI, CHINA

SHIPMENT: FROM SHANGHAI, CHINA TO HONGKONG NOT LATER THAN JULY. 30, 2016

DESCRIPTION OF GOODS AND/OR SERVICES:

COVERING 100PCT COTTON GREIGE PRINT CLOTH

ART. NO.3042 FIRST QUALITY

SIZE: 30×30 68×68 50″ EXPORT PACKING IN SEAWORTHY BALES

TOTAL QUANTITY: ABOUT 200,000YDS

PRICE @USD0.32 PER YARD CFR HONGKONG

DOCUMENTS REQUIRED: MANUALLY SIGNED COMMERCIAL INVOICE IN 4 COPIES SHOWING BREAKDOWN OF FREIGHT CHARGES AND FOB VALUE CERTIFYING THAT EACH CARTON/CASE OF THE GOODS CARRIES THE NAME OF COUNTRY OF ORIGIN PACKING LIST IN THREE FOLDS SHOWING G. W., N. W., AND MEAS. OF EACH PACKGE.

……

SEPCIAL CONDITION:

—INVOICE SHOULD BE MADE OUT IN THE NAME OF KUWAIT GARMENT CO., LTD INVOICE SHOULD BE CERTIFIED BY CHAMBER OF COMMERCE OR CCPIT ALL DOCUMENTS MUST BEAR THE L/C NO.

补充资料:

(1) SHIPPING MARKS: SAM/L/C NO. 123/HONGKONG/MADE IN CHINA/NO.1～166

(2) 实际出运 199200YDS, H.S. CODE: 52081100

(3) 包装明细:布包(IN BALE)

件号	货号	包装率	每包毛重	每包净重	每包尺码
1－166	3042	1200YDS/BALE	141 KGS	139 KGS	95×68×50

(4) 发票号:05AO－P001　　　　日期:2016 年 3 月 1 日

WUXI TEXTILES IMPORT & EXPORT CORPORATION
27 CHUNGSHAN ROAD. WUXI, CHINA
TEL:860510－65342517 FAX:860510－65724743

COMMERCIAL INVOICE

TO:

InvoiceNo.: ....
Date: ....

From .... To ....
L/C No. .... Issued by ....

Marks & Nos.	Descriptions	Quantity	Unit Price	Amount

WUXI TEXTILES IMPORT & EXPORT CORPORATION
27 CHUNGSHAN ROAD. WUXI, CHINA
TEL:860510－65342517　FAX:860510－65724743

PACKING LIST

TO:　　　　　　　　　　　　　　　　INVOICE NO:
　　　　　　　　　　　　　　　　　　DATE:

FAX:
TEL:
FROM　　　　TO　　　　BY

MARKS	DESCRIPTION	QUANTITY	PACKAGES (CTN)	N.W (KGS)	G.W (KGS)	MEAS.
TOTAL						

SAY TOTAL:

项目 4　制作订舱委托书和办理托运

4.1　学习目标

知识目标:熟悉出口订舱的流程,掌握订舱委托书的内容和制作要点。

能力目标:能够独立制作符合要求的订舱委托书,能够办理出口货物订舱。

4.2　工作任务

无锡蓝天进出口公司向加拿大的 KU TEXTILE CORPORATION 出口全棉女童连衣裙。2015 年 5 月 22 日,无锡蓝天进出口公司的业务员与国内工厂无锡星宇纺织有限公司在分析备货生产进程后,确认 2015 年 7 月 12 日货物能生产完毕并出运。该公司外贸单证员郭晓芳在收到无锡星宇纺织有限公司如下计划出运货物的信息和其他信息,准备好商业发票、装箱单后,着手制作订舱委托书,办理货物托运手续。

在本任务中,郭晓芳需要完成如下工作内容:

① 缮制订舱委托书。

② 办理出口托运手续。

4.3　操作范例

第一步:落实货运代理和运输公司

2015 年 6 月 22 日,无锡蓝天进出口公司的外贸业务员根据无锡星宇纺织有限公司提供的货物出货信息,决定本批出口货物采用集装箱班轮运输。故在落实信用证及备货时,外贸业务员即在网上向各家货运代理公司询价,最终确定委托上海运达国际货运代理有限公司(以下简称上海运达)向中远集装箱运输有限公司(COSCO Container Lines)代为订舱,以便及时履行交货和交单的任务。

第二步:订舱委托

在 6 月 22 日货物备齐后,郭晓芳填制订舱委托书,随附发票、装箱单等其他必要单据,委托上海运达代为订舱。订舱委托书是出口企业和货代公司之间委托代理关系的证明文件。

出口货物订舱委托书见表 4 - 1。

表 4-1 出口货物订舱委托书

日期:2015 年 6 月 1 日

发货人	信用证号码	123456		
WUXI BLUE SKY IMP&EXP. Co., LTD.. NO. 53 ZHIGONG STREET, WUXI, P. R. CHINA TEL:+86-510-82398888 FAX:+86-510-82398889	开证银行	HSBC BANK PLC, MONTREAL, CANADA		
	合同号码	K123	成交金额	USD65300
	装运口岸	SAHNGHAI	目的港	MONTREAL
收货人	转船运输	ALLOWED	分批装运	ALLOWED
TO ORDER	信用证有效期	AUG. 15, 2015	装船期限	July31, 2015
	运费	PREPAID	成交条件	CIF MONTREAL
	公司联系人	GUO XIAO FANG	电话/传真	+86-510-82398889
通知人	公司开户行	BANK OF CHINA, WUXI, CHINA	银行帐号	58625935148
KU TEXTILE CORPORATION 430 VTRA MONTREAL CANADA TEL+971-4-6666888FAX—971-4-6666889	标记唛码	KU/K123/MONTREAL/C/NO. 1-235		
	包装件数	总毛重	总净重	总体积
GIRL DRESS 100% COTTON	235 CTNS	2 285 KGS	2 070 KGS	45.385 M^3
备注				

请预订 1×40′(FCL)船,7 月 15 日前能够签发提单;提前通知产地装箱日期;提单提前传真我公司预审,正副本提单各 3 份;

提单上要显示:(1) FREIGHT PREPAID;(2) SHIPPED ON BOARD

第三步：订妥舱位

2015 年 6 月 1 日，郭晓芳把订舱委托书传真给上海运达国际货运代理有限公司，指示其向中远集装箱运输有限公司订船期为 2015 年 7 月 15 日，船名为 DONG FANG、航次为 V. 25 的一个 40 米集装箱整箱。

上海运达公司接到委托后，填制集装箱货物托运单（见表 4－2）向中远集装箱运输有限公司托运。

表 4－2　集装箱货物托运单

<table>
<tr><td colspan="3">Shipper
WUXIBLUE SKY IMP&EXP. Co., LTD..
NO.53 ZHIGONG STREET, WUXI, P.R. CHINA
TEL:＋86－510－82398888
FAX:＋86－510－82398889</td><td colspan="3" rowspan="5">D/R No.(编号)GUAN

集装箱货物托运单
第
一
联
货主留底</td></tr>
<tr><td colspan="3">Consignee
TO ORDER</td></tr>
<tr><td colspan="3">Notify Party
KU TEXTILE CORPORATION
430 VTRA MONTREAL CANADA
TEL:＋971－4－6666888
FAX:＋971－4－6666889</td></tr>
<tr><td>Pre carriage by</td><td colspan="2">Place of Receipt</td></tr>
<tr><td>Ocean vessel
DONG FANG</td><td>Voy. No.
V.25</td><td>Port of Loading
SAHNGHAI</td></tr>
<tr><td>Port of Discharge
MONTREAL</td><td colspan="2">Place of delivery</td><td colspan="3">Final Destination for Merchant's References</td></tr>
<tr><td>Container No.

COSU1007778</td><td>Seal No.
Mark & Nos.
KU
K123
MONTREAL
C/NO.1－235
seal No.5087002</td><td>No. of Containers or P'kgs.
ONE CONTAINER
235 CTNS</td><td>Kind of Packages; Description of Goods

GIRL DRESS
100% COTTON</td><td>Gross weight

2 285 kgs</td><td>Measurement

45.385 m³</td></tr>
<tr><td colspan="3">TOTAL NUMBER OF CONTAINERS OR PACKAGES(IN WORDS)</td><td colspan="3">SAY ONE CONTAINER ONLY</td></tr>
<tr><td>FREIGHT&CHARGES
FREIGHT PREPAID</td><td colspan="2">Revenue tons</td><td>Rate</td><td>Per</td><td>Prepaid</td></tr>
<tr><td colspan="6">Collect</td></tr>
<tr><td rowspan="2">Ex rate:</td><td colspan="2">Prepaid at</td><td colspan="2">Payable at</td><td>Place of Issue</td></tr>
<tr><td colspan="2">Total Prepaid</td><td colspan="2">No. of Original B(s)/L
THREE(3)</td><td></td></tr>
<tr><td colspan="2">Service Type on Receiving
□-CY, □-CFS, □-DOOR</td><td colspan="2">Service Type on delivery
□-CY, □-CFS, □-DOOR</td><td>Reefer Temperature Required.
Not Required</td><td>℉ ℃</td></tr>
</table>

（续表）

<table>
<tr><td rowspan="2">TYPE
OF
GOODS
（种类）</td><td>□Ordinary, □Reefer □Dangerous, □Auto.
（普通） （冷藏） （危险品） （裸装车辆）</td><td rowspan="2">危
险
品</td><td rowspan="2">Class:
Property:
IMDG Code
Page:
UN No.</td></tr>
<tr><td>□Liquid, □Live Animal, □Bulk, □______
（液体） （活动物） （散货）</td></tr>
<tr><td>Transhipment:
ALLOWED</td><td>Partial Shipment:
ALLOWED</td><td colspan="2" rowspan="4"></td></tr>
<tr><td>Date of Shipment
JUL 15, 2015</td><td>Period of Validity(有效期)
JUL 31, 2015</td></tr>
<tr><td colspan="2">Amount(USD):USD65 520.00</td></tr>
<tr><td colspan="2">制单日期:2015 年 7 月 15 日</td></tr>
</table>

上海运达订妥中远集运 2015 年 7 月 15 日自上海至蒙特利尔 1×40′舱位，中远集运在托运单上编制提单号码并盖章，将配舱回单和装货单等退还给上海运达。上海运达在确认配船和费用后，传真送货通知给无锡蓝天进出口公司，要求公司 7 月 13 日中午前将货物运至指定仓库(无锡星宇纺织有限公司仓库)。

第四步：集装箱货物装箱、集港

上海运达随即向中远集运箱管部门提出用箱申请，填写设备交接单，提取一个 40′空箱，同时通知无锡蓝天进出口公司做好装箱准备。12 月 29 日下午，集装箱被运至上海星宇纺织有限公司仓库，将货物装箱并封存。外贸单证员郭晓芳确认集装箱装箱单(见表 4-3)后签字，随后，上海运达将重箱运至上海港集港，港区仓库签发场站收据，以确认收到货物。

表 4-3 集装箱装箱单

<table>
<tr><td colspan="4">Reffer Temperature Required 冷藏温度
℃ ℉</td><td colspan="7" rowspan="2">CONTAINER LOAD PLAN
COSCO TIANJIN COMPANY
中远
装箱单
中远天津公司
Shipper's/Packer's Copy
发货人/装箱人 联</td></tr>
<tr><td>Class
等级</td><td>IMDG Page
危险页码</td><td>UN NO.
联合国编号</td><td>Flashpoint
闪点</td></tr>
<tr><td colspan="4">Ship's Name/Voy No. 船名/船次
DONGFANG V.25</td><td>Port of Loading
装港
TIANJIN</td><td colspan="2">Port of Discharge
卸港
DUBAI</td><td>Place of delivery
交货地</td><td colspan="3">SHIPPER'S/PACKER'S DECLARATIONS: We hereby declare that the container has been thoroughly cleaned without any evidence of cargoes of previous shipment prior to vanning andcargoes has been properly stuffed and seured.</td></tr>
<tr><td colspan="4">Container No. 箱号
COSU1007778</td><td>B/L NO.
提单号</td><td>Packages & Packing
件数与包装</td><td>Gross weight
毛重</td><td>Measure-ments
尺码</td><td>Description of Goods
货名</td><td colspan="2">Marks & Nos.
唛头</td></tr>
</table>

（续表）

<table>
<tr><td colspan="2">Seal No. 封号</td><td rowspan="4"></td><td rowspan="4">235
CTNS</td><td rowspan="4">2 285
KGS</td><td rowspan="4">45. 385 8
M^3</td><td rowspan="4">GIRL
DRESS</td><td rowspan="4">KU
K123
MONTREAL
C/NO. 1 - 235</td></tr>
<tr><td>Container Size
箱型
20′40′45′
20 GP</td><td>Cont. Type 箱类
GP＝普通箱 TK＝油罐箱
RF＝冷藏箱 PF＝平板箱
OT＝开顶箱 HC＝高箱
FR＝框架箱 HT＝挂衣箱</td></tr>
<tr><td colspan="2">ISO Code ForContainer Size/Type
箱型/箱类 ISO 标准代码
22G1</td></tr>
<tr><td colspan="2">Packer's Name/Address 装箱人名称/地址
北京星宇纺织有限公司
北京朝阳区十八里店路 39 号</td></tr>
</table>

<table>
<tr><td>Packing Date 装箱日期
2015 年 12 月 29 日</td><td>Received By Drayman
驾驶员签收及车号</td><td>Total Packages
总件数
235 CTNS</td><td>Total Cargo Wt
总货重
2 285 KGS</td><td>Total Meas
总尺码
45. 385 M^3</td><td rowspan="2">Remarks：</td></tr>
<tr><td>Packed by 装箱人签名
郭晓芳</td><td colspan="2">Received By Terminals/Date of Receipt
码头收箱签收和收箱日期</td><td>Cont Tare Wt
集装箱皮重</td><td>Cgo/Cont. Tare Wt
货/箱总重量</td></tr>
</table>

4.4 知识链接

1. 集装箱货物海运出口托运的流程（见图 4 - 1）（二维码）

从理论上说，出口商（受益人）可以直接向船公司托运订舱。但在我国目前的情况下，船公司一般不接受出口商的直接托运，大多只接受货代的间接托运，所以出口商只能通过货代向船公司托运订舱。

① 出口企业在货、证备齐后，填制订舱委托书，随附商业发票、装箱单等等其他必要单据，委托货运代理公司代为订舱。

② 货代公司接收订舱委托后，缮制集装箱货物托运单，随同相关单据向船公司办理订舱。

③ 船公司在接受订舱后，在集装箱货物托运单上加列船名、航次和编号（该编号就是事

后签发的提单号码)，同时在第五联(装货单)上加盖图章以示确认，然后将有关各联退还给货代，以便他们办理报关、装船和换取提单之用。

④ 整箱货的空箱由船公司送交货代。一般情况下，整箱货运输时，货代到集装箱堆场领取，拼箱货运输时，货运站工作人员到堆场领取。

⑤ 货代收到空箱后，即往厂家进行装箱，完毕后在集装箱的箱门上施加铅封。然后货代将重箱拖进堆场并将场站收据送交堆场工作人员，工作人员点收货物无误后，代表船方在场站收据上签字，并把它退还给货代。签过字的场站收据证明承运人已收到货物并开始承担责任。重箱到达堆场的最晚时间是货物装运前 48 小时。

拼箱货出口时，出口企业可将报关所需的单据连同货物一并送交货运站，货运站点收货物后，根据货物的性质、流向、目的港的不同进行拼装。货运站的工作人员点收货物无误后，代表船方在场站收据上签字，并把它退还给发货人或货代。出口货物到达货运站的最晚时间是货物装运前 72 小时。

⑥ 货代或者货运站接到可装船的通知后，于船舶开航前 3 天即可将重箱运入指定港区备装。通常情况下，重箱进港的最晚时间是船舶装前 24 小时。

⑦ 换取提单。如果是老三种术语(FOB/CFR 和 CIF)出口，货代要在重箱上船后，凭场站收据副本才能换取提单。如果采用新三种术语(FCA、CPT 和 CIP)出口，货代凭场站收据正本即可换得提单。在使用新三种术语的情况下，场站收据是承运人收货的凭证，也是货代公司代表出口商换取提单的唯一凭证。

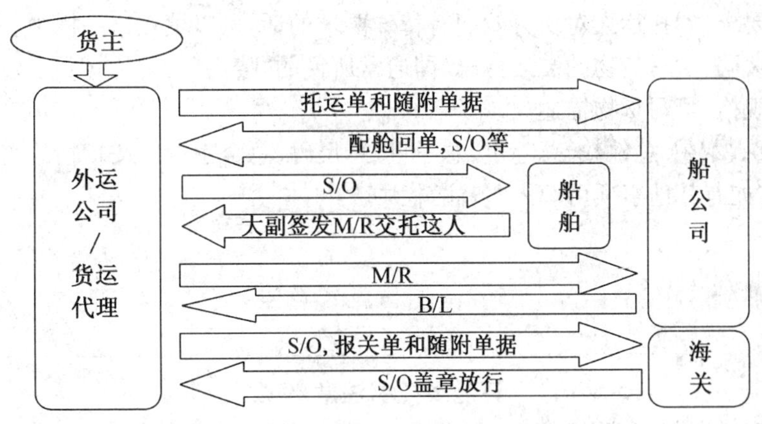

图 4-1 集装箱货物海运出口托运的流程

2. 订舱委托书各栏目的缮制要点和注意事项

订舱委托书(Shipping Note)是出口企业与货运代理公司之间委托代理关系的证明文件。出口企业委托对外贸易运输公司或货运代理公司向承运人或其代理人办理出口货物运输业务时需要向其提供订舱委托书。

订舱委托书各栏目内容的缮制要点如下：

① 发货人(托运人)：填写出口公司(信用证受益人)。

② 收货人：填写信用证规定的提单收货人。

③ 通知人：填写信用证规定的提单通知人。

一般在订舱委托书上会注明托运人、收货人、通知人这三栏为提单(B/L)项目要求。意即,将来船公司签发的提单上的相应栏目的填写也会参照订舱委托书的写法。因此,这三栏的填写应该按照信用证提单条款的相应规定填写。

④ 信用证号码:填写相关交易的信用证号码。

⑤ 开证银行:填写相关交易的信用证开证银行的名称。

⑥ 合同号码:填写相关交易的合同号码。

⑦ 成交金额:填写相关交易的合同总金额。

⑧ 装运口岸:填写信用证规定的起运地。如信用证未规定具体的起运港口,则填写实际装港名称。

⑨ 目的港:填写信用证规定的目的地。如信用证未规定的目的港口,则填写实际卸货港名称。

⑩ 转船运输:根据信用证条款,如允许分批,则填"YES",反之,则填"NO"。

⑪ 分批装运:根据信用证条款,如允许分批,则填"YES",反之,则填"NO"。如信用证未对转船和分批作具体的规定,则应该按照合同的有关填写。

⑫ 信用证效期:填写信用证的有效期。

⑬ 装运期限:填写信用证规定的装运期限。

⑭ 运费:根据信用证提单条款的规定填写"FREIGHT PREPAID"(运费预付)或"FREIGHT TO COLLECT"运费到付。

⑮ 成交条件:填写成交的贸易术语,如:"FOB""CIF""CFR"等。

⑯ 特别要求:如托运人对所订舱门有特殊要求的话,可以填在这一栏中。

⑰ 标记唛码:填写货物的装运标志,即通常所说的"唛头"。

⑱ 货号规格:填写货物描述。

⑲、⑳、㉑、㉒、㉓ 总件数、总毛重、总净重、总尺码、总金额——按货物的实际情况填写。

㉔ 备注:如有其他事项可填入"备注"栏中。

订舱委托书注意事项

① 确认委托书所载品名是否是危险品,是否是液体(对接载液体以及电池有特殊要求)确认品名的另外一个作用就是查明货物,是否对该产品存在海关监管条件。

② 确认件数,确认货物尺寸体积是否超过装载装箱能力,确认重量是否有单件货物超过3吨,如果超过3吨需要和仓库确认是否能有装箱能力。

③ 托书是预配舱单以及提单确认的初步依据,如果一次性正确可为提单确认省去许多麻烦。

④ 如需要投保,熏蒸、拍照、换单、买单、要在订舱委托书显要位置注明。

⑤ 所订船期受到外商订购合同,备货时间,商检时间等制约,根据时间合理安排订舱日期。

⑥ 遇到拼箱出口未能按时出运,并未按时撤载,会产生亏舱费。

3. 场站收据的组成和功能

在集装箱货物出口运输业务中，为简化手续，就以场站收据作为集装箱货物的托运单。

（1）场站收据的组成

场站收据(Dock Receipt;D/R)是集装箱运输重要的出口单证，其组成格式在许多资料上说法不一，不同港、站使用的也有所不同，其联数有 7 联、10 联、12 联不等。在实际业务中，比较常见的是 10 联的场站收据，我们这里以上海港的 10 联单(见表 4－4)为例进行说明。

表 4－4　场站收据各联名称与用途

顺序	名　称	颜色	主要用途
1	集装箱货物托运单——货主留底	白色	也称订舱单，托运合同，托留存备查
2	集装箱货物托运单——船代留底	白色	托运合同，据此编制装船清单
3	运费通知(1)	白色	计算运费
4	运费通知(2)	白色	运费收取通知
5	装货单——场站收据副本(1)	白色	关单、下货纸，报关单证之一，放行证明
6	大副联——场站收据副本(2)	粉红	报关单证之一，并证明货已装船
7	场站收据正本，俗称黄联	淡黄	报关单证之一，船代凭此签发提单
8	货代留底	白色	缮制货物流向单
9	配舱回单(1)	白色	货代缮制提单等
10	配舱回单(2)	白色	据回单批注修改提单

目前，上海洋山口岸实行出口货物电子放行，纳入电子放行试点范围的货物，通过审核后，现场接单关员无须在场站收据上加盖“放行章”。港务部门不再收取场站收据，仅验凭海关发送的电子放行信息办理货物装运手续。

（2）场站收据的功能和作用

场站收据是由承运人签发的证明已收到托运货物并对货物开始负有责任的凭证，场站收据一旦经承运人或其代理人签收，就表明承运人已收到货物，责任也随之产生。与传统件杂货运输使用的托运单证比较，场站收据是一份综合性单证，它把货物托运单(订舱单)、装货单(关单)、大副收据、理货单、配舱回单、运费通知等单证汇成一份，这对于提高集装箱货物托运效率和加快流转速度有很大意义。一般认为场站收据的功能和作用如下：

① 船公司或船代确认订舱并在场站收据上加盖有报关资格的单证章后，将场站收据交给托运人或其代理人，意味着运输合同开始执行；

② 是出口货物报关的凭证之一；

③ 是承运人已收到托运货物并对货物开始负有责任的证明；

④ 是换取海运提单或联运提单的凭证；

⑤ 是船公司、港口组织装卸、理货、配载的资料；

⑥ 是运费结算的依据；

⑦ 如信用证中有规定，可作为向银行结汇的单证。

4. 集装箱货物托运单的填制规范

集装箱货物托运单的填写，要求英文字母必须大写(委托人信息可以用中文缮制)。其具体填制规范如下：

① 发货人(Shipper)：托货人，或货主，或信用证上的卖方，或无船承运人等。

② 收货人(Consignee)：货主，或信用证上的买方，或无船承运人，或某某指示人。

③ 通知人(Notify Party)：详列通知方名称、地址、电话、传真等。当没有通知人时，以SAME AS CONSINGEE。

④ 场站收据号(D/R No.)：或称为关单号，为船代接受定舱时提供的号码，或作为提单号码。

⑤ 前程运输(Pre-carriage by)：联程运输时，相对收货地之前一段的货物运输承运方式或承运人填列在此栏中。一般海托运单中，此栏不填。

⑥ 收货地(Place of Receipt)：货物实际收货地点(一般以港口所在的城市)。

⑦ 船名/航次(Ocean Vessel/Voy. No.)：船代在接收订舱时，按照配船要求确定。

⑧ 装货港(Port of Loading)：货物实际装运海港名称。

⑨ 卸货港(Port of Discharge)：将货物卸下的港口(一般是船舶班轮航线上的港口。但未必是货物的交货地)。

⑩ 交货地(Place of Delivery)：承运人将货物实际交付的地点(可以是船舶班轮航线上的港口，也可以是通过其他船舶转运过去的交货港口，或通过铁路、公路运输方式转运过去的内路交货地点)。

⑪ 目的地(Final Destination for Merchant's Reference)：客户或印贸易文件要求需要在提单上显示的货物交付的最终目的地。因为承运人是以交货地作为联运的交货点，所以承运人一般在出具的提单上并不显示此项内容。

⑫ 集装箱号(Container No.)：此栏对应正本提单的相应栏，提单上显示的集装箱号显示在此栏的靠下空白部分。

⑬ 标记与号码(Seal No./Marks & Nos.)：贸易合同上、发票上、装箱单上标明的、信用证等文件规定的标记与号码。

⑭ 箱数或件数(No. of Containers or packages)：贸易合同上、发票上、装箱单上标明的、信用证等文件规定的货物件数。

⑮ 包装种类与货名(Kind of Packages: Description of Goods)：贸易合同上、发票上、装箱单上标明的、信用证等文件规定的货物的包装种类、商品名称、商品规格等。

⑯ 毛重(Gross Weight)：每一类货物的包装毛重，单位是公斤S(千克)；两类以上，要有合计数。

⑰ 尺码(Measurement)：每一类货物的包装尺码(体积)，单位是CBM(立方米)；两类以上要有合计数。

⑱ 集装箱或件数大写：若是多票托运单自拼整箱，则相应托单上根据货物的件数，包装用英文大写字母予以表示托单上的件数(如3票托单拼1＊40′HQ，其中1票的货物包装是20CTNS，则大写为SAY TWENTY CARTONS ONLY)；若是1票托单中多个集装箱，则用英文大写字母予以表示集装箱数量或包装数(如200CTNS，装3＊40′普箱，FCL CY/CY交接，可以表示为SAY THREE CONTAINERS ONLY；或SAY TWO HUNDRED

CARTONS ONLY)。

⑲ 运费与附加费(Freight & Charges):一般在此栏填写与集装箱海关有关的海运运费和海运附加费的结算金额,或由货代填写、或又船代确认后填写货主与船公司约定的运价协议号(船公司以运价协议号的形式,确定与货主的运费结算标准,如S/C、SHA0451)。

此外,货物的交接方式(如CY-CY,CFS-CFS等)、货物的类型(如普通货、冷藏货等)、运输要求等按照实际运输情况填制。

5. 集装箱装箱单的组成与功能

集装箱装箱单(Container Load Plan, CLP)以箱为单位制作,由装箱人填制并经装箱人签署后生效。装箱单一般一式数份,分别由货主、货运站、装箱人留存和交船代、海关、港方、理货公司使用,另外,还需准备足够份数交船方随船带往卸货港以便交接货物、报关、拆箱等用。制作装箱单时,装箱人员负有装箱单内容与箱内货物一致的责任。如需理货公司对整箱货物理货时,装箱人员应会同理货人员共同制作装箱单。集装箱装箱单记载内容必须与场站收据保持一致;所装货物如品种不同必须按箱子前部到箱门的先后顺序填写。

(1) 集装箱装箱单的组成

目前各港口使用的装箱单有的一式4联,也有一式5联甚至一式10联,但是内容上基本大同小异。上海港使用的集装箱装箱单一式五联,由码头联、船代联、承运人联各1联、发货人/装箱人联共2联组成。装箱单的流转程序如下:

① 装箱人将货物装箱,缮制实际装箱单一式五联,并在装箱单上签字。

② 联装箱单随同货物一起交付给拖车司机,指示司机将集装箱送至集装箱堆场,在司机接箱时应要求司机在装箱单上签字并注明拖车号。

③ 集装箱送至堆场后,司机应要求堆场收箱人员签字并写明收箱日期,以作为集装箱已进港的凭证。

④ 堆场收箱人在5联单上签章后,留下码头联、船代联和承运人联(码头联用以编制装船计划,船代联和承运人联分送给船代和承运人用以缮制积载计划和处理货运事故),并将发货人/装箱人联退还给发货人或货运站。发货人或货运站除留一份发货人/装箱人联备查外,将另一份送交发货人,以便发货人通知收货人或卸箱港的集装箱货运站,供拆箱时使用。

(2) 集装箱装箱单的主要功能

集装箱装箱单是根据已装进集装箱内的货物制作的,是详细记载每一个集装箱内所装货物详细情况的唯一单据,所以在以集装箱为单位进行运输时,是一张极其重要的单据。每个载货集装箱都要制作这样的单据,是集装箱运输的辅助货物舱单。不论是由发货人自己装箱的(FCL),还是由集装箱货运站负责装箱的(LCL),负责装箱的一方都要制作装箱单。集装箱装箱单的主要作用如下:

① 作为发货人、集装箱货运站与集装箱码头堆场之间货物的交接单证;

② 作为向船方通知集装箱内所装货的明细表;

③ 单据上所记载货与集装箱总重量是计算船舶吃水差、稳性的基本数据;

④ 在卸货地点是办理集装箱保税运输的单据之一;

⑤ 当发生货损时,是处理索赔事故的原始单据之一;

⑥ 卸货港集装箱货运站安排拆箱、理货的单据之一。

4.5 能力实训

实训 1 根据发票和信用证中相关的规定填写“出口货物订舱委托书”

1. 相关信用证资料

SOME MSG FROM THE L/C (ISSUED BY BNP PARIBAS (CANADA))

DOC. CREDIT NUMBER	* 20:63211020049
DATE OF ISSUE	31 C: 20150129
EXPIRY	* 31 D: DATE 050410 PLACE IN BENEFICIARY'S COUNTRY
APPLICANT	* 50:FASHION FORCE CO., LTD P. O. BOX 8935 NEW TERMINAL, ALTA, VISTA OTTAWA, CANADA
BENEFICIARY	* 59:NANJING TANG TEXTILE GARMENT CO., LTD. HUARONG MANSION RM2901 NO. 85 GUANJIAQIAO, NANJING 210005, CHINA
... ...	
PARTIAL SHIPMTS	43 P: NOT ALLOWED
TRANSSHIPMENT	43 T:ALLOWED
FOR TRANSPORT TO ...	44 B:MONTREAL
LATEST DATE OF SHIP.	44 C:20150325
DOCUMENTS REQUIRED	46 A:

+FULL SET OF ORIGINAL MARINE BILLS OF LADING CLEAN ON BOARD
FLUS 2 NON NEGOTIABLE COPIES MADE OUT OR ENDORSED TO ORDER
OF BNP PARIBAS (CANADA) MARKED FREIGHT PREPAID AND NOTIFY APPLICANT'S
FULL NAME AND ADDRESS.

... ...

2. 商业发票

<table>
<tr><td colspan="2">ISSUER
NANJING TANG TEXTILE GARMENT CO., LTD.
HUARONG MANSION RM2901 NO. 85 GUANJIAQIAO,
NANJING 210005, CHINA</td><td colspan="3">商业发票

COMMERCIAL INVOICE</td></tr>
<tr><td colspan="2">TO
FASHION FORCE CO., LTD
P. O. BOX 8935 NEW TERMINAL, ALTA,
VISTA OTTAWA, CANADA</td><td colspan="2">NO.
NT01FF004</td><td>DATE
Mar. 9, 2015</td></tr>
<tr><td colspan="2" rowspan="2">TRANSPORT DETAILS
SHIPMENT FROM SHANGHAI TO MONTREAL BY VESSEL</td><td colspan="2">S/C NO.
F01LCB14127</td><td>L/C NO.
63211020049</td></tr>
<tr><td colspan="3">TERMS OF PAYMENT
L/C AT SIGHT</td></tr>
<tr><td>Marks and Numbers</td><td>Number and kind of package Description of goods</td><td>Quantity</td><td>Unit Price</td><td>Amount</td></tr>
<tr><td>FASHION FORCE
F01LCB05127
CTN NO.
MONTREAL
MADE IN CHINA</td><td>LADIES COTTON BLAZER
(100% COTTON,
40S×20/140×60)</td><td>2 550 PCS</td><td>USD12.80 CIF MONTREAL, CANADA</td><td>USD32 640.00</td></tr>
</table>

Total:

2 550 PCS　　**USD32 640.00**

SAY TOTAL: USD THIRTY TWO THOUSAND SIX HUNDRED AND FORTY ONLY

SALES CONDITIONS: CIF MONTREAL/CANADA
SALES CONTRACT NO. F01LCB05127
LADIES COTTON BLAZER (100% COTTON, 40S×20/140×60)

STYLE NO.	PO NO.	QTY/PCS	USD/PC
46 - 301A	10 337	2 550	12.80

PAKAGE	N. W.	G. W.
85CARTONS	17 KGS	19 KGS

TOTAL PACKAGE: 85 CARTONS
TOTAL MEAS: 21.583 CBM

NANJING TANG TEXTILE GARMENT CO., LTD.
唐明生

3. 补充资料

出口公司的相关情况如下：

电话:025－58818844;传真:025－58818855

开户银行:中国银行;银行账号:586259351483

4. 训练要求:格式及内容完整和正确

出口货物订舱委托书见表 4－5。

表 4－5　出口货物订舱委托书　　　　年　　月　　日

1）发货人	4）信用证号码			
	5）开证银行			
	6）合同号码		7）成交金额	
	8）装运口岸		9）目的港	
2）收货人	10）转船运输		11）分批装运	
	12）信用证有效期		13）装船期限	
	14）运费		15）成交条件	
	16）公司联系人		17）电话/传真	
3）通知人	18）公司开户行		19）银行账号	
	20）特别要求			

21）标记唛码	22）货号规格	23）包装件数	24）毛重	25）净重	26）数量	27）单价	28）总价

	29）总件数	30）总毛重	31）总净重	32）总尺码	33）总金额

34）备注

实训 2　根据信用证中的有关内容填制“集装箱货物托运单”

设本信用证项下货物的交接方式为 CY—CY，整批货被装在 2 个 20 米普通货柜，编号分别为 EASU982341、EART520152 的集装箱内，由 YINHU A3032 号船于 8 月 30 日装运出海。该批货物的合同号为 BEIT0112，体积为 66.4 CBM，每个纸箱重 0.15 KGS，唛头由受益人自行设计。

ISSUING BANK: FIRST ALABAMA BANK

106 ST. FRANCIS STREET MOBILE ALABAMA 36602 USA

BENEFICIARY: XIAMEN YINCHENG ENTERPRISE GENERAL CORP.
176 LUJIANG ROAD XIAMEN, CHINA(厦门银城企业总公司)
TELEX: 93052 IECTA CN, TEL: 86-592-2046841
FAX: 86-592-2020396

APPLICANT: BAMA SEA PRODUCTS. INC.
1499 BEACH DRIVE S. E. ST PELERSBURG. FL 33701, USA

ADVISING BANK: THE BANK OF EAST ASIA LIMITED XIAMEN BRANCH
G/F & 1/F HUICHENG BUILDING 837 XIAHE ROAD, XIAMEN, CHINA
TELEX: 93132 BEAXM CN　FAX: 86-592-5064980

DATE: AUGUST 1, 2015

FORM OF DC: IRREVOCABLE L/C AT SIGHT

AMOUNT: USD 170,450.00

PARTIAL SHIPMENT: PERMITTED

TRANSSHIPMENT: PERMITTED ONLY FROM XIAMEN CHINA FOR TRANSPORTATION TO LONG BEACH, CA. USA. WITH FINAL PORT OF DESTINATION TAMPA, FL, USA.

SHIPMENT CONSISTS OF: 34000KGS CHINESE SAND SHRIMP OR BIG HARD SHELL SHRIMP. BLOCK FROZEN SHRIMP (PTO), PACKED 5X2KGS/CTN. (RAW, PEELED, TAIL ON)

CONSISTING OF:

KGS.	SIZE(MM)	UNIT PRICE(/KGS)	TOTAL
3 000	71/90	USD6.60	USD19 800.00
5 000	91/110	USD6.35	USD31 750.00
6 000	111/130	USD5.45	USD32 700.00
8 000	131/150	USD4.55	USD36 400.00
12 000	151/200	USD4.15	USD49 800.00

TOTAL AMOUNT OF USD170450.00 CFR TAMPA FL. U.S.A.

THE LATEST SHIPMENT DATE IS AUGUST 31. 2015

DOCUMENTARY　REQUIREMENTS:

1) FULL SET(3/3) CLEAN ON BOARD COMBINED TRANSPORT BILLS OF LADING CONSIGNED TO THE ORDER OF BAMA SEA PRODUCTS INC., 1499 BEACH DRIVE S. E., ST, PELERSBURG, FL. 33701 MARKED "FREIGHT PREPAID" NOTIFYING WILLIAMS CLARKE, INC., 603 NORTH FRIES AVENUE, WILMINGTON, CA 90744, USA. AND MUST INDICATE CONTAINER(S) NUMBER AND STATE THAT CONTAINER(S) HAVE BEEN MAINTAINED AT ZERO DEGREES FAHRENHEIT OR BELOW. IF COMBINED TRANSPORT BILL OF LADING IS PRESENTED, MUST BE INDICATE VESSEL NAME.

2) BILLS OF LADING MUST ALL FREIGHT CHARGES PREPAID, INCLUDING FUEL ADJUSTMENT FEES (FAF)

<table>
<tr><td colspan="3">Shipper</td><td colspan="4" rowspan="5">D/R No.(编号)GUAN

集装箱货物托运单
第
一
联
货主留底</td></tr>
<tr><td colspan="3">Consignee</td></tr>
<tr><td colspan="3">Notify Party</td></tr>
<tr><td colspan="3">Pre carriage by   Place of Receipt</td></tr>
<tr><td colspan="3">Ocean vessel   Voy. No.   Port of Loading</td></tr>
<tr><td colspan="3">Port of Discharge   Place of delivery</td><td colspan="4">Final Destination for Merchant's References</td></tr>
<tr><td>Container No.</td><td>Seal No.
Mark & Nos.</td><td>No. of Containers or P'kgs.</td><td>Kind of Packages;
Description of Goods</td><td>Gross weight</td><td colspan="2">Measurement</td></tr>
<tr><td colspan="3">TOTAL NUMBER OF CONTAINERS OR PACKAGES(IN WORDS)</td><td colspan="4"></td></tr>
<tr><td>FREIGHT&CHARGES</td><td>Revenue tons</td><td>Rate</td><td>Per</td><td>Prepaid</td><td colspan="2">Collect</td></tr>
<tr><td rowspan="2">Ex rate:</td><td>Prepaid at</td><td colspan="2">Payable at</td><td colspan="3">Place of Issue</td></tr>
<tr><td>Total Prepaid</td><td colspan="2">No. of Original B(s)/L</td><td colspan="3"></td></tr>
<tr><td>Service Type on Receiving
□-CY, □-CFS, □-DOOR</td><td>Service Type on delivery
□-CY, □-CFS, □-DOOR</td><td colspan="3">Reefer Temperature Required.
Not Required</td><td>°F</td><td>℃</td></tr>
<tr><td rowspan="2">TYPE OF GOODS(种类)</td><td colspan="2">□Ordinary, □Reefer □Dangerous, □Auto.
(普通) (冷藏) (危险品) (裸装车辆)</td><td rowspan="2">危险品</td><td colspan="3" rowspan="2">Class:
Property:
IMDG Code Page:
UN No.</td></tr>
<tr><td colspan="2">□Liquid, □Live Animal, □Bulk, □______
(液体) (活动物) (散货)</td></tr>
<tr><td>Transhipment:</td><td colspan="2">Partial Shipment:</td><td colspan="4" rowspan="4"></td></tr>
<tr><td>Date of Shipment</td><td colspan="2">Period of Validity(有效期)</td></tr>
<tr><td colspan="3">Amount(USD):</td></tr>
<tr><td colspan="3">制单日期:</td></tr>
</table>

项目5　制作出境货物报检单和办理报检手续

5.1　学习目标

知识目标：熟悉的流报检程，熟悉换证单和通关单的用途，了解商品检验检疫基本知识。

能力目标：能够根据合同条款和信用证条款准确填制出境货物报检单和报检委托书。

5.2　工作任务

无锡蓝天进出口公司向与加拿大的 KU TEXTILE CORPORATION 出口全棉女童连衣裙。无锡蓝天进出口公司的业务员与国内工厂无锡星宇纺织有限公司在备货生产进程后，确认 2015 年 5 月 20 日货物能生产完毕并出运。该公司外贸单证员郭晓芳在收到无锡星宇纺织有限公司计划出运货物的信息和其他信息，准备好商业发票、装箱单后，制作出境货物报检单和报检委托书。

思考：该笔业务是否需要报检，如果需要，应该准备哪些单证，如何填制和操作呢？

根据相关规定，女童连衣裙（HS 编码 61044200.00），监管条件为"B"（出境货物通关单），属于法定检验的商品范围；最迟在出口报关或装运前 7 天报检，应在产地报检。本批货物准备从上海吴淞港报关出境，由于产地（无锡）与报关地（上海）不一致，应换证放行。

2015 年 5 月 21 日，郭晓芳制作报检委托书和出境货物报检单，随附商业发票、装箱单等，委托无锡星宇纺织有限公司（供货商）向无锡商检局报检，申请签发《出境货物换证凭条》。

为了委托上海海州国际货运代理公司办理上海口岸的换证放行、报关手续，无锡蓝天进出口公司（出口商）出具了报检委托书，连同其他海关所需要的单证，交给货代。

2015 年 5 月 24 日，此批货物进检验合格，无锡商检局出具《出境货物换证凭条》。当天，无锡星宇纺织有限公司将《出境货物换证凭条》的号码通知无锡蓝天进出口公司指定的货代。

2015 年 5 月 25 日，由货代在上海办理换证放行手续。

1. 商业发票

COMMERCIAL INVOICE

<table>
<tr><td rowspan="3">1) SELLER
WUXIBLUE SKY IMP&EXP. Co., LTD.
NO. 53 ZHIGONG STREET, WUXI, P. R. CHINA</td><td>3) INVOICE NO.
ZYIE1502</td><td>4) INVOICE DATE
MAY20, 2015</td></tr>
<tr><td>5) L/C NO.
123456</td><td>6) DATE
MAY20, 2015</td></tr>
<tr><td colspan="2">7) ISSUED BY
HSBC BANK PLC, MONTREAL, CANADA</td></tr>
<tr><td rowspan="3">2) BUYER
KU TEXTILE CORPORATION
430 VTRA MONTREAL CANADA</td><td>8) CONTRACT NO.
K123</td><td>9) DATE
9-APRIL-15</td></tr>
<tr><td>10) FROM
SHANGHAI</td><td>11) TO
MONTREAL</td></tr>
<tr><td>12) SHIPPED BY
TUO HE V. 25</td><td>13) PRICE TERM
CIFMONTREAL</td></tr>
</table>

14) MARKS&NOS. 15) DESCRIPTIONS OF GOODS 16) QTY 17) UNIT PRICE 18) AMOUNT

GIRL DRESS 100% COTTON

AS PER SALES COMTRACT NO. K123 DATED APR. 9, 2015

KU	11574	2 400 PCS	US$6.50	US$15 600.00
K123	11575	3 000 PCS	US$5.50	US$16 500.00
MONTREAL	11576	2 400 PCS	US$8.50	US$20 400.00
C/NO. 1-235	11577	1 600 PCS	US$8.00	US$12 800.00
	TOTAL	9 400 PC		US$65 300.00

TOTAL AMOUNT IN WORDS:

SAY US DOLLARS SIXTY FIVE THOUSAND THREE HUNDRED ONLY.

WE HEREBY CERTIFY THAT GOODS ARE OF CHINA ORIGIN.

19) ISSUEDY BY

WUXI BLUE SKY IMP&EXP. Co., LTD.

郭晓芳

2. 装箱单

PACKING LIST

1) SELLER WUXI BLUE SKY IMP&EXP. Co., LTD. NO.53 ZHONGSHAN ROAD, WUXI, CHINA	3) INVOICE NO. ZYIE1502	4) INVOICE DATE MAY20, 2015
	5) FROM SHANGHAI	6) TO MONTREAL
	7) TOTAL PACKAGES (IN WORDS) SAY TWO HUNDRED AND THIRTY-FIVE CARTONS ONLY	
2) BUYER KU TEXTILE CORPORATION 430 VTRA MONTREAL CANADA	8) MARKS&NOS. KU K123 MONTREAL C/NO.1－235	

9) C/NOS.	10) NOS.&KINDS OF PKGS	11) ITEM	12) QTY	13) G.W.	14) N.W.	15) MEAS(M3)
	GIRL DRESS 100% COTTON					
1－60	60 CARTONS	11574	2 400 PCS	600.000	540.000	12.660
61－135	75CARTONS	11575	3 000 PCS	825.000	750.000	15.825
136－195	60CARTONS	11576	2 400 PCS	600.000	540. 000	12.660
196－235	40CARTONS	11577	1 600 PCS	260.00	240.000	4.240
TOTAL:	235CARTONS		9 400 PCS	2 285.00	2 070.000	45.385

ART.NO.	G.W.(KG)	N.W.(KG)	MEAS(M3)	OF EACH PACKAGE
11574	10.000	98.000	0.211	PER CARTON
11575	11.000	10.000	0.211	PER CARTON
11576	10.000	9.000	0.211	PER CARTON
11577	6.500	6.000	0.106	PER CARTON

DOCUMENTARY CREDIT NO.: 123456
DATE OF ISSUE: 150520
NAME OF ISSUING BANK: HSBC BANK PLC, MONTREAL, CANADA

16) ISSUEDY BY
WUXI BLUE SKY IMP&EXP. Co., LTD.
郭晓芳

3. 其他信息

信用证“46A 所要求提供的单据”

CERTIFICATE OF QUALITY ISSUED BY CIQ IN DUPLICATE.(质量证书一式两份,由中国出入境检验检疫局出具和签署)

货物存放地址:无锡市东亭路 88 号

报检单位登记号 9823412345

生产厂家:无锡星宇纺织有限公司(1990023489)

在本任务中,郭晓芳需要完成以下内容:

① 制作报检委托书。

② 制作出境货物报检单。

③ 办理报检手续。

5.3 操作范例

第一步:制作报检委托书

代理报检委托书

无锡市出入境检验检疫局:

本委托人郑重声明,保证遵守出入境检验检疫法律、法规的规定。如有违法行为,自愿接受检验检疫机构的处罚并负法律责任。

本委托人委托受委托人向检验检疫机构提交"报检申请单"和各种随附单据。具体委托情况如下:

本单位将于2015 年 7 月间进口/出口如下货物:

品名	女童连衣裙	HS 编码	661044200
数(重)量	235 箱	合同号	K123
信用证号	123456	审批文号	
其他特殊要求			

特委托上海海州国际货运代理公司(单位/注册登记号),代表本公司办理下列出入境检验检疫事宜:

☑ 1. 办理代理报检手续;

☑ 2. 代缴检验检疫费;

☑ 3. 负责与检验检疫机构联系和验货;

☑ 4. 领取检验检疫证单;

☐ 5. 其他与报检有关的相关事宜。

请贵局按有关法律法规规定予以办理。

上海海州国际货运公司业务专用章

无锡蓝天进出口公司业务专用章

委托人(公章)　　　　　　　　受委托人(公章)
×××　　　　　　　　　　　　×××
2015 年 5 月 21 日　　　　　　2015 年 5 月 21 日

① 报检委托书是委托人与受委托人之间的一份协议，规定双方的义务。
② 委托人制作报检委托书各项栏目的内容必须真实，且不得有误。
③ 报检委托书必须由双方签章，否则不能生效。

第二步：根据以上资料，填制出境货物报检单

中华人民共和国出入境检验检疫
出境货物报检单

报检单位(加盖公章)：×××　　　　*编　号 120400309015677
报检单位登记号 9823412345　联系人：××　电话：8888888　报检日期：2015 年 5 月 25 日

<table>
<tr><td rowspan="2">发货人</td><td colspan="5">(中文)无锡蓝天进出口公司</td></tr>
<tr><td colspan="5">(外文)WUXI BLUE SKY IMP&EXP. Co., LTD.</td></tr>
<tr><td rowspan="2">收货人</td><td colspan="5">(中文)</td></tr>
<tr><td colspan="5">(外文)KU TEXTILE CORPORATION</td></tr>
<tr><td>货物名称(中/外文)</td><td>H.S.编码</td><td>产地</td><td>数/重量</td><td>货物总值</td><td>包装种类及数量</td></tr>
<tr><td>GIRL DRESS
100% COTTON
全棉女童连衣裙</td><td>661044200</td><td>中国
无锡</td><td>9 400 件</td><td>65 300 美元</td><td>235 箱</td></tr>
</table>

<table>
<tr><td>运输工具名称号码</td><td>DONGFANG V. 25</td><td>贸易方式</td><td>一般贸易</td><td>货物存放地点</td><td>东亭路 88 号</td></tr>
<tr><td>合同号</td><td>K123</td><td>信用证号</td><td>123456</td><td>用途</td><td>其他</td></tr>
<tr><td>发货日期</td><td>20150715</td><td>输往国家(地区)</td><td>加拿大</td><td>许可证/审批号</td><td>***</td></tr>
<tr><td>启运地</td><td>上海</td><td>到达口岸</td><td>蒙特利尔</td><td>生产单位注册号</td><td>1990023489</td></tr>
<tr><td>集装箱规格、数量及号码</td><td colspan="5">1×40′整箱</td></tr>
</table>

（续表）

<table>
<tr><td>合同、信用证订立的检验检疫条款或特殊要求</td><td>标记及号码</td><td colspan="3">随附单据（划“✓”或补填）</td></tr>
<tr><td></td><td>KU
K123
MONTREAL
C/N:1 - 235</td><td colspan="2">☑合同
☑信用证
☑发票
☐换证凭单
☑装箱单
☐厂检单</td><td>☐包装性能结果单
☐许可/审批文件
☐
☐
☐
☐</td></tr>
<tr><td colspan="3">需要证单名称（划“✓”或补填）</td><td colspan="2">＊检验检疫费</td></tr>
<tr><td rowspan="3">☑品质证书 __正__副
☐重量证书 __正__副
☐数量证书 __正__副
☐兽医卫生证书 __正__副
☐健康证书 __正__副
☐卫生证书 __正__副
☐动物卫生证书 __正__副</td><td colspan="2" rowspan="3">☐植物检疫证书__正__副
☐熏蒸/消毒证书__正__副
☐出境货物换证凭单
☑出境货物通关单</td><td>总金额
（人民币元）</td><td></td></tr>
<tr><td>计费人</td><td></td></tr>
<tr><td>收费人</td><td></td></tr>
<tr><td colspan="2" rowspan="3">报检人郑重声明：
1. 本人被授权报检。
2. 上列填写内容正确属实，货物无伪造或冒用他人的厂名、标志、认证标志，并承担货物质量责任。
签名：×××</td><td colspan="3">领取证单</td></tr>
<tr><td>日期</td><td colspan="2"></td></tr>
<tr><td>签名</td><td colspan="2"></td></tr>
</table>

第三步：出境货物换证凭条

出境货物换证凭条

<table>
<tr><td>转单号</td><td colspan="3">7832490498623412</td><td>报检号</td><td>120400309015677</td></tr>
<tr><td>报检单位</td><td colspan="5">无锡蓝天进出口公司</td></tr>
<tr><td>品名</td><td colspan="5">全棉女童连衣裙</td></tr>
<tr><td>合同号</td><td colspan="3">K123</td><td>HS 编码</td><td>661044200</td></tr>
<tr><td>数(重)量</td><td>9 400 件</td><td>包装件数</td><td>235 箱</td><td>金额</td><td>65 300 美元</td></tr>
<tr><td colspan="6">评定意见：
贵单位报检的该批货物，经我局检验检疫，已合格。请执此单至上海局办理出境验证业务。本单有效期截止于年 7 月 27 日。
上海局本部　2015 年 5 月 28 日</td></tr>
</table>

第四步：出境货物通关单

中华人民共和国出入境检验检疫
出境货物通关单

编号：

<table>
<tr><td colspan="3">1. 发货人
无锡蓝天进出口公司</td><td colspan="2" rowspan="3">5. 标记及号码
KU
K123
MONTREAL
C/N: 1 - 235</td></tr>
<tr><td colspan="3">2. 收货人
KU TEXTILE CORPORATION</td></tr>
<tr><td colspan="2">3. 合同/信用证号
K123/123456</td><td>4. 输往国家或地区
加拿大</td></tr>
<tr><td colspan="2">6. 运输工具名称及号码
DONG FANGV. 25***</td><td>7. 目的地
蒙特利尔</td><td colspan="2">8. 集装箱规格及数量
1×40′GP</td></tr>
<tr><td>9. 货物名称及规格
全棉女童连衣裙***</td><td colspan="2">10. H.S.编码
61 044 200.00</td><td>11. 申报总值
USD65 300.00 美元</td><td>12. 数/重量、包装数量及种类
* 9 400 件* 235 箱*</td></tr>
<tr><td colspan="5">上述货物业经检验检疫，请海关予以放行。
本通关单有效期至 2015 年 7 月 18 日

签字：许浩　　　　日期：2015 年 5 月 28 日</td></tr>
<tr><td colspan="5">13. 备注</td></tr>
</table>

第五步：商检局签发数量、重量检验证书

中华人民共和国出入境检验检疫
ENTRY-EXIT INSPECTION AND QUARANTINE OF
THE PEOPLE'S REPUBLIC OF CHINA
数量检验证书

QUANTITY CERTIFICAT

编号
No.：76890333654

发货人：WUXI BLUE SKY IMP&EXP. Co., LTD.
Consignor
收货人：***
Consignee

品名：GIRL DRESS 100% COTTON
Description of Goods
报检数量/重量：9 400 PCS
Quantity/Weight Declared

标记及号码
Mark & No.

KU
K123

包装种类及数量：
Number and Type of Packages

MONTREAL
C/NO: 1 - 235

运输工具：BY SEA
Means of Conveyance

检验结果：
RESULTS OF INSPECTION:
SAMPLES WERE DRAWN AT RANDOM FROM THE WHOLE LOT OF GOODS AND INSPECTED STRICTLY ACCORDING TO THE S/C NO. K123.
THE ABOVE RESULT OF INSPECTION ARE IN CONFORMITY WITH THE REQUIREMENTS IN THE SAID CONTRACT.
我们已尽所知最大能力实施上述试验，不能因我们签发本证书而免除卖方或其他方面根据合同和法律所承担的产品质量责任和其他责任。
All inspections are carried out conscientiously to the best of our knowledge and ability. This certificate does not in any respect absolve the seller and other related parties from his contractual and legal obligations especially when product quality is concerned.

印章 签证地点SHANGHAI 签证日期2015年5月30日 签名郭晓芳
Stamp Official Place of Issue Date of Issue Signature

5.4　知识链接

出境货物报检单的制作规范见表5-1。

表5-1　出境货物报检单的制作规范

项目顺序号	填写内容	要点提示
(1) 编号	检验检疫机构受理本批货物报检后生成的正式报检号	由检验检疫机构的受理人员填写
(2) 报检单位	填写报检单位的中文名称	加盖报检单位公章或已向检验检疫机构备案的“报检专用章”
(3) 报检单位登记号	10位数字登记证号码	报检单位在国家质检总局的登记证号码
(4) 报检日期	以阿拉伯数字表示	检验检疫机构接受报检当天的日期
(5) 发货人	出口商的名称	一般只填写名称不填写地址
(6) 收货人	外贸合同的收购商，或商业发票的受票人	一般只填写名称不填写地址
(7) 货物名称(中/外)	商品名称	按照合同、信用证、商业发票中所列商品名称填写
(8) H.S编码	商品编码	以当年海关公布的商品税则编码为准
(9) 产地	出境货物生产地的中文名称	
(10) 数/重量	实际出运的数量或重量	应与装箱单和提单的数量或重量一致
(11) 货物总值	出境货物的商业总值及币种	应与合同、发票或报关单上所列货物总值一致
(12) 包装种类及数量	实际运输外包装的种类及对应的数量	
(13) 运输工具名称号码	实际出境运输工具的名称及编号	与实际运输方式相符
(14) 合同号	合同号	
(15) 贸易方式	“一般贸易”“来料加工贸易”“进料加工贸易”等	与实际情况一致的海关规范贸易
(16) 货物存放地点	具体地点、仓库	
(17) 发货日期	货物实际出境的日期	
(18) 输往国际(地区)	输往国家/地区的中文名称	货物最终的销售国
(19) 许可证号/审批号	许可证号/审批号	无须许可证或审批文件的出境货物本栏免报

（续表）

项目顺序号	填写内容	要点提示
(20) 生产单位注册号	实际生产单位注册号	
(21) 启运地	出境货物最后离境的口岸或所在地的中文名称	
(22) 到达口岸	出境货物运往境外的最终目的地	
(23) 集装箱规格、数量及号码	实际集装箱数量	如 1×40′ FCL
(24) 合同、信用证订立检验检疫条款或特殊要求	在合同、信用证订立有关的检验检疫条款的特殊要求及其他要求填写	
(25) 标记和号码	具体的唛头； 没有唛头填 N/M	此栏不能留空； 应与其他单据的唛头保持一致
(26) 用途	填写实际出境货物的用途	
(27) 随附单据	按照实际随附的单据种类选择	
(28) 签名	报检人手签	
(29) 检验检疫费用	计费人员核对后填写	
(30) 领取证单	领证日期与领证人签名	

开动脑筋

货物先经过海运经新加坡到荷兰鹿特丹，再陆运至瑞士。报检单中“到达口岸”填什么？

超链接

商品的报检

1. 商品检验的定义

商品检验是指商品检验机构对商品的品种、数量（重量）、包装、安全性能、卫生指标、残损情况、货物装运技术条件等进行检验和鉴定，从而确定货物的品质、数量（重量）和包装等是否与合同条款相一致，是否符合交易国家有关法律和法规的规定。

7. 商检与法检的区别以及进出口操作流程

2. 货物的报检范围

① 国家法律、行政法规规定须经检验检疫机构检验出证的货物；

② 入境国家或地区规定必须凭检验检疫机构出具的证书方准入境的货物；

③ 对外贸易合同、信用证规定由检验检疫机构检验的货物；

④ 有关国际条约规定须经检验检疫机构检验、检疫的货物；

⑤ 申请签发普惠制产地证或一般原产地证的货物；

⑥ 对外贸易关系人申请的鉴定业务或委托检验业务；

⑦ 报检单位对检验检疫机构出具的检验检疫结果有异议的，可申请复验。

3. 出境报检的时间、地点

出境货物最迟应于报关或出境装运前7天向检验检疫机构申请报检；出境动物应在出境前60天预报，隔离前7天报检；出入境的运输工具应在出境前向口岸检验检疫机关报检或申报。

4. 出境报检时应提供的单证、资料

① 报检单位必须在检验检疫机构注册登记，报检时填写登记号；报检员在报检时应该出示报检员证。

② 每份报检单限填一批货物，特殊情况下，对批量小的同一类货物，以同一运输工具，运往同一地点，同一收货、发货人，同一报关单的货物，可填写同一份报检单。

③ 出境报检时，应提供对外贸易合同(销售确认书或订单)、信用证、发票及装箱单等必要的单证；生产经营部门出具的厂检结果单原件；检验检验机构签发的《出境货物包装性能检验结果单》正本；出口生产企业代外贸出口单位报检的，须有外贸出口单位委托出口生产企业向检验检疫局报检的委托书。

④ 凭样成交的货物，应提供经买、卖双方确认的样品。

⑤ 产地与报关地不一致的出境货物，在向报关地检验检疫机构申请出境货物通关单时，应提交检验检疫机构签发的出境货物换证凭单(正本)。

5. 出境报检的工作流程

出境报检的工作流程是报检—抽样—检验—签证放行(见图5-1)。

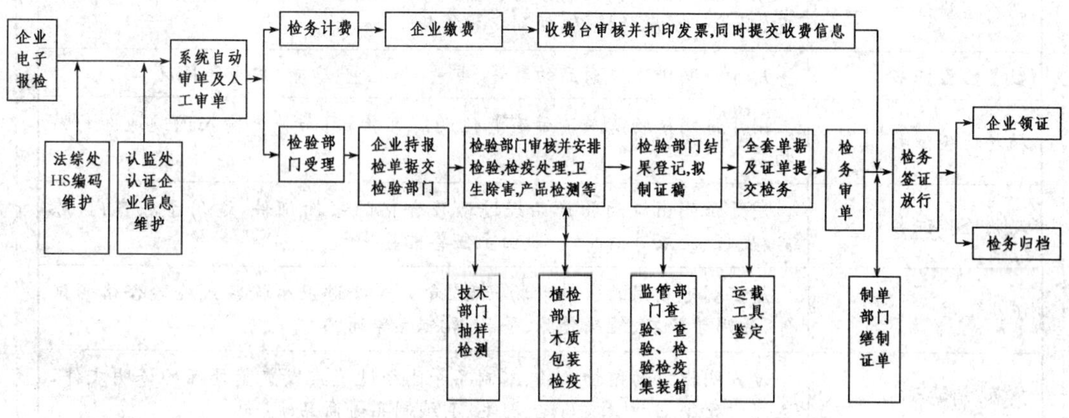

图5-1　出境报检业务的工作流程

6. 国外著名的商品检验机构及其业务范围

① 瑞士通用公证书(SGS)。当今世界上最大的检验鉴定公司，于1878年成立，拥有悠久的历史，总部设在日内瓦，在全球140多个国家和地区拥有超过1 650家分支机构和实验

室，是专门从事检验、实验、质量认证的国际性检验鉴定公司。

② 英国英子杰检验集团(IITS)。英国英子杰检验集团是一个国际性的商品检验组织，总部设在伦敦。为了加强其在世界贸易领域中的竞争地位，IITS通过购买世界上有名望、有实力的检验机构，组建自己的检验集团。IITS集团中包括嘉碧集团、天祥国际公司、安那实验室、英之杰劳埃德代理公司(汉基国际集团、马修斯但尼尔公司)、英特泰克服务公司及英特泰克国际服务有限公司等。IITS与中国CCIC有多年的友好往来，并签订有委托检验协议。

③ 日本海事鉴定协会(NKKK)。日本海事检定协会创立于1913年，是日本最大的综合性商品检验鉴定机构。总部设在东京，NKKK在国内外设立的分支机构有70多个，业务范围很广，主要检验项目有：舱口检视、积载鉴定、状态检验、残损鉴定、水尺计重、液体计量、衡重衡量及理化检验等，还接受从厂家到装船或从卸货到用户之间的连续检验。NKKK与中国商品检验机构签订长期委托检验协议，多年来，双方有着密切的相互委托检验业务和频繁的技术交流

④ 美国安全实验所。美国安全实验所，又称为美国保险人实验室，其宗旨是采用科学的测试方法来研究各种材料、装置、产品、建筑等对生命财产有无危害和危害的程度，确定编写、发行相应的标准和资料，从而确保安全的可靠性。UL公司除在美国本土设有分支机构外，还与加拿大、德国、瑞典、英国、日本、中国等国家的检验机构建立了业务关系。UL在中国的业务由中国进出口商品检验总公司(CCIC)及其下属分公司承办。

检验检疫证书的种类见表5-2。

表5-2 检验检疫证书的种类

检验检疫证书种类	适用范围
品质检验证书	用于证明出口商品的品名、规格、等级、成分、性能等产品质量的实际情况，用于证明履约情况、便利交接货物
数量检验证书	用于证明进出口商品的数量、重量，如毛重、净重、皮重等情况
植物检验证书	用于证明植物基本不带有其他的有害物，因而符合输入国或地区的植物要求
动物检验证书	用于证明出口动物产品经过检疫合格的书面证件，适用于冻畜肉、冻禽、皮张、肠衣等商品，一般由主任兽医签署
卫生证书	是证明可食用的出口动物产品、食品等经过卫生检疫或检验合格的证件，适用于肠衣、罐头食品、蛋品、乳制品等商品
熏蒸/消毒证书	是证明出口动植物产品、木制品等已经过消毒或熏蒸处理的证明文件，适用于猪鬃、针叶林、马尾、羽毛、羽绒制品等商品
出境货物运输包装性能鉴定结果单	用于证明出境货物的包装已经检验并合格，适用于运输
残损鉴定证书	用于证明进口商品残损情况，供索赔时使用

（续表）

检验检疫证书种类	适用范围
包装检验证书	用于证明进出口商品包装情况
温度检验证书	用于证明出口冷冻商品的温度符合合同或有关规定
船舶检验证书	用于证明承运出口商品船舶清洁、牢固、冷藏效能及其他装运条件符合保护承载商品的质量和数量完整与安全要求
货载衡量检验证书	是证明进出口商品的重量、体积、吨位的证书，是计算运费和制订配载计划的依据

5.5　能力实训

实训 1　根据提供的信息判断填制出境货物报检单有关内容的正误

SALES CONFIRMATION

The Buyer: Yi Yang Trading Corporation
88 Marshall Ave
Doncaster Vic 3108 Canada

The Seller: Shanghai Knitwear and Manufactured Goods Import and Export Trade Corporation 321, Zhougshan Road, Shanghai, China

NAME OF COMMODITY	QUANTITIES		UNIT PRICE	AMOUNET
			CIF	MONTREAL
COTTON TEATOWELS	10 * 10 INCHES	6 000 DOZ	USD1.31/DOZ	USD7 860
	20 * 20 INCHES	6 000 DOZ	USD2.51/DOZ	USD15 060
	30 * 30INCHES	11 350 DOZ.	USD4.73/DOZ..	USD53 685.50.
	TOTAL	23 350 DOZ		USD76 605.50.

Packing: In cartons

Port of Loading: Yang Shan Port, Shanghai, China

Port of Destination: Montreal Port

Shipping Mark: Yi yang/L/C No. Th2015/Montreal/C/NO.1－734

Date of Shipment: Not Later Than 31, OCT.15

Terms of payment: L/C(N0.: TR0069)

Documents Required: Certificate of Quality issued by CIQ indicating the L/C No.

判断一下说法是否正确：

(1) 收货人(外文)栏“Yi Yang Trading Corporation”。　（　　）

(2) 信用证号码栏填写“Th2015”。　（　　）

(3)“货物总值”栏填写“76 605.50 元”。 (　　)

(4)“合同、信用证订立的检验检疫条款或特殊要求”栏填写“无”。 (　　)

(5)“需要证单名称”栏填写“品质证书”。 (　　)

(6)“包装种类及数量”栏填写“23350 DOZ/734 箱”。 (　　)

(7)“输往国家(地区)”栏填写“加拿大”。 (　　)

(8)“标记及号码”栏填写“C/NO.1－734”。 (　　)

实训 2　根据给出的条件制作出境货物报检单

信用证材料

ISSUING BANK: THE PUNJAB NATIONAL BANK, INDIA

L/C NO.: AV123

ISSUING DATE: MAR.7 2015

BENEFICIARY: WUXI TIANYI TRADING Co. Ltd

NO.118 HONGQI ROAD, WUXI, CHINA

APPLICANT: ORANGE COMOANY, INDIA

702/1, BEHIND ACHAR FACTORY, PANIPA－132(INDIA)

AMOUNT: USD6 080

SHIPMENT FROM SHANGHAI FOR TRANSPORTATION TO MUMBAI

6400 CANS OF CHEN BRAND CANNED SWEET CORN, 360 GRAMMS/CAN, 8CANS IN A CARTON, TTL 800 CARTONS

N.W.:2.88KGS/CARTON, G.W.:3.8KGS/CARTON　MEAS:8M3

S/C NO.: WX001

TRADE TERM: CIF MUMBAI

附加信息:

唛头:WX
　　WX001
　　MUMBAI
　　NO.1－800

发票号码:DE123

发票日期:2015 年 4 月 15 日

生产厂家:无锡新绿公司

商品名称:甜玉米罐头

船名:DAHAI V.001

集装箱号码:1×20′FCL APLU1234567

商品编码:20058000　FORM A 号码: SD12/999/1234

总毛重:3 040 千克

中华人民共和国出入境检验检疫
出境货物报检单

报检单位(加盖公章)： 编号________

报检单位登记号： 联系人： 电话： 报检日期： 年 月 日

发货人	(中文)
	(外文)
收货人	(中文)
	(外文)

货物名称(中/外文)	H.S.编码	产地	数/重量	货物总值	包装种类及数量

运输工具名称及号码		贸易方式		货物存放地点	
合同号		信用证号		用途	
发货日期		输往国家(地区)		许可证/审批号	
启运地		到达口岸		生产单位注册号	
集装箱规格、数量及号码					

合同、信用证订立的检验检疫条款或特殊要求	标记及号码	随附单据(划"✓"或补填)	
		□合同 □信用证 □发票 □换证凭单 □装箱单 □厂检单	□包装性能结果单 □许可/审批文件 □ □

(续表)

需要证单名称(划"✓"或补填)		检验检疫费	
□品质证书 _正_副 □重量证书 _正_副 □数量证书 _正_副 □兽医卫生证书 _正_副 □健康证书 _正_副 □卫生证书 _正_副 □动物卫生证书 _正_副	□植物检疫证书 _正_副 □熏蒸/消毒证书 _正_副 □出境货物换证凭单 _正_副 □出境货物通关单 _正_副 □ □ □	总金额(人民币元) 计费人 收费人	
报检人郑重声明: 1. 本人被授权报检。 2. 上列填写内容正确属实,货物无伪造或冒用他人的厂名、标志、认证标志,并承担货物质量责任。 签名:______		领取证单 日期 签名	

实训 3　根据给出的信息制作出境货物报检单

1. 合同

SALES CONFIRMATION

S/C NO.: FFF04027

DATE: 03 APR., 2004

THE SELLER:
FFF TRADING CO., LTD.
3TH FLOOR KINGSTAR MANSION,
676 JINLIN RD., SHANGHAI CHINA

THE BUYER:
JAMES BROWN & SONS
#304 - 310 JALAN STREET,
TORONTO, CANADA

ART. NO.	COMMODITY	QUANTITY	UNIT PRICE	AMOUNT
HX1115 HX2012 HX4405 HX4510	CHINESE CERAMIC DINNERWARE 35PCS DINNERWARE & TEA SET 20PCS DINNERWARE SET 47PCS DINNERWARE SET 95PCS DINNERWARE SET	542SETS 800SETS 443SETS 254SETS	CIFC5 TORONTO USD23.50/SET USD20.40/SET USD23.20/SET USD30.10/SET	USD12 737.00 USD16 320.00 USD10 277.60 USD7 645.40
	TOTAL	2 039SETS		USD46 980.00
TOTAL CONTRACT VALUE: SAY US DOLLARS FORTY SIX THOUSAND NINE HUNDRED EIGHTY ONLY.				

PACKING: HX2012 IN CARTONS OF 2 SETS EACH AND HX1115, HX4405 AND

HX4510 TO BE PACKED IN CARTONS OF 1 SET EACH ONLY.
TOTAL: 1639 CARTONS.

PORT OF LOADING & DESTINATION: FROM SHANGHAI TO TORONTO.

TIME OF SHIPMENT: TO BE EFFECTED BEFORE THE END OF APRIL 2004 WITH PARTIAL SHIPMENT NOT ALLOWED AND TRANSSHIPMENT ALLOWED.

TERMS OF PAYMENT: THE BUYER SHALL OPEN THROUGH A BANK ACCEPTABLE TO THE SELLER AN IRREVOCABLE L/C AT 30 DAYS AFTER SIGHT TO REACH THE SELLER BEFORE APRIL 10, 2004 VALID FOR NEGOTIATION IN CHINA UNTIL THE 15TH DAY AFTER THE DATE OF SHIPMENT.

INSURANCE: THE SELLER SHALL COVER INSURANCE AGAINST ALL RISKS AND WAR RISKS FOR 110% OF THE TOTAL INVOICE VALUE AS PER THE RELEVANT OCEAN MARINE CARGO OF P.I.C.C. DATED 1/1/1981.

THE SELLER: THE BUYER:
FFF TRADING CO., LTD. JAMES BROWN & SONS
++++ **********

2. 信用证

RECEIVED FROM: THE ROYAL BANK OF CANADA
BRITISH COLUMBIA INT'L CENTRE
1055 WEST GEORGIA STREET, VANCOUVER, B.C. CANADA

MESSAGE TYPE: MT700 ISSUE OF A DOCUMENTARY CREDIT

:27: SEQUENCE OF TOTAL
1/1

:40A: FORM OF DOC. CREDIT
IRREVOCABLE

:20: DOC. CREDIT NUMBER
04/0501-FTC

:31C: DATE OF ISSUE
040408

:31D: EXPIRY
DATE 040515 PLACE CHINA

:50: APPLICANT
JAMES BROWN & SONS
#304-310 JALAN STREET,
TORONTO, CANADA

:59: BENEFICIARY
FFF TRADING CO., LTD.
3TH FLOOR KINGSTAR MANSION,
676 JINLIN RD., SHANGHAI CHINA

:32B: AMOUNT
CURRENCY USD AMOUNT 46 980 00

:41D: AVAILABLE WITH/BY
ANY BANK
BY NEGOTIATION

:42C: DRAFTS AT ...
30 DAYS AFTER SIGHT

:42D: DRAWEE
US

:43P: PARTIAL SHIPMENTS
PROHIBITED

:43T: TRANSSHIPMENT
ALLOWED

:44A: LOADING IN CHARGE
SHANGHAI, CHINA

:44B: FOR TRANSPORT TO ...
TORONTO, CANADA

:44C: LATEST DATE OF SHIP.
04043 0

:45A: DESCRIPT. OF GOODS
4 ITEMS OF CHINESE CERAMIC DINNERWARE AS FOLLOW:
HX1115: 542SETS OF 35PCS DINNERWARE & TEA SET AT USD23.50/SET;
HX2012: 800SETS OF 20PCS DINNERWARE SET AT USD20.40/SET;
HX4405: 443SETS OF 47PCS DINNERWARE SET AT USD23.20/SET;
HX4510: 254SETS OF 95PCS DINNERWARE SET AT USD30.10/SET.
CIF TORONTO, CANADA. AS PER S/C NO.: FFF04027
PACKING:STANDARD EXPORT PACKING

:46A: DOCUMENTS REQUIRED
+SIGNED COMMERCIAL INVOICE IN 5 COPIES.
+PACKING LIST INDICATING THE INDIVIDUAL WEIGHT AND MEASUREMENT OF EACH ITEM. +FULL SET OF CLEAN ON BOARD OCEAN BILLS OF LADING MADE
OUT TO ORDER OF SHIPPER AND ENDORSED IN BLANK, MARKED FREIGHT PREPAID NOTIFY APPLICANT.

+CERTIFICATE OF ORIGIN ISSUED BY CHINA COUNCIL FOR THE PROMOTION OF INTERNATIONAL TRADE.

+INSURANCE POLICY OR CERTIFICATE FOR 110 PERCENT OF INVOICE VALUE COVERING INSTITUTE CARGO CLAUSES (A) AND WAR RISKS AS PER I.C.C. DATED 1/1/1982

+CANADA CUSTOMS INVOICE OF DEPARTMENT OF NATIONAL REVENUE/CUSTOMS AND EXCISE IN DUPLICATE.

+BENEFICIARY'S FAX COPY OF SHIPPING ADVICE TO APPLICANT AFTER SHIPMENT ADVISING L/C NO. SHIPMENT DATE, VESSEL NAME, NAME, QUANTITY AND WEIGHT OF GOODS.

:47A: ADDITIONAL COND.

A DISCREPANCY HANDLING FEE OF USD50.00(OR EQUIVALENT) AND THE RELATIVE TELEX/SWIFT COST WILL BE DEDUCTED FROM THE PROCEEDS NO MATTER THE BANKING CHARGES ARE FOR WHOEVER ACCOUNT.

:71B: DETAILS OF CHARGES

ALL BANKING CHARGES OUTSIDE LC ISSUING BANK ARE FOR ACCOUNT BENEFICIARY INCLUDING OUR REIMBURSEMENT CHARGES.

:48: PRESENTATION PERIOD

WITHIN 15 DAYS AFTER THE DATE OF SHIPMENT BUT WITHIN THE CREDIT VALIDITY.

:49: CONFIRMATION ... WITHOUT

:78: INSTRUCTIONS

1. DOCUMENTS MUST BE SENT THROUGH NEGOTIATING BANK TO OUR ADDRESS: THE ROYAL BANK OF CANADA, BRITISH COLUMBIA INT'L CENTRE, 1055 WEST GEORGIA STREET, VANCOUVER, B.C. CANADA IN 1 LOT BY COURIER SERVICE.
2. UPON RECEIPT OF COMPLIANT DOCUMENTS, WE SHALL REIMBURSE YOU AS INSTRUCTED.
3. EACH DRAWING/PRESENTATION MUST BE ENDORSED ON THE REVERSE OF THE CREDIT.

项目 6　制作和申请原产地证

6.1　学习目标

知识目标:熟悉产地证书的类型和作用。

能力目标:能够正确填制一般原产地证书和普惠制产地证书。

6.2　工作任务

无锡蓝天进出口公司向加拿大出口女士羊毛衫,根据信用证的规定,G.S.P. CERTIFICATE OF ORIGIN FORM A IN DUPLICATE ISSUED BY CIQ,该要求需要出口商提供正本正式的由中国出入境检验检疫局签发的普惠制原产地证。

在本任务中,郭晓芳需要依据相关资料及信用证的要求缮制相关普惠制原产地证书。

6.3　操作范例

1. Goods consigned from (Exporter's business name, address, country) WUXIBLUE SKY IMP&EXP. Co., LTD. NO.53 ZHONGSHAN ROAD, WUXI, CHINA	Reference No. **GENERALIZED SYSTEM OF PREFERENCE CERTIFICATE OF ORIGIN** (Combined declaration and certificate) FORM A
2. Goods consignee to (Consignee's name, address, country) KU TEXTILE CORPORATION 430 VTRA MONTREAL CANADA	Issued in **THE PEOPOE'S REPUBLIC OF CHINA** (Country) See Noted Overleaf
3. Means of transport and route(as far as known) FROM SHANGHAI, CHINA TO MONTREAL CANADA	4. For official use

5. Item number	6. Mrks and number of packages	7. Number and kind of packages; description of goods	8. Origin criterion (seeNotes overleaf)	9. Gross weight or other quantity	10. Number and date of invoices
1		SAY TWO HUNDRED AND THIRTY-FIVE CARTONS ONLY ******************************	P	2.285M/T	ZYIE1502 MAY20, 2015

（续表）

11. Certification It is hereby certified on the basis of control carried out, the declaration by the exporter is correct. Place and date. signature and stamp of certifying authority	12. Declaration by the exporter he undersigned hereby declares that the above detail and statements are correct that the goods were produce in ----------------CHINA-------------------- and that they comply with the original requirements specified for those goods in the Generalized System of Preferences for goods exported to CANADA (import country) Place and date, SHANGHAI MAY 25,2015 signature of authorized signatory

开动脑筋

① 若提单上的收货人为“ TO ORDER ”,原产地证上的收货人应与其保持一致吗?

② 普惠制和一般原产地证的日期是早于、晚于还是等于提单日期?

6.4 知识链接

1. 普惠制原产地证书的填制规范(见表 6－1)

表 6－1　普惠制原产地证书的填制规范

项目顺序号	填写内容	要点提示
Certificate No. (1) 证书号码 Reference	填写证书号码	G＋年份后两位＋单位注册号九位＋流水号四位(中间不得加空格)如 G082100001230001
Goods consigned from (2) 出口方 Exporter	填写最终收货方的名称、详细地址及国家	按外贸合同的卖方或发票抬头填写
Goods consigned to (3) 收货人 Consignee	此栏应填写给惠国的最终收货人名称	如信用证规定未明确最终收货人,可以填写商业发票的抬头人,但不可填写中间商的名称
(4) 运输路线和方式 Means of transport and route	填写从装货港到目的港的详细运输路线	如 SHIPPED FROM GUANGZHOU TO HAMBURG W/T HONGKONG, IN TRANST TO SWITZERLAND

（续表）

项目顺序号	填写内容	要点提示
(5) 目的地国家/地区 Country/region of destinagion	目的地国家/地区的名称	最终运抵港，一般与最终收货人或最终目的港国别一致，不得填写中间商国别
(6) 签证机构用栏 For certifying authority	正常情况下证书申领单位应将此栏留空	由签证机构在签发后发证、补发证书或加注其他声明时使用
(7) 运输标志 Marks and numbers	与发票相同	不可简单填写“按照发票”（As Per Invoice No ×××）或者按照提单（As Per B/L No ×××）货物如无唛头，应填写“NO MARK”字样，此栏不得留空
(8) 包装数量及种类、商品描述 Number and kind of packages; description of goods	按发票填写，包括商品的件数和货物描述，并应加结束符	① 包装件数必须用大小写同时表示； ② 商品名称要填写具体，可以用统称，但不能过于笼统； ③ 如货物为散装，在商品名称后加注“IN BULK”
(9) 商品编码 H.S. Code	此笔业务的商品海关编码，应与报关单一致	若同一证书包含几种商品，则应将相应的税目号全部填写。此栏不得留空
(10) 数量 Quantity	出口商品的数量及计量单位	以重量计算的则填毛重，填净重亦可，但要标上 N. W.
(11) 发票号码及日期 Number and kind of packages; description of goods	填写商业发票的号码和日期	商业发票的号码和日期与申请签证时随附的发票号一致
(12) 出口商申明 Declaration by the exporter	由申请单位的手签人员签字并盖章，填制申报地点、时间	此栏日期不得早于发票日期
(13) 签证机构证明、签字盖章 Certification	签证地点、日期，签证机构签证人经审核后在此栏（正本）签名，并签证盖章	签发日期不得早于发票日期和申请日期

2. 一般原产地证书的填制规范（见表 6-2）

表 6-2　一般原产地证书的填制规范

项目顺序号	填写内容	要点提示
(1) 证书号码 Certificate No.	填写证书号码	
(2) 出口方 Exporter	填写最终收货方的名称、详细地址及国家	按外贸合同的卖方或发票抬头填写
(3) 收货人 Consignee	此栏应填最终收货人名称（即信用证上规定的提单通知人或特别声明的受货人）	如信用证规定所有单证收货人一栏留空，在这种情况下，此栏应加注“To Whom It May Concern”或“To Order”，但此栏不得留空

（续表）

项目顺序号	填写内容	要点提示
(4) 运输路线和方式 Means of transport and route	填写从装货港到目的港的详细运输路线	如 SHIPPED FROM GUANGZHOU TO HAMBURG W/T HONGKONG, IN TRANST TO SWITZERLAND
(5) 目的地国家/地区 Country/region of destination	目的地国家/地区的名称	最终运抵港，一般与最终收货人或最终目的港国别一致，不得填写中间商国别
(6) 签证机构用栏 For certifying authority	正常情况下证书申领单位应将此栏留空	由签证机构在签发后发证、补发证书或加注其他声明时使用
(7) 运输标志 Marks and numbers	与发票相同	不可简单填写"按照发票"(As Per Invoice No ×××)或者按照提单(As Per B/L No ×××)货物如无唛头，应填写"NO MARK"字样，此栏不得留空
(8) 包装数量及种类、商品描述 Number and kind of packages; description of goods	按发票填写，包括商品的件数和货物描述，并应加结束符	① 包装件数必须用大小写同时表示； ② 商品名称要填写具体，可以用统称，但不能过于笼统； ③ 如货物为散装，在商品名称后加注"IN BULK"
(9) 商品编码 H. S. Code	此笔业务的商品海关编码，应与报关单一致。	若同一证书包含几种商品，则应将相应的税目号全部填写。此栏不得留空
(10) 数量 Quantity	出口商品的数量及计量单位	以重量计算的则填毛重，填净重亦可，但要标上 N. W.
(11) 发票号码及日期 Number and kind of packages; description of goods	填写商业发票的号码和日期	商业发票的号码和日期与申请签证时随附的发票号一致
(12) 出口商申明 Declaration by the exporter	由申请单位的手签人员签字并盖章，填制申报地点、时间	此栏日期不得早于发票日期
(13) 签证机构证明、签字盖章 Certification	签证地点、日期，签证机构签证人经审核后在此栏(正本)签名，并签证盖章	签发日期不得早于发票日期和申请日期

小贴士

填制原产地证书的注意点

① 如合同是通过中间商达成的，货物直运最终用户所在国，原产地证书的收货人应填写最终收货人的名称和地址，出于商业秘密，中间商可能不会告知出口商真正的最终买主，在这种情况下可以填写"To whom it may concern"或"TO order"，不能填

写成中间商。

② 唛头一定要严格按照发票或提单填写，并且要与发票或提单中的唛头一致，不能简单地填写“As per invoice No. ××”, “As per B/L No. ××”。

③ 目的国国家、地区应该填写为最终用户所在国或所在地区名称，不能填写中间商所在国、所在地区名称。

④ 货物描述最后不要漏打“*** ”以示结束。

⑤ 注意原产地证书生几个日期的逻辑关系，申领日期不能早于发票日期，可略晚，最早可以与发票日期同一天；签发日期不能早于申领日期，可略晚，最早可以与申领日期相同，同时注意签发日期也不能晚于装运日期。

超链接

8. 申请原产地证时常见的问题

1. 一般原产地证书

原产地证(CERTIFICATE OF ORIGIN，简称 C/O)，是出口国的特定机构出具的证明其出口货物为该国家(或地区)原产的一种证明文件。其作用包括：证明出口货物产地的书面文件；是进口国海关作为实施差别关税、进口限制、不同进口配额和不同税率的依据；是进出口通关和贸易统计的重要依据。

9. 外贸企业如何利用原产地证成功提价

(1) 产地证的类别

一般原产地证书是出口国根据一定原产地规则签发的证明货物原产地的证明书。在我国，一般原产地证书有以下四种形式：

① 国家出入境检验检疫局设在各地的出入境检验检疫机构出具的《中华人民共和国原产地证明书》；

② 贸促会及其分会出具的《中华人民共和国原产地证书》；

③ 出口商出具的《原产地证书》；

④ 生产厂家出具的《原产地证书》。

注：商检机构出具的原产地证最权威，最有说服力。贸促会出具的产地证书有一定的声誉和说服力。

(2) 一般原产地证书的签发程序及所需材料

① 出口企业根据合同或信用证填写一般原产地证书及其申请书。

② 出口企业应在货物出运(报关)前 3 天持填好的下述资料到出入境检验检疫局或贸促会办理一般原产地签发手续：

a. 《中华人民共和国出口货物原产地证明书、加工装配证明书申请书》；

b. 《中华人民共和国出口货物原产地证明书》一式四份(一正三副)；

c. 正式出口商业发票正本一份，如发票内容不全，另附装箱单(盖章，不得涂改)；

d. 含有进口成分的产品，必须提交《产品成本明细表》；

e. 签证机构认为必要的其他证明文件，如：“加工工序清单”等。

(3) 签发机构只签发原产地证正本一份，副本三份，其中一正二副交申请企业。另一副本、申请书、商业发票等有关文件，由签证机构存档。

2. 普惠制原产地证书

普惠制是发达国家给予发展中国家或地区在经济、贸易方面的一种非互利的特别优惠待遇。即发展中国家向发达国家出口制成品或半制成品(包括某些初级产品)普遍的、非歧视性的、非互惠的一种关税优惠制度。

(1) 普惠制产地证的定义

普惠制产地证(Generalized System of Preferences/Certificate of Origin，简称 G. S. P 证、Form A 证)是一种受惠国有关机构就本国出口商向给惠国出口受惠商品签发的用以证明原产地的文件。在我国，普惠制产地证是由检验检疫机构签发的。

目前给予我国普惠制待遇的国家共 40 个，即欧盟 28 国(比利时、丹麦、英国、德国、法国、爱尔兰、意大利、卢森堡、荷兰、希腊、葡萄牙、西班牙、奥地利、芬兰、瑞典、波兰、捷克、斯洛伐克、拉脱维亚、爱沙尼亚、立陶宛、匈牙利、马耳他、塞浦路斯、斯洛文尼亚、罗马尼亚、保加利亚和克罗地亚)、其他 12 国(挪威、瑞士、土耳其、俄罗斯、白俄罗斯、乌克兰、哈萨克斯坦、日本、加拿大、澳大利亚、新西兰和列支敦士登公国)。

普惠制原产地证格式包括格式 A、格式 59A 和格式 APR，其中，格式 A(Form A)的使用范围最广。

(2) 普惠制原产地证书的签发程序及所需材料

① 出口企业根据合同或信用证填写普惠制原产地证书(Form A)及其申请书。

② 出口企业应在货物出运(报关)前 5 天持填好的下述资料到出入境检验检疫局或贸促会办理普惠制原产地证书签发手续：

a. 填制正确、清楚的《普惠制原产地证书申请书》一份；

b. 填制正确、清楚的并经申请单位手签人员手签并加盖公章的《普惠制原产地证明书(Form A)》一套(一正二副)；

c. 正式出口商业发票正本一份，如发票内容不全，另附装箱单(盖章，不得涂改)；

d. 含有进口成分的产品，必须提交《含进口成分受惠商品成本明细表》；

e. 必要时，申请单位还应提交信用证、合同、提单及报关单等。

3. 区域经济集团互惠原产地证书

区域经济集团互惠原产地证书，是具有法律效力的在协定成员国之间就特定产品享受互惠减免关税待遇的官方凭证。

4. 专用原产地证书

专用原产地证书是国际组织和国家根据政策和贸易措施的特殊需要，针对某一特殊行业的特定产品规定的原产地证书。

① 纺织品产地证书(Certificate of Origin Textile Product)输欧盟纺织品产地证书(EEC 纺织品产地证书)输欧盟纺织品产地证，由外经贸部签发，是中国向欧盟等国家出口配额或非配额纺织品时需提供的产地证，其栏目用英、法两种文字对照。它是针对纺织品和服装出口到欧盟国家清关必需的一种证书，这是我国与欧盟国家达成的一种协议。

② 中国东盟自由贸易区原产地证，又称为格式 E 或 Form E。它是根据中国与东盟签署的《中国—东盟全面经济合作框架协议货物贸易协定》(以下简称《货物贸易协定》)的规定签署的一种优惠性原产地证明书。证书为棕色，一式四份。在中国，由国家质检总局设在各

地的检验检疫机构负责签发这种原产地证书。

相关链接

1. 输欧盟纺织品产地证；	2. 输欧盟手工制品产地证；
3. 输欧盟丝麻制品产地证；	4. 输土耳其纺织品产地证；
5. 输土耳其丝麻制品产地证；	6. 一般原产地证(C/O)；
7. 东盟产地证 FORM E；	8. 智利产地证 FORM F；
9. 中国—巴基斯坦原产地证 FTA(简称中巴产地证)；	
10. 亚太产地证 FORM M；	11. 中国—新西兰原产地证；
12. 中国—秘鲁原产地证。	

③ 对美国出口的原产地证书(Declaration of Country Origin，简称 DCO 产地证书)又称为美国产地证，凡是出口到美国的纺织品，出口商必须向进口商提供该类原产地声明书，作为进口商清关的单据之一。声明书主要包括 A、B、C 三种格式。格式 A 为单一国家产地声明书，一般适用于本国原材料并由本国生产的产品；格式 B 为多国产地声明书，一般用于来料加工、来件装配的产品，由多国生产；格式 C 为非多种纤维纺织品声明书，一般适用于纺织品原料的主要价值或重量是丝、麻类或其中羊毛含量不超过 17%的纺织品。

6.5 能力实训

实训 1 根据给出的信用证填写原产地证书

FM: STANDARD CHARTERED BANK DUBLIN
TO: BANK OF CHINA, ZHBRANCH, HANGZHOU CHINA.

SEQUENCE OF TOTAL	27:1/1
FORM OF DOC. CREDIT	40A: IRREVOCABLE
DATE OF ISSUE	31C: 050512
EXPIRY	31D: 050812 PLACE CHINA
APPLICANT	50: BEST S EJIANG ELLER COMPANY WATERFORD BUILDING 22 FLOOR NO. 998 FINECALL STREET DUBLIN IRELAND.
BENEFICIARY	59: ZHEJIANG SECOND LIGHT INDUSTRY NO. 74 YOU SHENG GUAN ROAD HANGZHOU CHINA.
AMOUNT	32B: USD AMOUNT 20 000. 00 (SAY UNITED STATES DOLLARS TWENTY THOUSAND ONLY).
AVAILABLE WITH/BY	41D: STANDARD CHARTERED BANK DUBLIN BY ACCEPTANCE

DRAPTS AT　　42C: DRAPTS AT 30 DAYS AFTER SIGHT

DRAWEE:　　42A: STANDARD CHARTERED BANK DUBLIN

PARTIAL SHIPMENT　　43P: PROHIBITED

TRANSSHIPMENT　　43T: PERMITTED

LOADING IN CHARGE　　44A: SHANGHAI CHINA

FOR TRANSPORT TO　　44B: DUBLIN IRELAND

DESCRIPT. OF GOODS:　　45A

DRAWER SLIDES AND HANDLES

CIF DUBLIN IRELAND

DOCUMENTS REQUIRED　　46A:

+SIGNED INVOICE IN TRIPLICATE.

+FULL SET OF CLEAN ON BOARD MARINE BILLS OF LADING CONSIGNED TO ORDER, BLANK ENDORSED, MARKED FREIGHT PREPAID AND NOTIFY APPLICANT.

+INSURANCE POLICY/CERTIFICATE BLANK ENDORSED COVERING ALL RISKS FOR 10 PERCENT ABOVE THE CIF VALUE.

+CERTIFICATE OF CHINA ORIGIN ISSUED IN DUPLICATE

+PACKING LIST INTRIPLICATE.

ADDITIONAL CONDITIONS:

PLEASE FORWARD ALL DOCUMENTS TO US (STANDARD CHARTERED BANK LTD, TRADE FINANCE SERVICES, CARRISBROOK HOUSE BALLSBRIDGE DUBLIN 500.)

IF BILLS OF LADING ARE REQUIRED ABOVE, PLEASE FORWARD DOCUMENTS IN TWO MAILS, ORIGINALS SEND BY COURIER AND DUPLICATES BY REGISTERED AIRMAIL.

DETAILS OF CHARGES　　71B

+BANK CHARGES EXCLUDING ISSUING BANK ARE FOR ACCOUNT OF BENEFICIARY.

PRESENTATION PERIOD　　48:

+DOCUMENTS TO BE PRESENTED WITHIN 21 DAYS FROM SHIPMENT DATE BUT WITHIN THE VALID OF THE CREDIT.

CONFIRMATION　　49: WITHOUT

有关资料:

发票号码:2015ZH8898　　发票日期:2015 年 7 月 10 日

H. S. 号码:7306. 2000　　货物装箱情况:800SETS/40CARTONS

净　重:25 KGS/CTN　　毛　重:28 KGS/CTN

尺　码:(50×40×20)CM/CTN

唛　头:B. C. /DUBLIN/NOS:1－40/MADE IN CHINA

一般原产地证书

ORIGINAL

<table>
<tr><td colspan="3">1. Exporter</td><td colspan="2">**Certificate No.**

CERTIFICATE OF ORIGIN

OF

THE PEOPLE'S REPUBLIC OF CHINA</td></tr>
<tr><td colspan="3">2. Consignee</td></tr>
<tr><td colspan="3">3. Means of transport and route</td><td colspan="2" rowspan="2">5. For certifying authority use only</td></tr>
<tr><td colspan="3">4. Country/region of destination</td></tr>
<tr><td>6. Marks and numbers</td><td colspan="2">7. Number and kind of packages; description of goods</td><td>8. H.S. Code</td><td>9. Quantity</td><td>10. Number and date of invoices</td></tr>
<tr><td colspan="3">11. Declaration by the exporter
The undersigned hereby declares that the above details and statements are correct, that all the goods were produced in China and that they comply with the Rules of Origin of the People's Republic of China.

Place and date, signature and stamp of certifying authority</td><td colspan="3">12. Certification
It is hereby certified that the declaration by the exporter is correct.

Place and date, signature and stamp of authorized signatory</td></tr>
</table>

实训 2　根据所给的资料填写普惠制产地证书申请表和普惠制产地证书

SEQUENCE OF TOTAL	27:1/1
FORM OF DOC. CREDIT	40A: IRREVOCABLE
DATE OF ISSUE	31C: 151210
EXPIRY	31D: 160215 PLACE CHINA
APPLICANT	50: GOODS BROTHER RESOURCES CO. LTD.,

	29 HIGHWAY DRIVE TRAIL BRITISH COLOMBIA, CANDAN
	FAX: 001-234 786 2456
BENEFICIARY	59: WUXI HUISHAN XINGASHUN TRDING CORP. NO. 444 WEST INXING ROAD, WUXI, JIANGSU, P.R.C.
AMOUNT	32B: USD 165,000.00
AVAILABLE WITH/BY	41D: ANY BANK IN BENEFICIARY'S COUNTRY BY NEGOTIATION.
DRAPTS AT	42C: SIGHT FOR 100% OF INVOICE VALUE
DRAWEE:	42A: NORTHEST AMERICA BANK OF CANDAD
PARTIAL SHIPMENT	43P: ALLOWED
TRANSSHIPMENT	43T: ALLOWED
LOADING IN CHARGE	44A: SHANGHAI CHINA
FOR TRANSPORT TO	44B: MONTREAL, CANDAN

LATEST DATE OF SHIPMENT　160131

DESCRIPT. OF GOODS:　45A

100M/T/100 BAGS OF SILICON METAL

Si: 99% MIN.　Fe: 0.4% MAX. Al: 0.4% MAX.　Ca: 0.1% MAX.

Size: 10-100 MM 90% MIN.

UNIT PRICE: USD 1650/MT CIF MONTREAL, CANDAN

AS PER SALES CONTRACT NO. QWE123

PACKED IN PLASTIC WOVEN BAGS OF ABOUT 1000 KGS NET EACH.

DOCUMENTS REQUIRED　46A:

+SIGNED INVOICE IN TRIPLICATE.

+FULL SET OF CLEAN ON BOARD MARINE BILLS OF LADING CONSIGNED TO ORDER OF NORTHEST AMERICA BANK OF CANDAD NOTIFYING APPLICANT EVIDENCING SHIPMENT FROM SHANGHAI TO MONTREAL BY VESSEL.

+INSURANCE POLICY/CERTIFICATE BLANK ENDORSED COVERING ALL RISKS FOR 10 PERCENT ABOVE THE CIF VALUE.

+CERTIFICATE OF ORIGINGSP FORM A ISSUED BY CORREPONDING AUTHORITY IN DUPLICATE

+PACKING LIST INTRIPLICATE.

ADDITIONAL CONDITIONS: 47A

+ALL DOCUMENTS MUST BEAR THIS CREDIT NUMBER AND DATE.

+SHIPMENT DATE PRIOR TO L/C'S ISSUING DATE IS PROHIBITED.

+5 PCT MORE OR LESS IN QUANTITY AND AMOUNT ARE ACCEPTABLE.

+IF DOCUMENT PRESENT UNDER THIS L/C ARE FOUND TO BE DISSCRPEPANT, WE SHALL GIVE ITS NOTICE OF REFUSAL AND SHALL HOLD

DOCUMENTS AT YOUR DISPOSAL SUBJECT TO THE FOLLOWING CONDITION:"IF WE HAVE NOT RECEIVED YOUR DISPOSAL INSTRUCTIONS FOR THE DISCREPANT DOCUMENTS PROIR TO RECEIPT OF THE APPLICANT'S WAIVER OF DISCREPANCIES, WE WILL RELEASE DOCUMENTS TO APPLICANT WITHOUT NOTICE TO YOU.

DETAILS OF CHARGES 71B:

+BANK CHARGES EXCLUDING ISSUING BANK ARE FOR ACCOUNT OF BENEFICIARY.

PRESENTATION PERIOD:

+DOCUMENTS TO BE PRESENTED WITHIN 21 DAYS FROM SHIPMENT DATE BUT WITHIN THE VALID OF THE CREDIT.

PRESENTATION PERIOD 48: WITHIN 15 DAYS AFTER THE DATE OF SHIPMENT BUT WITHIN THE VALIDITY OF THE CREDIT.

CONFIRMATION 49: WITHOUT

有关资料:

发票号码:2015ZH8898 发票日期:2016 年 1 月 10 日

金属硅 H.S.编码:2804690000

净重:100 M/T,毛 重:100.8 M/T,体积:40 M^3

唛头:按要求设计

普惠制产地证明书申请书

申请人单位（盖章）：　　　　　　　　　　　　　　　　　　证书号：________

申请人郑重声明：　　　　　　　　　　　　　　　　　　　　注册号：________

本人是被正式授权代表出口单位办理和签署本申请书的。

本申请书及普惠制产地证格式A所列内容正确无误，如发现弄虚作假，冒充格式A所列货物，擅改证书，自愿接收签证机关的处罚及负法律责任。现将有关情况申报如下：

<table>
<tr><td>生产单位</td><td colspan="3"></td><td colspan="2">生产单位联系人电话</td><td colspan="2"></td></tr>
<tr><td>商品名称
（中英文）</td><td colspan="3"></td><td colspan="2">H.S税目号
（以六位数码计）</td><td colspan="2"></td></tr>
<tr><td colspan="2">商品（FOB）总值（以美元记）</td><td colspan="3"></td><td>发票号</td><td colspan="2"></td></tr>
<tr><td>最终销售国</td><td colspan="2"></td><td colspan="2">证书种类划“✓”</td><td>加急证书</td><td colspan="2">普通证书</td></tr>
<tr><td colspan="2">货物拟出运日期</td><td colspan="6"></td></tr>
<tr><td colspan="8">贸易方式和企业性质（请在适用处划“✓”）</td></tr>
<tr><td>正常贸易C</td><td>来进料加工
L</td><td>补偿贸易
B</td><td>中外合资
H</td><td>中外合作
Z</td><td>外商独资
D</td><td>零售
Y</td><td>展卖
M</td></tr>
<tr><td></td><td></td><td></td><td></td><td></td><td></td><td></td><td></td></tr>
<tr><td colspan="3">包装数量或毛重或其他数量</td><td colspan="5"></td></tr>
<tr><td colspan="8">原产地标准：
本项商品系在中国生产，完全符合该给惠国给惠方案规定，其原产地情况符合以下第　　条；
(1) “P”（完全国产，未使用任何进口原材料）；
(2) “W”其H.S税目号为……………………（含进口成分）；
(3) “F”（对加拿大出口产品，其进口成分不超过产品出厂价值的40%）。
本批产品系：1. 直接运输从……………到……………………；
　　　　　　2. 转口运输从……………中转国（地区）……………到…………；</td></tr>
<tr><td colspan="8">申请人说明
　　　　　　　　　　　　　　　　领证人（签名）
　　　　　　　　　　　　　　　　电　话：
　　　　　　　　　　　　　　　　日期　　　年　　月　　日</td></tr>
</table>

现提交中国出口商业发票副本一份，普惠制产地证明书格式A（FORM　A）一正二副，以及其他附件　　　份，请予审核签证。

注：凡含有进口成分的商品，必须按要求提交《含进口成分受惠商品成本明细单》。

ORIGINAL

<table>
<tr><td colspan="3">Goods consigned from (Export's business, address, country) (1)</td><td colspan="3" rowspan="2">Reference No. 981898699

GENERALIZED SYSTEM OF PREFERENCES
CERTIFICATE OF ORIGIN
(Combined declaration and certificate)
FORM A
Issued in THE PEOPLE'S REPUBLIC OF CHINA
(country)
See Notes overleaf</td></tr>
<tr><td colspan="3">Goods consigned to (Consignee's name, address, country) (2)</td></tr>
<tr><td colspan="3">Means of transport and route (as far as known) (3)</td><td colspan="3">For official use</td></tr>
<tr><td>Item number (4)</td><td>Marks and number of packages (5)</td><td>Number and Kind of packages; description of goods (6)</td><td>Origin criterion (see Notes overleaf) (7)</td><td>Gross weight or other quantity (8)</td><td>Number and date of invoices (9)</td></tr>
<tr><td colspan="3">Certification
It is hereby certified, on the basis of control carried out, that the declaration by the exporter is correct</td><td colspan="3">Declaration by the exporter
The undersigned hereby declares that the above details and statements are correct; that all the goods were produced in
CHINA
and that they comply with origin requirements specified for those goods in the Generalized System of Preferences for goods exported to (10)
Place and date. Signature and stamp of certifying authority</td></tr>
<tr><td colspan="3">Place and date. Signature and stamp of certifying authority</td><td colspan="3"></td></tr>
</table>

项目 7　制作和办理报关单

7.1　学习目标

知识目标：熟悉一般进出口货物报关单的含义和分类；掌握进出口货物报关单填报的一般要求和填制规范。

能力目标：能够正确填写一般进出口货物报关单。

7.2　工作任务

无锡蓝天进出口公司（社会信用代码：31010100018****）出口一批全棉女童连衣裙，于2015 年 7 月 13 日抵达上海吴淞，次日无锡蓝天进出口公司委托上海运达国际货运代理有限公司（社会信用代码：91310113630425****）向上海吴淞海关申报（关区代码 2202）。全棉女童连衣裙的法定计量单位为：条/千克。

报关材料包括以下几项：

① 装箱单。

② 商业发票。

③ 合同。

郭晓芳接到这笔业务后，要根据以上材料完成该批服装的出口报关工作，具体工作任务如下：

① 完成出口申报。帮客户进行代理报关时，要确定具体申报需要哪些材料，并进行网上申报和现场申报。

② 如果有海关查验通知，要配合海关查验。

③ 按规定办理缴纳税款的手续。

④ 海关放行后，要提取货物。

7.3 操作范例

中华人民共和国海关出口货物报关单

预录入编号：

海关编号：5213788990766××××××

收发货人 无锡蓝天进出口公司 31010100018****	出口口岸 上海吴淞海关 2202	出口日期 20150715	申报日期 20150714
生产销售单位 无锡蓝天进出口公司 31010100018****	运输方式 江海运输	运输工具名称 DONG FANG V. 25	提运单号 COSOOTEC192
申报单位 上海运达货代 91310113630425****	监管方式 一般贸易 0110	征免性质 一般征税 101	备案号

贸易国(地区) 加拿大	运抵国(地区) 加拿大	指运港 蒙特利尔	境内货源地 无锡市东亭路 88 号

许可证号	成交方式 CIF	运费 USD1 700	保费 USD198	杂费
合同协议号 K123	件数 235	包装种类 纸箱	毛重(公斤) 2 285	净重(公斤) 2 070
集装箱号 COSOOTEC192	随附单证			

标记唛码及备注
KU/K123/MONTREAL/C/N:1－235

项号	商品编号	商品名称、规格型号	数量及单位	最终目的国(地区)	单价	总价	币制	征免
1.	661044200	全棉女童连衣裙	2 400 件 600 千克	加拿大	6.5	15 600	美元	照章征税(0)
2.	661044200	全棉女童连衣裙	3 000 件 825 千克	加拿大	5.5	16 500	美元	照章征税(0)
3.	661044200	全棉女童连衣裙	2 400 件 600 千克	加拿大	8.5	20 400	美元	照章征税(0)
4.	661044200	全棉女童连衣裙	1 600 件 260 千克	加拿大	8.0	12 800	美元	照章征税(0)

特殊关系确认:是　价格影响确认:否　支付特许权使用费确认:是

录入员　录入单位	兹申明对以上内容承担如实申报、依法纳税之法律责任	海关批注及签章

报关人员　李湘　　　申报单位(签章)

上海运达国际货运代理有限公司

7.4 知识链接

1. 报关单各栏目的填制规范

(1) 预录入编号

本栏目填报预录入报关单的编号，预录入编号规则由接受申报的海关决定。

(2) 海关编号

本栏目填报海关接受申报时给予报关单的编号，一份报关单对应一个海关编号。

报关单海关编号为 18 位，其中第 1～4 位为接受申报海关的编号(海关规定的《关区代码表》中相应海关代码)，第 5～8 位为海关接受申报的公历年份，第 9 位为进出口标志(“1”为进口，“0”为出口；集中申报清单“I”为进口，“E”为出口)，后 9 位为顺序编号。

(3) 收发货人

本栏目填报在海关注册的对外签订并执行进出口贸易合同的中国境内法人、其他组织或个人的名称及编码。编码可选填 18 位法人和其他组织统一社会信用代码或 10 位海关注册编码任一项。

(4) 进口口岸/出口口岸

本栏目应根据货物实际进出境的口岸海关，填报海关规定的《关区代码表》中相应口岸海关的名称及代码。特殊情况填报要求如下：

进口转关运输货物应填报货物进境地海关名称及代码，出口转关运输货物应填报货物出境地海关名称及代码。按转关运输方式监管的跨关区深加工结转货物，出口报关单填报转出地海关名称及代码，进口报关单填报转入地海关名称及代码。

在不同海关特殊监管区域或保税监管场所之间调拨、转让的货物，填报对方特殊监管区域或保税监管场所所在的海关名称及代码。

其他无实际进出境的货物，填报接受申报的海关名称及代码。

(5) 进口日期/出口日期

进口日期填报运载进口货物的运输工具申报进境的日期。

出口日期指运载出口货物的运输工具办结出境手续的日期。本栏目供海关签发打印报关单证明联用，在申报时免予填报。

无实际进出境的报关单填报海关接受申报的日期。

本栏目为 8 位数字，顺序为年(4 位)、月(2 位)、日(2 位)。

(6) 申报日期

申报日期指海关接受进出口货物收发货人、受委托的报关企业申报数据的日期。以电子数据报关单方式申报的，申报日期为海关计算机系统接受申报数据时记录的日期。以纸质报关单方式申报的，申报日期为海关接受纸质报关单并对报关单进行登记处理的日期。

申报日期为 8 位数字，顺序为年(4 位)、月(2 位)、日(2 位)。本栏目在申报时免予填报。

(7) 消费使用单位/生产销售单位

消费使用单位填报已知的进口货物在境内的最终消费、使用单位的名称；生产销售单位填报出口货物在境内的生产或销售单位的名称。

(8) 运输方式

运输方式包括实际运输方式和海关规定的特殊运输方式，前者指货物实际进出境的运输方式，按进出境所使用的运输工具分类；后者指货物无实际进出境的运输方式，按货物在境内的流向分类。

本栏目应根据货物实际进出境的运输方式或货物在境内流向的类别，按照海关规定的《运输方式代码表》选择填报相应的运输方式。

(9) 运输工具名称

本栏目填报载运货物进出境的运输工具名称或编号。填报内容应与运输部门向海关申报的舱单(载货清单)所列相应内容一致。

(10) 航次号

本栏目填报载运货物进出境的运输工具的航次编号。

(11) 提运单号

本栏目填报进出口货物提单或运单的编号。

一份报关单只允许填报一个提单或运单号，一票货物对应多个提单或运单时，应分单填报。其具体填报要求如下：

① 直接在进出境地或采用区域通关一体化通关模式办理报关手续的如下。

水路运输：填报进出口提单号。如有分提单的，填报进出口提单号＋“*”＋分提单号。

公路运输：启用公路舱单前，免予填报；启用公路舱单后，填报进出口总运单号。

铁路运输：填报运单号。

航空运输：填报总运单号＋“_”＋分运单号，无分运单的填报总运单号。

邮件运输：填报邮运包裹单号。

② 转关运输货物的报关单如下：

a. 进口。

水路运输：直转、中转填报提单号。提前报关免予填报。

铁路运输：直转、中转填报铁路运单号。提前报关免予填报。

航空运输：直转、中转货物填报总运单号＋“_”＋分运单号。提前报关免予填报。

其他运输方式：免予填报。

以上运输方式进境货物，在广东省内用公路运输转关的，填报车牌号。

b. 出口。

水路运输：中转货物填报提单号；非中转货物免予填报；广东省内汽车运输提前报关的转关货物，填报承运车辆的车牌号。

其他运输方式：免予填报。广东省内汽车运输提前报关的转关货物，填报承运车辆的车牌号。

采用“集中申报”通关方式办理报关手续的，报关单填报归并的集中申报清单的进出口起止日期〔按年(4位)月(2位)日(2位)年(4位)月(2位)日(2位)〕。

无实际进出境的，本栏目免予填报。

(12) 申报单位

自理报关的，本栏目填报进出口企业的名称及编码；委托代理报关的，本栏目填报报关企业名称及编码。

本栏目可选填18位法人和其他组织统一社会信用代码或10位海关注册编码任一项。

本栏目还包括报关单左下方用于填报申报单位有关情况的相关栏目，包括报关人员、申报单位签章。

(13) 监管方式

监管方式是以国际贸易中进出口货物的交易方式为基础，结合海关对进出口货物的征税、统计及监管条件综合设定的海关对进出口货物的管理方式。其代码由 4 位数字构成，前两位是按照海关监管要求和计算机管理需要划分的分类代码，后两位是参照国际标准编制的贸易方式代码。

本栏目应根据实际对外贸易情况按海关规定的《监管方式代码表》选择填报相应的监管方式简称及代码。一份报关单只允许填报一种监管方式。

(14) 征免性质

本栏目应根据实际情况按海关规定的《征免性质代码表》选择填报相应的征免性质简称及代码，持有海关核发的《征免税证明》的，应按照《征免税证明》中批注的征免性质填报。一份报关单只允许填报一种征免性质。

(15) 备案号

本栏目填报进出口货物收发货人、消费使用单位、生产销售单位在海关办理加工贸易合同备案或征、减、免税备案审批等手续时，海关核发的《加工贸易手册》《征免税证明》或其他备案审批文件的编号。

一份报关单只允许填报一个备案号。

(16) 贸易国(地区)

本栏目填报对外贸易中与境内企业签订贸易合同的外方所属的国家(地区)。进口填报购自国，出口填报售予国。未发生商业性交易的填报货物所有权拥有者所属的国家(地区)。

本栏目应按海关规定的《国别(地区)代码表》选择填报相应的贸易国(地区)或贸易国(地区)中文名称及代码。

无实际进出境的，填报“中国”(代码 142)。

(17) 启运国(地区)/运抵国(地区)

启运国(地区)填报进口货物起始发出直接运抵我国或者在运输中转国(地)未发生任何商业性交易的情况下运抵我国的国家(地区)。

运抵国(地区)填报出口货物离开我国关境直接运抵或者在运输中转国(地区)未发生任何商业性交易的情况下最后运抵的国家(地区)。

不经过第三国(地区)转运的直接运输进出口货物，以进口货物的装货港所在国(地区)为启运国(地区)，以出口货物的指运港所在国(地区)为运抵国(地区)。

经过第三国(地区)转运的进出口货物，如在中转国(地区)发生商业性交易，则以中转国(地区)作为启运/运抵国(地区)。

本栏目应按海关规定的《国别(地区)代码表》选择填报相应的启运国(地区)或运抵国(地区)中文名称及代码。

无实际进出境的，填报“中国”(代码 142)。

(18) 装货港/指运港

装货港填报进口货物在运抵我国关境前的最后一个境外装运港。

指运港填报出口货物运往境外的最终目的港；最终目的港不可预知的，按尽可能预知的目的港填报。

本栏目应根据实际情况按海关规定的《港口代码表》选择填报相应的港口中文名称及代码。装货港/指运港在《港口代码表》中无港口中文名称及代码的，可选择填报相应的国家中文名称或代码。

无实际进出境的，本栏目填报“中国境内”(代码142)。

(19) 境内目的地/境内货源地

境内目的地填报已知的进口货物在国内的消费、使用地或最终运抵地，其中最终运抵地为最终使用单位所在的地区。最终使用单位难以确定的，填报货物进口时预知的最终收货单位所在地。

境内货源地填报出口货物在国内的产地或原始发货地。出口货物产地难以确定的，填报最早发运该出口货物的单位所在地。

本栏目按海关规定的《国内地区代码表》选择填报相应的国内地区名称及代码。

(20) 许可证号

本栏目填报以下许可证的编号：进(出)口许可证、两用物项和技术进(出)口许可证、两用物项和技术出口许可证(定向)、纺织品临时出口许可证。

一份报关单只允许填报一个许可证号。

(21) 成交方式

本栏目应根据进出口货物实际成交价格条款，按海关规定的《成交方式代码表》选择填报相应的成交方式代码。

无实际进出境的报关单，进口填报CIF，出口填报FOB。

(22) 运费

本栏目填报进口货物运抵我国境内输入地点起卸前的运输费用，出口货物运至我国境内输出地点装载后的运输费用。

运费可按运费单价、总价或运费率三种方式之一填报，注明运费标记(运费标记“1”表示运费率，“2”表示每吨货物的运费单价，“3”表示运费总价)，并按海关规定的《货币代码表》选择填报相应的币种代码。

(23) 保费

本栏目填报进口货物运抵我国境内输入地点起卸前的保险费用，出口货物运至我国境内输出地点装载后的保险费用。

保费可按保险费总价或保险费率两种方式之一填报，注明保险费标记(保险费标记“1”表示保险费率，“3”表示保险费总价)，并按海关规定的《货币代码表》选择填报相应的币种代码。

(24) 杂费

本栏目填报成交价格以外的、按照《中华人民共和国进出口关税条例》相关规定应计入完税价格或应从完税价格中扣除的费用。可按杂费总价或杂费率两种方式之一填报，注明杂费标记(杂费标记“1”表示杂费率，“3”表示杂费总价)，并按海关规定的《货币代码表》选择填报相应的币种代码。

应计入完税价格的杂费填报为正值或正率，应从完税价格中扣除的杂费填报为负值或负率。

(25) 合同协议号

本栏目填报进出口货物合同(包括协议或订单)编号。未发生商业性交易的免予填报。

(26) 件数

本栏目填报有外包装的进出口货物的实际件数。

(27) 包装种类

本栏目应根据进出口货物的实际外包装种类,按海关规定的《包装种类代码表》选择填报相应的包装种类代码。

(28) 毛重(千克)

本栏目填报进出口货物及其包装材料的重量之和,计量单位为千克,不足 1 千克的填报为“1”。

(29) 净重(千克)

本栏目填报进出口货物的毛重减去外包装材料后的重量,即货物本身的实际重量,计量单位为千克,不足 1 千克的填报为“1”。

(30) 集装箱号

本栏目填报装载进出口货物(包括拼箱货物)集装箱的箱体信息。一个集装箱填一条记录,分别填报集装箱号(在集装箱箱体上标示的全球唯一编号)、集装箱的规格和集装箱的自重。非集装箱货物填报为“0”。

(31) 随附单证

本栏目根据海关规定的《监管证件代码表》选择填报除本规范第十八条规定的许可证件以外的其他进出口许可证件或监管证件代码及编号。

本栏目分为随附单证代码和随附单证编号两栏,其中,代码栏应按海关规定的《监管证件代码表》选择填报相应证件代码;编号栏应填报证件编号。

① 加工贸易内销征税报关单,随附单证代码栏填写“c”,随附单证编号栏填写海关审核通过的内销征税联系单号。

② 优惠贸易协定项下进出口货物。

有关优惠贸易协定项下报关单填制要求将另行公告。

(32) 标记唛码及备注

(33) 项号

本栏目分两行填报及打印。第一行填报报关单中的商品顺序编号;第二行专用于加工贸易、减免税等已备案、审批的货物,填报和打印该项货物在《加工贸易手册》或《征免税证明》等备案、审批单证中的顺序编号。

有关优惠贸易协定项下报关单填制要求将另行公告。

(34) 商品编号

本栏目填报的商品编号由 10 位数字组成。前 8 位为《中华人民共和国进出口税则》确定的进出口货物的税则号列,同时也是《中华人民共和国海关统计商品目录》确定的商品编码,后 2 位为符合海关监管要求的附加编号。

(35) 商品名称、规格型号

本栏目分两行填报及打印。第一行填报进出口货物规范的中文商品名称,第二行填报规格型号。

(36) 数量及单位

本栏目分三行填报及打印。

① 第一行应按进出口货物的法定第一计量单位填报数量及单位,法定计量单位以《中华人民共和国海关统计商品目录》中的计量单位为准。

② 凡列明有法定第二计量单位的,应在第二行按照法定第二计量单位填报数量及单位。无法定第二计量单位的,本栏目第二行为空。

③ 成交计量单位及数量应填报并打印在第三行。

④ 法定计量单位为"千克"的数量填报。

⑤ 成套设备、减免税货物如需分批进口,货物实际进口时,应按照实际报验状态确定数量。

⑥ 具有完整品或制成品基本特征的不完整品、未制成品,根据《商品名称及编码协调制度》归类规则应按完整品归类的,按照构成完整品的实际数量填报。

⑦ 加工贸易等已备案的货物,成交计量单位必须与《加工贸易手册》中同项号下货物的计量单位一致,加工贸易边角料和副产品内销、边角料复出口,本栏目填报其报验状态的计量单位。

⑧ 优惠贸易协定项下进出口商品的成交计量单位必须与原产地证书上对应商品的计量单位一致。

⑨ 法定计量单位为立方米的气体货物,应折算成标准状况(即零度及 1 个标准大气压)下的体积进行填报。

(37) 原产国(地区)

原产国(地区)应依据《中华人民共和国进出口货物原产地条例》《中华人民共和国海关关于执行〈非优惠原产地规则中实质性改变标准〉的规定》以及海关总署关于各项优惠贸易协定原产地管理规章规定的原产地确定标准填报。同一批进出口货物的原产地不同的,应分别填报原产国(地区)。进出口货物原产国(地区)无法确定的,填报"国别不详"(代码 701)。

本栏目应按海关规定的《国别(地区)代码表》选择填报相应的国家(地区)名称及代码。

(38) 最终目的国(地区)

最终目的国(地区)填报已知的进出口货物的最终实际消费、使用或进一步加工制造国家(地区)。不经过第三国(地区)转运的直接运输货物,以运抵国(地区)为最终目的国(地区);经过第三国(地区)转运的货物,以最后运往国(地区)为最终目的国(地区)。同一批进出口货物的最终目的国(地区)不同的,应分别填报最终目的国(地区)。进出口货物不能确定最终目的国(地区)时,以尽可能预知的最后运往国(地区)为最终目的国(地区)。

本栏目应按海关规定的《国别(地区)代码表》选择填报相应的国家(地区)名称及代码。

(39) 单价

本栏目填报同一项号下进出口货物实际成交的商品单位价格。无实际成交价格的,本栏目填报单位货值。

(40) 总价

本栏目填报同一项号下进出口货物实际成交的商品总价格。无实际成交价格的,本栏目填报货值。

(41) 币制

本栏目应按海关规定的《货币代码表》选择相应的货币名称及代码填报，如《货币代码表》中无实际成交币种，需将实际成交货币按申报日外汇折算率折算成《货币代码表》列明的货币填报。

(42) 征免

本栏目应按照海关核发的《征免税证明》或有关政策规定，对报关单所列每项商品选择海关规定的《征减免税方式代码表》中相应的征减免税方式填报。

加工贸易货物报关单应根据《加工贸易手册》中备案的征免规定填报；《加工贸易手册》中备案的征免规定为“保金”或“保函”的，应填报“全免”。

(43) 特殊关系的确认

本栏目根据《中华人民共和国海关审定进出口货物完税价格办法》(以下简称《审价办法》)第十六条的规定，填报确认进出口行为中买、卖双方是否存在特殊关系，有下列情形之一的，应当认为买、卖双方存在特殊关系，在本栏目应填报“是”，反之则填报“否”：

① 买、卖双方为同一家族成员的；

② 买、卖双方互为商业上的高级职员或者董事的；

③ 一方直接或者间接地受另一方控制的；

④ 买、卖双方都直接或者间接地受第三方控制的；

⑤ 买、卖双方共同直接或者间接地控制第三方的；

⑥ 一方直接或者间接地拥有、控制或者持有对方5%以上(含5%)公开发行的有表决权的股票或者股份的；

⑦ 一方是另一方的雇员、高级职员或者董事的；

⑧ 买、卖双方是同一合伙的成员的。

买、卖双方在经营上相互有联系，一方是另一方的独家代理、独家经销或者独家受让人，如果符合前款的规定，也应当视为存在特殊关系。

(44) 价格影响确认

本栏目根据《审价办法》第十七条的规定，填报确认进出口行为中买、卖双方存在的特殊关系是否影响成交价格，纳税义务人如不能证明其成交价格与同时或者大约同时发生的下列任何一款价格相近的，应当视为特殊关系对进出口货物的成交价格产生影响，在本栏目应填报“是”，反之则填报“否”：

① 向境内无特殊关系的买方出售的相同或者类似进出口货物的成交价格；

② 按照《审价办法》倒扣价格估价方法的规定所确定的相同或者类似进出口货物的完税价格；

③ 按照《审价办法》计算价格估价方法的规定所确定的相同或者类似进出口货物的完税价格。

(45) 支付特许权使用费确认

本栏目根据《审价办法》第十三条的规定，填报确认进出口行为中买方是否存在向卖方或者有关方直接或者间接支付特许权使用费。特许权使用费是指进出口货物的买方为取得知识产权权利人及权利人有效授权人关于专利权、商标权、专有技术、著作权、分销权或者销售权的许可或者转让而支付的费用。如果进出口行为中买方存在向卖方或者有关方直接或者间接支付特许权使用费的,在本栏目应填报"是",反之则填报"否"。

(46) 版本号

本栏目适用加工贸易货物出口报关单。本栏目应与《加工贸易手册》中备案的成品单耗版本一致,通过《加工贸易手册》备案数据或企业出口报关清单提取。

(47) 货号

本栏目适用加工贸易货物进出口报关单。本栏目应与《加工贸易手册》中备案的料件、成品货号一致,通过《加工贸易手册》备案数据或企业出口报关清单提取。

(48) 录入员

本栏目用于记录预录入操作人员的姓名。

(49) 录入单位

本栏目用于记录预录入单位名称。

(50) 海关批注及签章

本栏目供海关作业时签注。

本规范所述尖括号(〈〉)、逗号(,)、连接符(-)、冒号(:)等标点符号及数字,填报时都必须使用非中文状态下的半角字符。

一般进出口货物报关单填制的注意要点

一般进出口货物报关单的填制中要注意备案号为空,监管方式、征免性质和征免的配合。监管方式为一般贸易时,对应的征免性质为一般征税,征免填照章征税。

收发货人填对外签约的企业及其18位信用编码;生产消费使用单位填收货单位或生产单位,及其18位社会信用编码,新增的贸易国填报国外签约国。

运、保费填报的方法是,进口:成交方式+运费+保费=CIF,出口:成交方式-运费-保费=FOB,件数的优先顺序为托盘、包装、集装箱,散装和裸装按实际填报。

报　关

1. 报关的含义及期限

报关是指进出口贸易的有关当事人或其代理人、进出境工具负责人、进出境物品的所有人在规定的有效期内向海关办理有关货物、运输工具、物品进出境手续的全过程。按照《中华人民共和国海关法》的规定,所有进出境的货物和运输工具必须通过设有海关的地方进境或出境,并接受海关的监督。只有经过海关放行后,货物才能提取或装运出口。

2. 报关单位

报关单位分为报关企业和进出口收发货人。报关企业分为报关公司和货运代理公司。

3. 报关员

报关员是指取得资格证书,按照规定程序在海关办理注册进出口货物报关业务的人员。我国海关规定进出口货物的报关必须由经海关批准的专业人员代表收发货人或报关企业向海关办理。这些人员就是报关员。

4. 进出口货物报关的流程

为了确保进出口货物合法进出境,海关根据国家有关法律法规的不同要求,对进出口货物的报关规定了一系列特定的手续和步骤。遵守这些规定的程序是保管人的法定义务,否则将承担相应的法律责任。根据时间的先后顺序和海关管理要求的不同,报关可以分为前期报关程序和进出境报关程序和后续报关程序。

(1) 前期报关程序

前期报关程序是指进出口货物在实际进出境之前,进出口货物发货人或其代理人向海关说明进出境货物的情况,申请适用特定的报关程序。

(2) 进出境报关程序

进出境报关程序是指进出口货物在进出境环节须向海关履行的手续。进出境报关程序是任何进出口货物通关时都必须履行经过的环节。一般进出口货物的报关只需履行进出境报关程序即可,主要包括进出口申报、陪同检验、缴纳税费、提取或装运货物等。通关流转程序如图7-1所示:

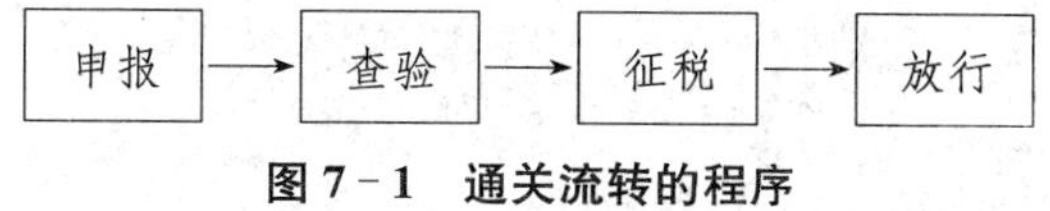

图7-1　通关流转的程序

(3) 后续报关程序

后报关程序则主要指进出口货物实际进出境以后,进出口货物收发货人或其代理人根据海关管理的要求向海关办理的旨在证明有关进出口、在境内合规使用并已经完成有关海关监管义务的手续。

7.5　能力实训

实训1　根据资料填制出口货物报关单一份

1) THE SELLER: DALIAN HAITIAN GARMENT CO., LTD.中韩合资大连海天服装有限公司(2115930064)

2) THE BUYER: WAN DO APPAREL CO. LTD, 550-17, YANGCHUN-GU, SEOUL, KOREA

3) PORT OF LOADING: DALIAN CHINA, FINAL DESTINATION: INCHON KOREA, CARRIER: DAIN/431E

4) TERMS OF PAYMENT: DOCUMENTS AGAINST ACCEPTANCE

5)

NO.S OF PACKAGES	DESCRIPTION	QTY/UNIT	UNIT PRICE	AMOUNT FOB DALIAN CHINA
260CTNS	LADY'S JUMPER	1 300PCS	@＄11.00	USD14 300.00
	MAN'S JUMPER	1 300PCS	@＄11.00	USD14 300.00

TOTAL:USD28 600.00

6) B/L NO.: DAINE 431227, INVOICE NO.: HT01A08

7) NW: 2 600KGS, GW: 3 380KGS, 1×40′CONTAINER NO.: EASU9608490.

8) 该公司在来料加工合同 9911113 项下出口男、女羽绒短上衣，分列手册（编号 B09009301018）第 2、3 项，外汇核销单编号：215157263，计量单位：件/千克。

9) 大连亚东国际货运有限公司于 2014 年 3 月 25 日向大连海关申报出口，提单日期为 2004 年 3 月 26 日。

10) 该男、女羽绒短上衣的商品编码分别为 6201.9310、6202.1310。

中华人民共和国海关出口货物报关单

预录入编号：　　　　　　　　　　　　　　　　　　海关编号：

<table>
<tr><td colspan="3">收发货人</td><td colspan="2">出口口岸</td><td colspan="2">出口日期</td><td colspan="2">申报日期</td></tr>
<tr><td colspan="3">生产销售单位</td><td>运输方式</td><td colspan="3">运输工具名称</td><td colspan="2">提运单号</td></tr>
<tr><td colspan="3">申报单位</td><td colspan="2">监管方式</td><td colspan="2">征免性质</td><td colspan="2">备案号</td></tr>
<tr><td colspan="2">贸易国(地区)</td><td colspan="2">运抵国(地区)</td><td colspan="3">指运港</td><td colspan="2">境内货源地</td></tr>
<tr><td colspan="2">许可证号</td><td>成交方式</td><td colspan="2">运费</td><td colspan="2">保费</td><td colspan="2">杂费</td></tr>
<tr><td colspan="2">合同协议号</td><td colspan="2">件数</td><td colspan="2">包装种类</td><td colspan="2">毛重(公斤)</td><td>净重(公斤)</td></tr>
<tr><td colspan="2">集装箱号</td><td colspan="7">随附单证</td></tr>
<tr><td colspan="9">标记唛码及备注</td></tr>
<tr><td>项号</td><td>商品编号</td><td>商品名称、规格型号</td><td>数量及单位</td><td>最终目的国(地区)</td><td>单价</td><td>总价</td><td>币制</td><td>征免</td></tr>
<tr><td colspan="9">1.</td></tr>
<tr><td colspan="9">2.</td></tr>
<tr><td colspan="9">3.</td></tr>
<tr><td colspan="9">4.</td></tr>
<tr><td colspan="9">5.</td></tr>
<tr><td colspan="9">6.</td></tr>
<tr><td colspan="9">7.</td></tr>
<tr><td colspan="9">8.</td></tr>
<tr><td colspan="3">特殊关系确认：</td><td colspan="3">价格影响确认：</td><td colspan="3">支付特许权使用费确认：</td></tr>
<tr><td colspan="2">录入员　　　　录入单位</td><td colspan="3">兹申明对以上内容承担如实申报、依法纳税之法律责任</td><td colspan="4">海关批注及签章</td></tr>
<tr><td colspan="2">报关人员</td><td colspan="7">申报单位(签章)</td></tr>
</table>

实训 2　根据资料填制进口报关单一份

上海顺景贸易公司(社会信用代码:31010100018 ****)委托上海服装进出口公司(社会信用代码:31011500012 ****),进口羊毛连衣裙和男式羊毛衬衫一批,于 2016 年 1 月 28

日抵达上海吴淞,次日上海服装进出口公司委托上海奔腾国际物流公司(社会信用代码:91310113630425 ****)向上海吴淞海关申报(关区代码 2202)。羊毛连衣裙的法定计量单位为:条/千克,男式羊毛衬衫的法定计量单位为:件/千克。

提供的单证材料如下:

MBA ENTERPRISE CORP.

KOYANG CITY KYONGGIDO KOREA

PACKING/WEIGHT LIST

SHIPPER MBA ENTERPRISE CORP. KOYANG CITY KYONGGIDO KOREA	**INCIOCE NO:** KH063812－1	**DATE:** JAN.18.2016
	L/C NO;	DATE
FOR ACCOUNT & RISK OF MESSES TIANJIN CLOTHING IMP. &EXP.CO. LTD 28 HAIDE ROAD WUSONG SHANGHAI, CHINA	**B/L NO**: KSAA186842	
	L/C ISSU BANK: T/T BASE	
	TERM: CFR WUSONG	
	SAILING ON OR ABOUT: JAN.28,2014	

SHIPPED FROM: INCHON KOREA **TO:** WUSONG CHINA **PER:** TITANNIKE/0088

MARKS & NOS	**DESCRIPTION**	**Q'NT**	**N.W**	**G.W**
N/M 40 FT TWO CONTAINER CONTAINER NO: ABLU386948 ABLU386956 TAREWGT 4 800 KG MADE IN KOREA		50 DOZENS 600PCS	200 KGS	210 KGS
	DRESSES OF WOOL HS CODE:62044100			
		30 DOZENS 360 PCS	300 KGS	310 KGS
TOTAL: 50 CARTONS / 960 PCS / 80 DOZENS			500 KGS	520 KGS

MBA ENTERPRISE CORP.

MBA ENTERPRISE CORP.

KOYANG CITY KYONGGIDO KOREA

COMMERCIAL INVOICE

<table>
<tr><td rowspan="2">SHIPPER
MBA ENTERPRISE CORP. KOYANG CITY KYONGGIDO KOREA</td><td>INVOICE NO:
KH063812－1</td><td>DATE: JAN.18.2016</td></tr>
<tr><td colspan="2">L/C NO; DATE</td></tr>
<tr><td rowspan="4">FOR ACCOUNT & RISK
OF MESSES TIANJIN CLOTHING IMP. & EXP.CO. LTD 28 HAIDE ROAD WUSONG, SHANGHIA, CHINA</td><td colspan="2">B/L NO: KSAA186842</td></tr>
<tr><td colspan="2">L/C ISSU BANK: T/T BASE
BY T/T</td></tr>
<tr><td colspan="2">TERM: CFR TANGGU</td></tr>
<tr><td colspan="2">SAILING ON OR ABOUT: JAN.28,2014</td></tr>
<tr><td colspan="3">SHIPPED FROM: INCHON KOREA　TO: TIANJIN CHINA　PER: TITANNIKE/0088</td></tr>
</table>

<table>
<tr><td>MARKS & NOS
N/M</td><td>DESCRIPTION</td><td>Q'NT</td><td>UNIT.P</td><td>AMOUNT</td></tr>
<tr><td></td><td>DRESSES OF WOOL
HS CODE: 62044100</td><td>50 DOZENS
600 PCS</td><td>@USD120</td><td>USD6 000</td></tr>
<tr><td colspan="5">MADE IN KOREA</td></tr>
<tr><td></td><td>BOY'S SHIRTS OF WOOL
HS CODE: 62051000</td><td>30 DOZENS
360 PCS</td><td>@USD180</td><td>USD5 400</td></tr>
<tr><td colspan="4">TOTAL: 50 CARTONS / 960 PCS / 80 DOZENS</td><td>USD11 400</td></tr>
</table>

INSURANCE: USD 500

MBA ENTERPRISE CORP.

CONTRACT

NO: KOR063828
DATE: SEP.26, 2010
SIGNED IN KOREA

THE BUYER: SHANGHIA CLOTHING IMP. &EXP. CO. LTD
28 HAIDE ROAD, WUSONG, SHANGHAI, CHINA

THE SELLER: MBA ENTERPRISE CORP. KOYANG CITY KYONGGIDO KOREA

1. This contract is made by and between the buyer and seller whereby the buy agree to buy and the seller agree to sell the under mentioned commodities according to the terms and condition stipulated below:

Goods	Quantity	Unit Price	Amount
1. DRESSES OF WOOL	50 Dozens 600 pcs	@USD 120	USD 6 000
2. BOYS' SHIRTS OF WOOL	30 Dozens 360 pcs	@USD 180	USD 5 400
TOTAL: 50 CARTONS/960 PCS/80 DOZENS			USD 11 400
SAY US DOLLARS ELEVEN THOUSAND FOUR HUNDRED ONLY			

2. **Country of origin:** R. OF KOREA
3. **Price term:** CFR WUSONG, CHINA
4. **Shipping marks:** at seller's option
5. **Time of shipment:** to ship the ponies installment basis before March 10, 2011
6. **Port of shipment:** KOREA INCHON PORT
7. **Port of destination:** WUSONG. CHINA
8. **Insurance:** to be covered by seller
9. **Payment:** by T/T after shipment

This contract is made out in two original copies, one copy to be held by each party.

Buyer: Seller:

中华人民共和国海关进口货物报关单(最新版)

预录入编号：　　　　　　　　　　　　　　　　海关编号：

收发货人	进口口岸	进口日期 20160128	申报日期 20160129

消费使用单位	运输方式 水路运输	运输工具名称 TITANNIKE/0088	提运单号 KSAA186842

申报单位	监管方式	征免性质	备案号

贸易国(地区)	启运国(地区)	装货港	境内目的地

许可证号	成交方式	运费	保费	杂费

合同协议号	件数	包装种类	毛重(公斤)	净重(公斤)

集装箱号	随附单证

标记唛码及备注
随附单证号：

项号	商品编号	商品名称、规格型号	数量及单位	原产国(地区)	单价	总价	币制	征免

录入员　　录入单位	兹申明对以上内容承担如实申报、依法纳税之法律责任	海关批注及签章

报关人员　　　　　　　　　　申报单位(签章)

实训 3 根据资料填制进口报关单一份

苏州苏迈进出口公司(3112935072)从香港购进一批钢铆钉(HS CODE:73182300,计量单位:千克)。该商品列进料对口合同手册第 4 项。经营单位于 2013 年 3 月 21 日自行向沪机海关(上海机场海关)申报进口。该批货物的国外运费为 3 000 美元,保险费为 100 美元。

ORIENTAL PACIFIC LIMITED

Rm. 1605, Ho Lik Centre, 66A Sha Tsui Road

Tsuen Wan, N. T., Hong Kong

Tel: (825)2402 - 2121 Fax: (825)2491 - 8532

INVOICE

For Account of: No.: OPL0211

SUZHOU SUMIEC IMP. & EXP. CORPORATION Date: MAR. 19, 2003

5/F ZHUHUI COMMERCIAL BLDG, 180 ZHUHUI RD. Contract No.: 03HK0311201

SUZHOU, CHINA

To Supply:

HUCK FASTENING PRODUCTS

STEEL 5/8″ DIAMETER

GRIP: 0.75″～1.00″

CASE NO.	CODE NO.	QTY.	UNIT PRICE	AMOUNT
				CPT SHANGHAI
1	BOM-R20 - 12GA	3 240 PCS	USD2.98	USD9 655.20
2	BOM - 420 - 12GA	3 240 PCS	USD2.98	USD9 655.20
TOTAL:			6 480 PCS	USD19 310.40

SHIPMENT: FROM CHICAGO USA TO SHANGHAI CHINA BY AIRFREIGHT

PAYMENT: BY TELEGRAPHIC TRANSFER

COUNTRY OF ORIGIN: USA

SHIPPING MARKS: SUMIEC/SHANGHAI/C/NO.1 - 2

ORIENTAL PACIFIC LIMITED

GEORGE PETERSON

E. & O. E.

ORIENTAL PACIFIC LIMITED
Rm. 1605, Ho Lik Centre, 66A Sha Tsui Road
Tsuen Wan, N.T., Hong Kong
Tel: (825)2402-2121　Fax: (825)2491-8532

PACKING LIST

For Account of:　　　　No.: OPL0211
SUZHOU SUMIEC IMP. & EXP. CORPORATION　　　　Date: MAR. 19, 2003
5/F ZHUHUI COMMERCIAL BLDG, 180 ZHUHUI RD.　　　　Contract No.: 03HK0311201
SUZHOU, CHINA

To Supply:
HUCK FASTENING PRODUCTS

CASE NO.	CODE NO.	QTY.	DIMENSIONS	N. WT	G. WT.
1	BOM-R20-12GA	3 240 PCS	0.467 CBM	530 KGS	550 KGS
2	BOM-420-12GA	3 240 PCS	0.467 CBM	530 KGS	550 KGS
TOTAL:		6 480 PCS	0.934 CMB	1 060 KGS	1 100 KGS

PORT OF LOADING: CHICAGO, USA
ORIENTAL PACIFIC LIMITED
GEORGE PETERSON

中华人民共和国海关进口货物报关单(最新版)

预录入编号：　　　　　　　　　　　　　　　海关编号：

<table>
<tr><td colspan="2">收发货人</td><td colspan="2">进口口岸</td><td colspan="2">进口日期</td><td colspan="2">申报日期</td></tr>
<tr><td colspan="2">消费使用单位</td><td>运输方式</td><td colspan="3">运输工具名称</td><td colspan="2">提运单号</td></tr>
<tr><td colspan="2">申报单位</td><td colspan="2">监管方式</td><td colspan="2">征免性质</td><td colspan="2">备案号</td></tr>
<tr><td>贸易国(地区)</td><td colspan="2">启运国(地区)</td><td colspan="3">装货港</td><td colspan="2">境内目的地</td></tr>
<tr><td>许可证号</td><td>成交方式</td><td colspan="2">运费</td><td colspan="2">保费</td><td colspan="2">杂费</td></tr>
<tr><td>合同协议号</td><td>件数</td><td colspan="2">包装种类</td><td colspan="2">毛重(公斤)</td><td colspan="2">净重(公斤)</td></tr>
<tr><td>集装箱号</td><td colspan="7">随附单证</td></tr>
<tr><td colspan="8">标记唛码及备注
随附单证号：</td></tr>
<tr><td colspan="8">项号　商品编号　商品名称、规格型号　数量及单位　原产国(地区)　单价　总价　币制　征免</td></tr>
<tr><td colspan="8"></td></tr>
<tr><td colspan="8"></td></tr>
<tr><td colspan="8"></td></tr>
<tr><td colspan="8"></td></tr>
<tr><td colspan="2">录入员　　　　录入单位</td><td colspan="3">兹申明对以上内容承担如实申报、依法纳税之法律责任</td><td colspan="3">海关批注及签章</td></tr>
<tr><td colspan="8">报关人员　　　　　　　　　　申报单位(签章)</td></tr>
</table>

项目 8　制作投保单和办理保险

8.1　学习目标

知识目标：了解投保的流程；掌握投保单的填制规范；掌握保险单的内容和填制规范。

能力目标：能够办理投保手续；能够分析信用证条款和/或合同条款中的保险条款；熟练缮制投保单和保险单；能够根据据具体业务审查保险单是否合乎合同与信用证的要求。

8.2　工作任务

无锡蓝天进出口公司和 KU TEXTILE CORPORATION 公司所签订的货物出口合同和修改后的信用证有以下内容：Insurance Policy or Certificate endorsed in blank for 110 PCT of CIF value, covering All Risks and War Risk subject to the relevant Ocean Marine Clause of the People's Insurance Company of China, dated 1/1/1981（保险单或凭证，空白背书，以 CIF 金额的 110%投保一切险及战争险，依据中国人民保险公司 1981 年 1 月 1 日的相关海运保险条款）。

无锡蓝天进出口公司外贸单证员郭晓芳在货物完成托运、报检与报关手续并确认船期后，于货物装船前到保险公司办理国际货物运输投保手续。

外贸单证员郭晓芳需要完成的工作任务如下：

① 制作投保单。

② 向保险公司办理投保手续。

③ 审查保险单据内容是否正确。

8.3　操作范例

第一步：根据信用证条款和出口合同条款制作投保单

PICC　中国人民保险公司南京分公司

The People's Insurance Company of China Nanjing Branch

货物运输保险投保单

APPLICATION FORM FOR CARGO TRANSPORTATION INSURANCE

被保险人：

Insured: WUXI BLUE SKY IMP&EXP. Co., LTD

发票号(INVOICE NO.)ZYIE1502

合同号(CONTRACT NO.)K123
信用证号(L/C NO.)123456
发票金额(INVOICE AMOUNT)653 000 美元　投保加成(PLUS)10%
兹有下列物品向中国人民保险公司南京分公司投保。(INSURANCE IS REQUIRED THE FOLLOWING COMMODITIES:)

标记 MARKS & NOS.	包装及数量 QUANTITY	保险货物项目 DESCRIPTION OF GOODS	保险金额 AMOUNT INSURED
AS PER INVOICE NO: ZYIE1502	235CARTONS	GIRL DRESS 100% COTTON	USD71830.00

总保险金额:
TOTAL AMOUNT INSURED: U. S. DOLLARS SEVENTY-ONE THOUSAND AND EIGHT HUNDRD THIRTY ONLY
启运日期　装载运输工具:
DATE OF COMMENCEMENTAS PER B/L PER
CONVEYANCE: DONG FANG　V.25
自　经　至
FROM SHANGHAI, CHINA　VIA　TO MONTREAL, CANADA
提单号:　赔款偿付地点:
B/L NO. COSOOTEC192 CLAIM PAYABLE AT MONTREAL, CANADA
投保险别:(PLEASE INDICATE THE CONDITIONS &/OR SPECIAL COVERAGES)
CONERING ALL RISKS AND WAR RISK SUBJECT TO THE RELEVENT OCEAN MARINE CLAUSE OF THE PEOPLE'S INSURANCE COMPANY OF CHINA, DATED 1/1/1981.
请如实告知下列情况:(如"是"在[ ]中打"X")IF ANY,PLEASE MARK"X":
1. 货物种类袋装[ ]散装[ ]冷藏[ ]液体[ ]活动物[ ]机器/汽车[ ] 危险品[ ]
GOODS BGA/JUMBO BULK REEFER IQUID LIVE ANIMAL MACHINE/AUTO DANGEROUS CLASS
2. 集装箱种类 普通[ ]开顶[ ]框架[ ]平板[ ]冷藏[ ]
CONTAINER ORDIDARY OPEN FRAME FLAY RAFRIGERATOR
3. 转运工具　海轮[ ]　飞机[ ]　驳船[ ]　火车[ ]　汽车[ ]
BY TRANSIT SHIP　PLANE　BARGE　TRAIN　TRUCK
4. 船舶资料　船籍　船龄
PARTICULAR OF SHIP　RIGISTRY　AGE
备注:被保险人确认本保险合同条款和内容已经完全了解。投保人(签名盖章)
APPLOCANT'S SIGNATURE

无锡蓝天进出口公司
WUXI BLUE SKY IMP&EXP. Co., LTD.
郭晓芳

THE ASSURED CONFIRMS HEREWITH THE TERMS AND CONGITIONS THESE INSURANCE CONTRACT FULLY UNDERSTOOD。

投保日期:(DATE)MAY20,2015 电话(TEL)0510－82398888 地址:(ADD)无锡市中山路53号

本公司自用(FOR OFFICE USE ONLY)

费率　　　　　　　　　　保费

RATE　　　　　　　　　　PREMIUM

经办人　　　核保人　　　负责人　　　联系电话:　　　承保公司盖章

INSURANCE COMPANY'S SIGNATURE

第二步:用填制好的投保单,随附商业发票,向中保财产保险有限公司提出投保申请。保险公司核保、承保后,出具保单

PICC 中国人民保险公司

THE PEOPLE'S INSURANCE COMPANY OF CHINA

总公司设于北京　　　　一九四九年创立

HEAD OFFICE:BEIJING　　ESTABLISHED IN 1949

货物运输保险单

CARGO TRANSPOTATIONINSURANCE POLICY

保险单号次

Policy No: 14087639

发票号(Invoice No.): ZYIE1502

合同号(CONTRACT NO.): K123

信用证号(L/C NO.): 123456

被保险人:

Insured: WUXI BLUE SKY IMP&EXP. Co., LTD

中国人民保险公司(以下简称本公司)根据被保险人的要求,由被保险人向本公司缴付约定的保险费,按照本保险单承保险别和背面所载条款与下列特款承保下述货物运输保险,特立本保险单。

This policy of Insurance witnesses that The People's Insurance company of China (hereinafter called "The Company") At the request of the insured and in consideration of the agreed premium paying to the company by the insured, undertakes to insure the under mentioned goods in transportation subject to the conditions of the policy as per the Clauses printed overleaf and other special clauses attached hereon.

标记 Marks & nos.	包装及数量 Quantity	保险货物项目 Description of goods	保险金额 Amount insured
AS PER INVOICE NO: ZYIE1502	235CARTONS	GIRL DRESS	USD71830.00

总保险金额

(Total Amount Insured) U. S. DOLLARS SEVENTY-ONE THOUSAND AND EIGHT HUNDRD THIRTY ONLY

保费 费率 装载运输工具

Premium AS ARRANGED Rate AS ARRANGED Per conveyance S. S DONG FANG V. 25

开航日期 从 至

Sig. On or abt AS PER B/L From SHANGHAI, CHINA to MONTREAL, CANADA

承保险别

conditions.

COVERING ALL RISKS AND WAR RISK SUBJECT TO THE RELEVANT OCEAN MARINE CLAUSE OF THE PEOPLE'S INSURANCE COMPANY OF CHINA, DATED 1/1/1981.

所保货物,如遇出险,本公司凭本保险单及其他有关证件给付赔款。所保货物,如发生本保险单项下负责赔偿的损失或事故,应立即通知本公司下述代理人查勘。

Claims, if any, payable on surrender of this Policy together with other relevant documents. In the event of accident whereby loss or damage may result in a claim under this Policy immediate notice applying for Survey must be given to the company's agent as mentioned hereunder.

AIG Europe, S. A., Canada Branch

Via della Chiusa 2

20123 Canada

Tel: 48 369010

中国人民保险公司

THE PEOPLE'S INSURANCE COMPANY OF CHINA

×××

赔款偿付地点 日期

Claim payable at MONTREAL, IN USD DATE MAY 28, 2015

第三步:审查保险单据内容是否正确

外贸单证员郭晓芳依据买卖合同、L/C(信用证)条款对保险单据的具体要求,并对照提单、发票等单据,对中国人民保险公司出具的保险单进行审核。郭晓芳审核的重点是保险单据的种类、被保险人、唛头、包装及数量、货物名称、保险金额、运输工具名称、开航日期、运输起讫地、承保险别、保险单份数、赔付地点、保险单据签发日期、保险公司签章等是否符合合同及信用证的要求,是否与提单、发票等同类项目相一致,以及保险单据是否满足信用证上的其他附加条件。

8.4　知识链接

1. 办理国际货运保险的程序

在国际货物买卖过程中，由哪一方负责办理投保国际贸易运输保险，应根据买、卖双方商定的价格条件来确定。例如，按 FOB 条件和 CFR 条件成交，保险应由买方办理；按 CIF 条件成交，保险就应由卖方办理。

投保程序有逐笔投保和预约投保等方式。

(1) 逐笔投保程序

1) 确定投保金额

投保金额既是确定保险费的依据，又是货物发生损失后计算赔偿的依据。按照国际惯例，投保金额应按发票上的 CIF 的预期利润计算。但是，各国市场情况不尽相同，对进出口贸易的管理办法也各有不同。

2) 填写国际运输保险投保单

投保单是投保人向保险人提出投保的书面申请，其主要内容包括被保险人的姓名、被保险货物的品名、标记、数量及包装、保险金额、运输工具名称、开航日期及起讫地点、投保险别、投保日期及签章等。

3) 支付保险费，取得保险单

保险费按投保险别的保险费率计算。保险费率是根据不同的险别、不同的商品、不同的运输方式、不同的目的地，并参照国际上的费率水平而制定的。它分为"一般货物费率"和"指明货物加费费率"两种。前者是一般商品的费率，后者系指特别列明的货物(如某些易碎、易损商品)在一般费率的基础上另行加收的费率。交付保险费后，投保人即可取得保险单据。除非信用证另有规定，每笔保费及费率可以不具体表示，保险公司会在保险单据上印就"AS ARRANGED"(如约定)字样。保险公司签发的保险单据有以下几种：

① 保险单(Insurance Policy)。它俗称大保单，是保险人与被保险人之间订立保险合同的一种正式证明，具有法律效力，对双方当事人均具有约束力。在发生保险范围内的损失或灭失时，投保人可凭保险单要求赔偿。实践中，当信用证没有特别说明保险单份数时，出口商一般提交一套完整的保险单(一份正本 ORIGINAL，一份复联本 DUPLICATE)。当来证要求提供的保险单"IN DUPLICATE/IN TWO FOLDS/IN 2 COPIES"时，出口商提交给议付行的是正本保险单(ORIGINAL)和复联保险单(DUPLICATE)构成全套保险单。其中的正本保险单可经背书转让。

② 保险凭证(Insurance Certificate)。它是一种简化的保险单，与保险单有同等的法律效力，故又称为小保单。现实中很少使用。它只有正面，其背面是空白的，没有载明保险条款。

③ 暂保单(Cover Note)。它又称为临时保险单，是保险人签发正式保单前所出立的临时证明。暂保单的有效期一般为 30 天，当正式保险单出立后，暂保单就自动失效。

④ 保险批单(Endorsement)。它是保险公司在保险单开立后，根据投保人的需求，对保险内容补充或变更而出具的一种凭证。

(2) 预约投保程序

① 签订预约保险单。预约保险单主要适用于大量进出口货物运输保险，是一种长期性

的货物保险合同，上面载明保险货物的范围、承保险别、保险费率、每批运输货物的最高保险金额以及保险费的结付、赔款处理等项目，凡属预约保单规定范围内的进出口货物，一经起运，保险合同即自动按预约保单上的承保条件生效。预约保险单如下：

中国人民财产保险股份有限公司
货物运输预约投保保险单

被保险人名称：

保险货物种类：

包装/运输方式：桶装　袋装　散装/裸装　集装箱　冷藏/干冰货

其他方式＿＿＿＿＿＿＿＿

保险期限：1年，自　　年　月　日零时起至　　年　月　日二十四时止。

在此期间出运的货物(以提单日期为准)属本保险范围。

运输方式：海运　　空运　　陆运　　其他方式。

运输区域：

运输工具：海上货物运输使用的船舶须为协会船级条款规定的资格船。若资格船船龄超过协会船级条款规定以上的，乙方将按所附船舶加费费率表规定另加收老船加费。对非资格船，1 000 吨以下的承运船舶、拆解船、25 年船龄以上的资格船，本保单不予承保，除非保险双方就保险条件核费率等另有书面约定。

预计年度运输货物价值(美元)：投保加成：%

预计年度总保险金额(美元)：统保费率：%

航次限额：USD10 000 000。超过此限额，投保人须提前两天通知保险人，如果投保人未予通知，则保险人对每艘船舶每一航次的最高赔付金额为 USD10 000 000。

计重标准：双方约定，对保险标的为袋装、散装货物的重量，计量标准为＿＿＿＿＿＿。

每次事故免赔率：

保险费的结算：

保险险别：海运一切险　空运一切险　陆运一切险　战争险(战区除外)

罢工险　其他险别：＿＿＿＿＿＿

保险条件：《中国人民保险公司国际保险条款海洋运输货物保险条款》(1/1/1981)一切险

《中国人民保险公司国际保险条款海洋运输货物战争险条款》(1/1/1981)

《中国人民保险公司国际保险条款航空运输货物保险条款》(1/1/1981)一切险

《中国人民保险公司国际保险条款航空运输货物战争险条款》(1/1/1981)

《中国人民保险公司国际保险条款陆上运输货物保险条款(火车、汽车)》(1/1/1981)一切险

《中国人民保险公司国际保险条款陆上运输货物战争险条款(火车)》(1/1/1981)《中国人民保险公司国际保险条款邮包险条款》(1/1/1981)一切险

《中国人民保险公司国际保险条款邮包战争险条款》(1/1/1981)

签发日期：

签发地点：　　　　　　　　　　中国人民财产保险股份有限公司

授权签字

② 通知保险公司运输情况。预约保险下，被保险人在获悉每批保险货物起运时，应立即将货物装船的详细情况，包括货物的名称、数量、保险金额、运输工具的种类和名称、航程起讫点、开航或起运日期等情况通知保险人。

通知保险公司运输情况可以采用下表所示的预约保险起运通知书的方式，也可以采用发出如下表所示的保险声明书(Insurance Declaration)的方式。

中国人民保险公司运输险预约保险起运通知书

承保公司编号　　　　字第　　　号

承保公司　　　　　　　　　　　　　　　　被保险人编号　　字第　　　号

被保险人　　　　　　　　　　　　　　　　预约保险单　　字第　　　号

<table>
<tr><td colspan="9">根据运输险预约保险合同规定所开立的货物运输险</td></tr>
<tr><td colspan="2">运输工具</td><td rowspan="2">提(通知)单　号次</td><td colspan="4">保险货物</td><td colspan="2">保险金额</td></tr>
<tr><td>名称</td><td>号次</td><td>标记</td><td>品名</td><td>数量</td><td>单价</td><td>货物成本金额</td><td>货物运输费、税款、保险费金额</td></tr>
<tr><td></td><td></td><td></td><td></td><td></td><td></td><td></td><td></td><td></td></tr>
<tr><td></td><td></td><td></td><td></td><td></td><td></td><td></td><td></td><td></td></tr>
<tr><td></td><td></td><td></td><td></td><td></td><td></td><td></td><td></td><td></td></tr>
<tr><td colspan="9">总保险金额:(大写)　　　　　　　　　　　　开航日期:　　年　月　日</td></tr>
<tr><td colspan="9">运输路线:自　　　　起　　　　至</td></tr>
<tr><td colspan="9">投保运输险加保　　　　险　　　　费率:　　　　保险费(大写)</td></tr>
<tr><td colspan="5">承保公司签章

年　月　日</td><td colspan="4">投保人签章

年　月　日</td></tr>
</table>

保险声明书

DATONG TRADING CO.

INSURANCE DECLARATION

(SHIPMENT ADVICE)

To:PICC,JIANGSU

Open Policy No.:CA118　　　　L/C NO.: SIN186　　　　Aug. 10th, 2014

Dear Sirs,

We declare that the shipment under the captioned open policy has been made, the details of shipment are stated below, please cover insurance and send your acknowledgement direct to the Insured Party.

Commodity:FAP INSTRUMENTS

Quantity:300SETS/300CARTONS

Invoice No./Value:FP12078/USD120000.00(FOB)

Carry Vessel's Name: VICTORY V.052

Shipment Date:on or about Aug.15th,2014

Port of Loading:Hong Kong

Port of Destination:Shanghai

Cover Risks: CIC All Risks and War Risk

Kindly forward directly to the insured your Insurance Acknowledge.

DATONG TRADING CO.

×××

③ 确认保险生效。被保险人在预约保险时,一般只要通知保险人运输情况,保险即生效,甚至在运输工具离境后,通知保险公司,保险也可生效,即使已经发生货损。

实际操作中,如果采用信用证付款方式等,银行在付款时要求卖方提供保险单,因而,在实际业务中,出口货物的投保大多是逐笔出单。如果时间仓促,也可采用口头或电话方式向保险人申请投保,如获允许,保险也可生效,但随后一定要补填投保单。

为了简化单证,在实际业务中,对于长期的客户,保险人也可以同意投保人不单独填写投保单,而利用出口企业现成的发票副本代替,但发票副本上必须将投保单上所规定的内容补填齐全。

2. 投保单的填制要点

(1) 被保险人(INSURED)

此项填写被保险人全称。

在CIF或CIP价格条件下,被保险人的几种规定方法如下:

① 信用证方式下指的是受益人,托收方式下为委托人。但是实际发生货损时,索赔的权益是进口商,所以保险单以出口商为被保险人时,出口商要在保险单的背面进行背书,以示索赔权益转让给保险单的持有人,同时受让人则负担被保险人的义务。

② 买方有时要求以其为被保险人,如被保险货物出险,其可直接向保险公司索赔。这种做法对出口商来说有一定风险,应谨慎采用。

③ 信用证规定保险单为TO THE ORDER OF ××× BANK或IN THE FAVOUR OF ××× BANK,即应在被保险人处填写"××× IMPORT & EXPORT CO.LTD.,+HELD TO THE ORDER OF ××× BANK(或IN THE FAVOUR OF ××× BANK)"。

④《信用证》规定,保单抬头为第三者名称,即中性名义,应填写"被保险利益人"即填写"TO WHOM IT MAY CONCERN"。实务中,中性保单很少见。

⑤《信用证》规定,保单为空白抬头(TO ORDER),被保险人名称应填写"××× IMPORT & EXPORT CO.LTD.,FOR THE ACCOUNT OF WHOM IT MAY CONCERN"。

⑥ 如信用证有特殊要求,所有单据以×××为抬头人,那么应在被保险人栏以×××为被保险人,这种保险单就不要背书了。

如果以FOB和CFR价格条件成交,则由买方投保,被保险人应该填写买方名称。

(2) 唛头(MARKS AND NOS)

投保单唛头应与发票、提单上的同项内容等一致,如唛头比较复杂,也可只填"AS PER

INVOICE NO。×××”。因为无论是办理货款结算还是保险索赔时，发票也是必须提交的单据之一。如无唛头，可填 N/M。

(3) 包装及数量(PACKAGE AND QUANTITY)

如以包装件数计价者，则将最大包装的总件数填入；如以毛重或净重计价，可填件数及毛重或净重；如果是裸装货物，则表示其件数即可；如为散装货物则表示其重量，并在其后注明“IN BULK”字样。

(4) 保险货物项目(DESCRIPTION OF GOODS)

此项填写货物名称，此栏允许填写货物总称，但必须与发票、提单等一致。

(5) 保险货物金额(AMOUNT INSURED)

即投保金额，如信用证未具体规定，一般按照发票总金额的110%投保，此处填写保险金额的小写(投保单上保险金额的填法应该是“进一取整”，例如，经计算，保险金额为USD12 345.23，则在投保单上应填“USD12 346”)。此栏保险金额使用的货币应与信用证使用的货币相一致。如果从信用证或单据中可以得知最后的发票金额仅仅是货物总价值的一部分，如由于折扣、预付等，则必须以货物总价值为基础来计算保险金额。

(6) 总保险金额(TOTAL AMOUNT INSURED)

即保险金额的大写数字，以英文表示，末尾应加“ONLY”，以防涂改，注意大写、小写金额必须保持一致。

开动脑筋

保险金额的确定

一份发票上的货物总值为10万美金，其中电汇预付款为2万美金，则信用证方式下：

若付的金额为8万美金，则保险金额是多少？

若信用证金额为20万美元，货值为18万美元，广告材料费和成本为2万美元，则保险金额是多少？

若5万美元的货价包含1%的佣金和1%的折扣，则保险金额是多少？

若发票上CIF金额为USD9 999.80，未规定投保加成率，则保险金额是多少？

(7) 启运日期(DATE OF COMMENCEMENT)

一般填写提单的签发日期，也可填写提单签发日前后各五天之内任何一天的日期，或填“AS PER B/L(或 AIRWAY BILL等)”。

(8) 装载运输工具(PER CONVEYANCE)

此处填写装载船的船名及航次。当运输由两程运输完成时，应分别填写一程船名和二程船名。如再转运到内陆加 OTHER CONVEYANCE。如空运，则填“BY AIR”或“BY AIRPLANE”；如陆运，则填“BY TRAIN”或“BY RAILWAY”，最好再加上车号，如“BY TRAIN WAGON NO.××”；如以邮包寄送，则写“BY PARCEL POST”。

(9) 自经至(FROM ... VIA ... TO ...)

此处填写 FROM 装运港 VIA 转运港 TO 目的港。

(10) 赔款偿付地点(CLAIM PAYABLE AT)

此处按合同或信用证要求填制,如果信用证中并未列明确,一般将目的港作为赔付地点。如买方指定理赔代理人,理赔代理人必须在货物到达目的港的所在国内,便于到货后检验,赔款货币一般为投保额相同的货币。

(11) 投保险别(CONDITIONS)

本栏系投保单的核心内容,填写时应注意保险险别及文句与信用证严格一致,即使信用证中有重复语句,为了避免混乱和误解,最好按信用证规定的顺序填写。如信用证没有规定具体险别,或只规定"MARINE RISK""USUAL RISK"或"TRANSPORT RISK"等,则可投保一切险(ALL RISKS)、水渍险(WA 或 WPA)、平安险(FPA)三种基本险中的任何一种。如信用证中规定使用伦敦协会条款,包括修订前后或修订后的,可以按信用证规定投保,投保单应按要求填制。投保的险别除注明险别名称外,还应注明险别适用的文本及日期。

(12) 日期(DATE)

日期指投保日期。由于保险公司提供仓至仓(WAREHOUSE TO WAREHOUSE)服务,所以要求投保手续在货物离开出口方仓库前办理。投保日期也应是货物离开出口方仓库前的日期。

3. 审查保险单据应注意的事项

实务中,买卖合同、L/C(信用证)条款对保险单据的要求各式各样。由于保险单据是被保险人进行索赔的主要依据,且又属于有价证券范畴,故审查保险单据不可不慎,具体应注意以下几个问题:

① 保险单据的种类、内容要与合同、信用证条款要求严格相符,且保险单据必须在表面上看来是由保险公司或其代理人签发的,银行不接受由保险经纪人签发的暂保单。

如合同和信用证中比较常见的保险条款如下:

INSURANCE POLICY OR CERTIFICATE IN TWO FOLD PAYABLE TO THE ORDER OF COMMERCIAL BANK OF LONDON LT. COVERING MARINE INSTITUTE CARGO CLAUSES A (1. 1. 1982), INSTITUTE STRIKE CLAUSES CARGO (1. 1. 1982), INSTITUTE WAR CLAUSES CARGO(1. 1. 1982) FOR INVOICE VALUE PLUS 10% INCLUDING WAREHOUSE TO WAREHOUSE UP TO THE FINAL DESTINATION AT SWISSLAND, MARKED PREMIUM PAID, SHOWING CLAIM IF ANY, PAYABLE IN GERMANY, NAMING SETTLING AGENT IN GERMANY.

此保险单据要求做到以下几点:一是被保险人填写受益人,但向银行交单前做记名背书给"COMMERCIAL BANK OF LONDON LT.";二是投保险别应严格按证要求,包括伦敦保险协会货物保险的 A 险、伦敦保险协会货物保险的罢工险、伦敦保险协会货物保险的战争险;三是保险金额应该是发票金额加成 10%;四是保险的责任起讫为仓至仓并到最终目的地 SWISSLAND;五是注明保险费已付;六是注明如果有索赔应该在德国赔偿,注明德国的赔付代理人。

又如:

MARINE INSURANCE POLICY OR CERTIFICATE IN DUPLICATE AND ENDORSED IN BLANK FOR 110 PCT OF THE INVOICE VALUE STATING CLAIM

PAYABLE IN THAILAND COVERING FPA AS PER OCEAN MARINE CARGO CLAUSE OF THE PEOPLE'S INSURANCE COMPANY OF CHINA DATED 1/1 1981, INCLUDING T. P. N. D. LOSS AND/OR DAMADGE CAUSED BY HEAT, SHIP'SWEAT AND ODOR, HOOPRUST, NREAKAGE OF PACKING.

这张保险单据内容需要注意以下两点：一是保险金额应该是发票金额加成 10%；二是保险险别除了投保中国人民保险集团股份有限公司的平安险外还要投偷窃、提货不着险，受热船舱发汗，串味，铁箍锈损，包装破裂等附加险。

再如：

INSURANCE COVERED BY THE APPLICANT ALL SHIPMENT UNDER THIS CREDIT MUST BE ADVI SED BY THE BENEFICIARY AFTER SHIPMENT DIRECTLY TO THE PRAGATI INSURANCE LTD. JUBILEE ROAD BRANCH, CHITTAGONG, BANGLADESH AND APPLICANT ALSO TO US QUOTING OUR CREDIT NO. AND MARINE COVER NOTE NO. PIL/JBL/0102014 DATED AUG 01 2014 GIVING FULL DETAILS OF SHIPMENT AND COPY OF SUCH ADVICE MUST ACCOMPANY SHIPPING DOCUMENTS.

这是一个由买方负责投保的条款，其对保险的要求有三：一是保险由申请人负责；二是货装船后，受益人应发装船通知给 PRAGATI 保险公司、申请人和开证行。通知上标明信用证号码，2014 年 8 月 1 日签发的暂保单的号码（PIL/JBL/0102014）和详细的装船信息；三是装船通知副本要随整套单据一并交银行。

② 保险单上的运输标志、包装及数量、货名、船名、开航日期、装运港和目的港等项内容应与提单一致。不能把保险单上船名写错，或把运输路线等填错，必须将提单所示的运输工具（如船名、车号）、运输路线（包括全程运输）在保单上清楚、准确地表示出来。

③ 可以按照 CIC 条款签发保险单，也可以按照 ICC 条款签发保险单，但不允许在一份保单内部分险别是 CIC 条款，而部分险别又是 ICC 条款，二者不能混用。

④ 信用证规定"claims payable at destination in currency of the draft/credit"，保险单上要照抄，尽管保单的币别是信用证的币别或已经注明赔付代理在进口国。

⑤ 保险单据的出单日期不得晚于货物在信用证规定的地点装船、发运或接管（如适用的话）的日期，除非保险单据表明保险责任最晚于货物在信用证规定的地点装船、发运或接管（如适用的话）之日起生效。通常情况下，保险单的签发日期就是保险责任的生效日期。如果这一日期晚于运输单据上货物装船、发运或监管的日期，即货物已装船、发运或接受监管，保险还未生效，那么在此期间发生的货物的损害或灭失将不在保险时段内，被保险人将无法获得赔偿。

⑥ 若信用证对保单有特殊要求，应在单据的适当位置（空白处）加注。比如，信用证要求所有单据要加注信用证号、开证行名称、开证日期。

⑦ 保险单上擦拭和更动的地方不能过多。

⑧ 保险单有没有正确的背书。

⑨ 保险公司签章：保险单只有经保险公司或其代理签章后才生效。

10. 保单背书方法

8.5 能力实训

实训 1 翻译保险条款

Insurance policy or certificate in two fold covering marine institute cargo clauses A, institute war clauses cargo for invoice value plus 10%, marked premium paid, showing claims if any, payable in Germany.

Insurance effected by seller for account of buyer. We understand that the cost of insurance premium will be settled directly between buyer and seller outside the letter of credit.

Except in cases where the insurance is covered by the Buyers as arranged, insurance is to be covered by the Sellers with a Chinese insurance company. If insurance for additional amount and/or for other insurance terms is required by the Buyers, prior notice to this effect must reach the Sellers before shipment and is subject to the Sellers' agreement, and the extra insurance premium shall be for the Buyers' account.

Negotiable insurance policy/certificate in duplicate by People's Insurance Co. of China incorporating their ocean marine cargo clauses (all risks) and war risks from China to Waterloo Ontario for 110% of invoice value, plus 23% for duty, additional cost of insurance is for buyer's account and to be drawn under this credit.

实训 2 根据所给的制单资料制作投保单

1. 有关合同条款

这是上海市进出口公司与美国 COMETALS 公司签订的出售 200 吨金属铬的一笔业务。以 USD35 550.00/MT CIF BALTIMORE 价格成交，90%以即期不可撤销信用证结算，另外 10%以 D/P 即期结算。

货物由上海检验检疫局 2004 年 11 月 21 日检验合格出证，运往上海港出口。

货物的基本情况如下：

合同号：JZIE041101

发票日期：2004 年 11 月 22 日

净重：40 吨

每钢桶重：3 公斤

装运期：2004 年 11 月 28 日

船名/航次：BLUE SKY V.312E

提单号：BS04112823

体积：30 立方米

集装箱号/封号：20′ CBHU0611758/25783 CY/CY

20′ CBHU2765381/25784 CY/CY

保险索赔代理：ABCD THE UNITED STATES

议付行：CHINA CONSTRUCTION BANK, SHANGHAI BRANCH

H.S. CODE: 81122100

2. 信用证

APPLICANT HEADER: CHASUS33DXXXN 1555 192579 030328 0458 N

*JPMORCAN CHASE BANK NEW YORK, NY

SEQUENCE TOTAL *27: 1/2

FORM OF DOCUMENTARY CREDIT *40A IRREVOCABLE

LETTER OF CREDIT NUMBER *20 C-788520

DATE OF ISSUE 31C 040112

DATE AND PLACE OF EXPIRY *31D DATE 041210 PLACE IN CHINA

APPLICANT *50 COMETALS

222 BRIDGE PLAZA SOUTH FORT LEE, NJ 07024

BENEFICIARY *59 SHANGHAI IMPORT AND EXPORT CORPORATION

NO.29, ECTION 3, DONGFANG ROAD, SHANGHAI CHINA

CURRENCY CODE, AMOUNT *32B CURRENCY USD AMOUNT 7110.000,00

AVAILABLE WITH ... BY ... *41D AVAILABLE WITH ANY BANK BY NEGOTIATION

DRAFTS AT 42C SIGHT FOR 90 PCT OF INVOICE VALUE

DRAWEE 42D JPMORCAN CHASE BANK, NY

PARTIAL SHIPMENTS 43P PERMITTED

TRANSHIPMENT 43T PERMITTED

SHIPPING ON BOARD/DISPATCH/LOADING IN CHARGE AT/FROM 44A

CHINESE MAIN PORT

TRANSPORTATION TO 44B BALTIMORE, MD

LATEST DATE OF SHIPMENT 44C 041130

PERIOD FOR PRESENTATION 48

DOCUMENTS MUST BE PRESENTED WITHIN 15 DAYS AFTER SHIPPMENT BUT WITHIN THE VALIDITY OF THE LETTER OF CREDIT.

CONFIMATION INSTRUCTIONS *49 WITHOUT

INSTRUCTIONS TO THE PAYING/ACCEPTING/NEGOTIATING BANK: 78

1. ALL DOCUMENTS MUST BE FORWARDED TO US IN ONE AIRMAIL TO THE JPMORCAN CHASE BANK.

2. A DISCREPANT DOCUMENT FEE OF USD 75.00 BE DEDUCTED FROM PROCEEDS IF DOCUMENTS WITH DISCREPANCIES ARE ACCEPTED.

3. UPON RECEIPT OF ALL DOCUMENTS AND DRAFT IN CONFORMITY WITH THE TERMS AND CONDITIONS OF THIS CREDIT, WE SHALL REMIT THE PROCEEDS TO THE BANK DESIGNATED BY YOU.

"ADVISING THROUGH" BANK 57 D: BANK OF CHINA, SHANGHAI BR. NO 25 SEC 5 JIEFANG RD SHANGHAI CHINA

MSG TYPE: 700(ISSUE OF A DOCUMENTARY CREDIT)

APPLICANT HEADER: CHASUS33DXXXN 1555 192579 030328 0458 N

＊JPMORCAN CHASE BANK

＊NEW YORK, NY

SEQUENCE TOTAL ＊27: 2/2

LETTER OF CREDIT NUMBER ＊20 C-788520

DESCRIPTION OF GOODS OR SERVICES: 45A

200 METRIC TONS CHROMIUM METAL FROM MAIN CHINESE PORT TO BALTIMORE, MD AT USD35,550.00 PER METRIC TON

GOODS ARE SUPPLIED IN STEEL DRUMS OF 250KGS NET EACH ON FUMIGATED WOODEN PALLETS, IN SEAWORTHY OCEAN CONTAINERS

SHIPPING TERMS: CIF BALTIMORE

DOCUMENTS REQUIRED: 46A

+ORIGINAL SIGNED COMMERCIAL INVOICE IN 3 COPIES

+ORIGINAL PACKING LIST IN 3 COPIES.

+CERTIFICATE OF ORIGIN IN 2 COPIES

+CERTIFICATE OF WEIGHT IN DUPLICATE ISSUED BY CIQ.

+CERTIFICATE OF QUALITY IN 3 COPIES ISSUED BY CIQ.

+FUMIGATION(熏蒸) CERTIFICATE ISSUED BY CIQ

+INSURANCE POLICY IN TRIPLICATE FOR 110 PERCENT OF THE INVOICE VALUE SHOWING CLAIMS SETTING AGENT AT DESTINATION PORT AND THAT CLAMIS ARE PAYABLE IN THE CURRENCR OF THE DRAFT, COVERING ALL RISKS, WAR RISKS AND S.R.C.C.

++3/3 OF SIGNED CLEAN ON BOARD OCEAN BILLS OF LADING MADE OUT TO ORDER OF COMETALS, NOTIFYING JOHN S. CONNOR, INC. INDICATIING OUR LETTER OF CREDIT NUMBER AND MARKED "FREIGHT PREPAID"

ADDITIONAL INSTRUCTIONS: 47A

1. THIS L/C IS NON TRANSFERABLE

2. BOTH QUANTITY AND AMOUNT 10 PERCENT MORE OR LESS ARE ALLOWED.

3. ALL DOCUMENT MUST INDICATE THIS CREDIT NUMBER

4. SHIPPING MARKS ON EACH DRUM:

CHROMIUM METAL/PC-14228/COMETALS/MADE IN CHINA

5. BENEFICIARY'S STATEMENT INDICATES THAT A COPY OF SHIPPING ADVICE

DESPATCHED TO THE ACCOUNTEE IMMEDIATELY AFTER SHIPMENT.

CHARGES 71B

ALL BANKING CHARGES OUTSIDE THE OPENNING BANK ARE FOR BENEFICIARY'S ACCOUNT.

REIMBURSING BANK 53A

PNBPUS3NNYC

CORESTATES BANK INTERNATIONAL

NEW YORK, NY

180 MAIDEN LANE

SENDER TO RECEIVER INFORMATION 72

THIS CREDIT IS ISSUED SUBJECT TO UNIFORM CUSTOMS AND PRACTICE FOR DOCUMENTARY CREDITS (1993 REVISION) ICC PUBLICATION NO. 600.

实训 3　根据资料 1 和资料 2 审核资料 3 并提出修改建议

资料 1. 商业发票

杭州中丽化纤有限公司

HANGZHOU ZHONGLI CHEMICAL FIBER CO., LTD
YONGLIAN VILLAGE GUALI TOWN XIAOSHAN DISTRICT HANGZHOU, ZHEJIANG, CHINA FAX: +86-571-82571633

COMMERCIAL INVOICE

Invoice No: HH201507-1

Date: JULY. 01, 2015

TO:BIG IDEA CORPORATE (THAILAND) CO.,LTD.
5/70 Mooban Nantatawee 4 Resort, Moo 2, Mit Maitri 18/1,
Khu Fang Nuea, Nong Chok District, Bangkok, 10530, Thailand.

PORT OF LOADING:
From: NINGBO, CHINA

PORT OF DISCHARGE:
To: BANGKOK, THAILAND

PAYMENT:BY L/C AT SIGHT

Marks & Nos	Description & Quantities	Unit Price	Amount
BIC INV. NO.: HH201507-1 NOS.: 1-5 BKK	PIGMENT VIOLET 19 5 BARRELS	CIF BANGKOK USD473.00/BARREL	 USD2 365.00

资料 2. 出口销售合同和信用证中的相关条款

Time of Shipment: no later than July. 20. 2015

Shipping Mark: BIC/INV. NO.: HH201507－1/NOS: 1－5/BKK

Terms of Payment: By 100% confirmed, Irrevocable, Transferable and Divisible Letter of Credit to be available by sight draft and to remain valid for negotiation in China until the 15th day after the aforesaid Time of Shipment.

Insurance: marine insurance policies or certificates in negotiable form, for 110% full CIF invoice covering the risks of War & W. A. as per the People's Insurance Co. of China dated 1/1/1981, with extended cover up to Bangkok with claims payable in (at) Bangkok in the currency of draft (irrespective of percentage)

资料 3: 货物运输保险单

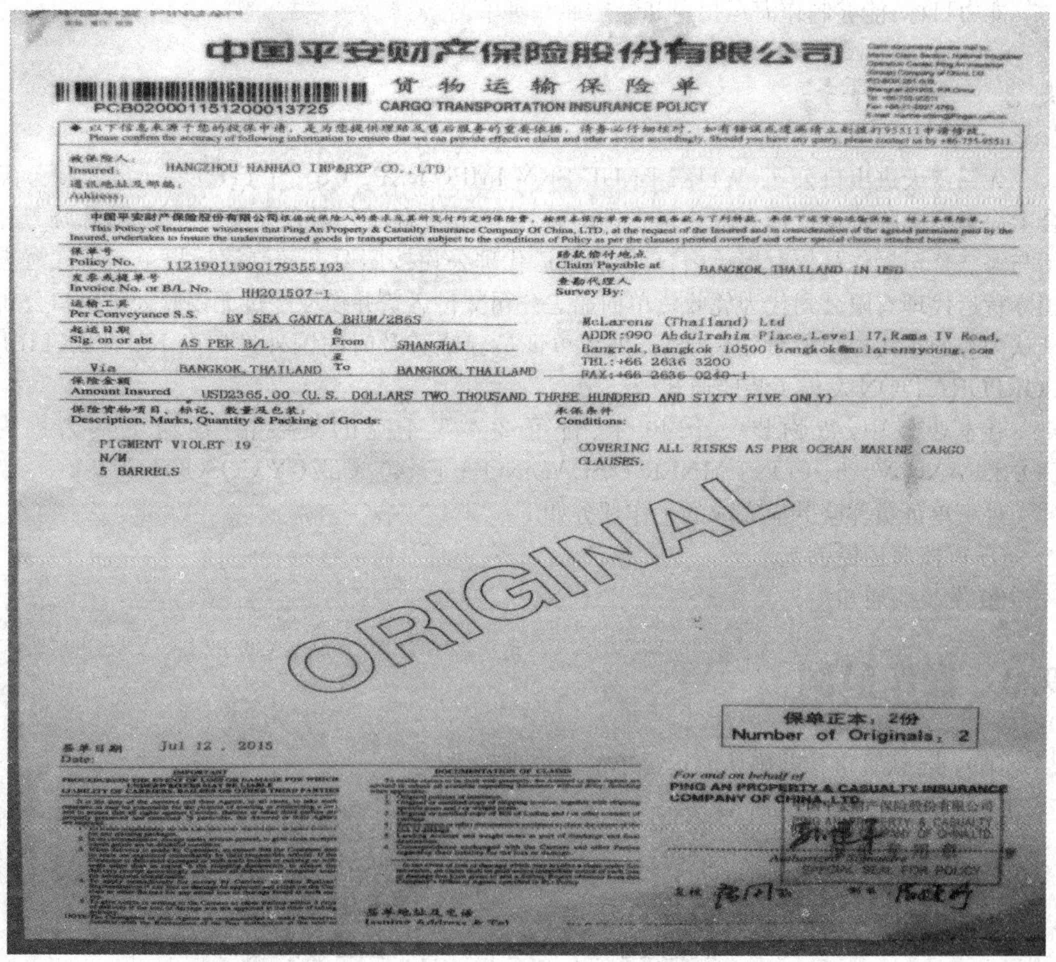

中国平安财产保险股份有限公司

货物运输保险单

CARGO TRANSPORTATION INSURANCE POLICY

PCB020001151200013725

被保险人: Insured: HANGZHOU HANHAO IMP&EXP CO., LTD

通讯地址及邮编: Address:

保单号 Policy No.: 11219011900179355193

赔款偿付地点 Claim Payable at: BANGKOK, THAILAND IN USD

发票或提单号 Invoice No. or B/L No.: HH201507-1

查勘代理人 Survey By:

运输工具 Per Conveyance S.S.: BY SEA GANTA BHUM/286S

McLarens (Thailand) Ltd
ADDR: 990 Abdulrahim Place, Level 17, Rama IV Road, Bangrak, Bangkok 10500
TEL: +66 2636 3200
FAX: +66 2636 0240-1

起运日期 Slg. on or abt: AS PER B/L　自 From: SHANGHAI

Via: BANGKOK, THAILAND　至 To: BANGKOK, THAILAND

保险金额 Amount Insured: USD2365.00 (U.S. DOLLARS TWO THOUSAND THREE HUNDRED AND SIXTY FIVE ONLY)

保险货物项目、标记、数量及包装: Description, Marks, Quantity & Packing of Goods:

PIGMENT VIOLET 19
N/M
5 BARRELS

承保条件 Conditions:

COVERING ALL RISKS AS PER OCEAN MARINE CARGO CLAUSES.

ORIGINAL

保单正本: 2份
Number of Originals: 2

签单日期 Date: Jul 12, 2015

For and on behalf of
PING AN PROPERTY & CASUALTY INSURANCE COMPANY OF CHINA, LTD.

SPECIAL SEAL FOR POLICY

项目9　制作运输单据

9.1　学习目标

知识目标：熟悉提单的种类和其他各种出口运输单据；掌握海运提单的内容和制作方法。

能力目标：能够制作海运提单和装船通知等单据。

9.2　工作任务

无锡蓝天进出口公司(WUXI BLUE SKY IMP&EXP. Co., LTD.)单证员郭晓芳配合上海运达国际货运代理有限公司安排调运、装船等事宜。公司有一票货装船后，郭晓芳开始与海杰公司操作员核对提单内容，协助货运代理公司按照要求缮制海运提单。浙江海杰国际货运代理有限公司代为凭收货单向船运公司交付运费并换取经过无锡蓝天进出口公司确认内容的正式提单。货物装船后，外贸单证员郭晓芳及时向国外进口商 KU TEXTILE CORPORATION 发出了装船通知。

在本业务中，货物装一个 40 米、自重 2 275 千克的集装箱；运输工具名称为 DONDFANG V.25; CONTAINER &SEAL NO.: 1×40′ CY/CY COSOOTEC192。

外贸单证员郭晓芳应完成的工作任务如下：

① 审核海运提单。

② 发装船通知。

9.3　操作范例

第一步：认真审核并确认海运提单的内容准确无误

11. 提单确认的项目

12. 海运提单的案例

<table>
<tr><td colspan="2">Shipper
B/L No. COSOOTEC192
WUXIBLUE SKY IMP&EXP. Co., LTD.
NO. 53 ZHONGSHAN ROAD, WUXI,
CHINA TEL: 0510 - 82398888</td><td colspan="3" rowspan="6">B/L No. COSOOTEC192

中国外运上海公司
SINOTRANS SHANGHAI COMPANY
OCEAN BILL OF LADING
SHIPPED on board in apparent good order and condition (unless otherwise indicated) the goods or packages specified herein and to be discharged at the mentioned port of discharge or as near thereto as the vessel may safely get and be always afloat.
The weight, measure, marks and numbers, quality, contents and value, being particulars furnished by the Shipper, are not checked by the Carrier on loading.
The Shipper, Consignee and the Holder of this Bill of Lading hereby expressly accept and agree to all printed, written or stamped provisions, exceptions and conditions of this Bill of Lading, including those on the back hereof.
IN WITNESS whereof the number of original Bills of Lading stated below have been signed, one of which being accomplished the other(s) to be void.</td></tr>
<tr><td colspan="2">Consignee or order
TO ORDER</td></tr>
<tr><td colspan="2">Notify address
KU TEXTILE CORPORATION
430 VTRA MONTREAL CANADA
+48 789065</td></tr>
<tr><td>Pre-carriage by</td><td>Port of loading
SHANGHAI</td></tr>
<tr><td>Vessel
DONDFANG V. 25</td><td>Port
of transshipment</td></tr>
<tr><td>Port of discharge
MONTREAL</td><td>Final destination</td></tr>
<tr><td>Container. seal No. or marks and Nos.</td><td>Number and kind of package</td><td>Description of goods</td><td>Gross weight (kgs.)</td><td>Measurement (m^3)</td></tr>
<tr><td>KU
K123
MONTREAL
C/No. 1 - 235
COSU 1007778
SEAL No. 5087802</td><td>235CTNS
ONE CONTAINER
1×40'Fcl</td><td>GIRL DRESS 100% COTTON
L/C NO. 123456
DATE: May 20, 2015
ISSINUG BANK: HSBC BANK PLC, MONTREAL, CANADA
ON BOARD</td><td>2 285 KGS</td><td>45.385 M^3</td></tr>
<tr><td colspan="3">Freight and charges
FREIGHT PREPAID</td><td colspan="2">REGARDING TRANSHIPMENT INFORMATION PLEASE CONTACT</td></tr>
<tr><td rowspan="2">Ex. rate</td><td>Prepaid at</td><td>Freight payable at</td><td colspan="2">Place and date of issue
SHANGHAI JULY 15, 2015</td></tr>
<tr><td>Total prepaid</td><td>Number of original Bs/L
THREE(3)</td><td colspan="2">Signed for or on behalf of the Master
SINOTRANS SHANGHAI COMPANY
As Agent</td></tr>
</table>

第二步:发装船通知

根据信用证的要求"SHIPPING ADVICE SHOWING B/L NO., GOODS NAME, QUANTITY AND AMOUNT OF GOODS NUMBER OF PACKAGES, NAME OF VESSEL AND VOYAGE NO., AND DATE OF SHIPMENT TO APPLICANT WITHIN 3 DAYS AFTER THE DATE OF BILL OF LADING",小郭在确认了提单内容后需要立即向进口商发出装船通知。不同公司装船通知的格式可能有所差异,但基本内容一致。无锡蓝天进出口公司的装船通知格式如下。

WUXIBLUE SKY IMP&EXP. Co., LTD.
NO.53 ZHONGSHAN ROAD, WUXI, CHINA
TEL: 86-510-82398888
SHIPPING ADVICE

TO:	KU TEXTILE CORPORATION 430 VTRA MONTREAL CANADA	ISSUE DATE:	JULY 15, 2015
		S/C NO.:	K123
		L/C NO.:	123456
		L/C DATE:	MAY20, 2015
		ISSUE BANK:	HSBC BANK PLC, MONTREAL, CANADA

Dear Sir or Madam,

We are pleased to advise you that the following mentioned goods have been shipped. Full details are shown as follows:

Invoice No.:	ZYIE1502
Bill of Lading no.:	COSOOTEC192
OceanVessel:	DONGFANG, V25
Port of Loading:	SHANGHAI, CHINA
On Board Date:	JULY 15, 2015
Port of Discharge:	MONTREAL
Estimated Date of Arrival:	AUGUST8, 2015
Containers/Seals No.:	COSU100778/5087002
Description of Goods:	GIRL DRESS 100% COTTON
Number of Packages:	235 CARTONS
Shipping Marks:	KU K123 MONTREAL C/N: 1-235
Quantity:	9 400PCS

（续表）

Total Value:	USD65 300.00
Thank you for your patronage. We look forward to the pleasure of receiving your valuable repeat orders. Sincerely yours.	
We hereby certify that the content of the shipping advice is true. WUXIBLUE SKY IMP&EXP. Co., LTD. 郭晓芳	

9.4 知识链接

1. 提单概述

《中华人民共和国海商法》第 71 条规定："提单，是指用以证明海上货物运输合同和货物已经由承运人接收或者装船，以及承运人保证据以交付货物的单证。提单中载明的向记名人交付货物，或者按照指示人的指示交付货物，或者向提单持有人交付货物的条款，构成承运人据以交付货物的保证。"

货物由承运人接收或者装船后，承运人应当签发提单。不同的承运人签发的提单格式有所不同，但都包含货物的品名、标志、包装数或者件数、重量或者体积，以及运输危险货物时对危险性质的说明；承运人的名称和主营业所；船舶名称；托运人的名称；收货人的名称；装货港和在装货港接收货物的日期；卸货港；多式联运提单增列接收货物地点和交付货物地点；提单的签发日期、地点和份数；运费的支付；承运人或者其代表的签字。即使提单缺少一项或者几项，但只要符合《中华人民共和国海商法》第 71 条的规定就不影响提单的性质。

外贸实践中，提单虽然由承运人或其代理人缮制，但货主必须审核提单原件。提单一经审核签章后，若货主发现提单内容有误，则须向承运人提出更改申请，并交纳相应的费用。

为适应贸易新环境，运用电子商务、近洋贸易和跨国公司开展公司内贸易的需要，方便及时提货，国际上许多船公司都印有海运单供货主选用。海运单(Sea Waybill)与海运提单有许多共同点，如都是货物收据、运输合同证明，都是处理买卖、保险、索赔、海事等问题或纠纷的证明，单据要式项目相同。不同之处在于，海运单不是物权凭证，收货人一栏采用记名式，不能为指示式；海运单下提货时无须出示海运单，只要证明是单据上指明的收货人即可。若收货人一面提货，一面挑剔单据拒付，出口人则会"钱货两空"。

2. 提单的种类(见表 9-1)

表 9-1　提单的种类

区别点	种　类	中文名	适用情况或特点
是否有背面条款	Long Form B/L	全式提单	有背面条款，银行可接受
	Blank Back B/L	简式提单	无背面条款，常用于租船提单，须附租船合同，否则银行不接受

（续表）

区别点	种　类	中文名	适用情况或特点
是否已装船	On Board B/L	已装船提单	装船后签发，银行可接受
	Received for Shipment B/L	收妥备运提单	已收货，未装船，银行不接受
是否有不良批注	Clean B/L	清洁提单	无不良批注，银行可接受
	Unclean B/L	不清洁提单	有不良批注，银行不接受
收货人（提单抬头）不同	Straight B/L	记名式提单	确定收货人，不可背书转让
	Open B/L	来人式提单	收货人留空或制成“to bearer”无须背书即可转让
	Qrder B/L	指示提单	收货人制成“to order”或“to order of ××”，背书后可转让
运营方式不同	Liner B/L	班轮提单	班轮方式下采用，是全式提单
	Charter Party B/L	租船合同提单	租船方式下采用，受租船合同约束
提单的签发人不同	Master B/L	船公司提单	船公司签发
	House B/L	无船承运人提单	无船承运人签发
运输方式不同	Direct B/L	直达提单	直运时采用
	TransshipmentB/L	转船提单	转船时采用
	Combined Transport B/L	多式联运提单	海运和其他运输方式结合时采用
—	Advanced B/L	预借提单	货未装船，为符合装运日要求，提前签发的已装船清洁提单
—	Anti-dated B/L	倒签提单	货已装船，超过规定装运日，提单上的签发日期提前到规定日期前
—	Stale B/L	过期提单	超过规定装运日，交单日提单晚于货物到达目的港
—	On Deck B/L	舱面提单	货物直接置于舱面（集装箱直接置于舱面的提单不视作舱面提单）
—	SurrenderedB/L	电放提单	托运人申请“电放”，出具保函、缴费后，承运人收回原提单，重新签发提单，注明“电放”

13. 清洁提单与不清洁提单

14. 船公司提单与无船承运人提单的区别

15. 电放提单

表9-1所列的各类提单中，哪些提单交到银行，银行可以接受？

3. 提单主要栏目的填制说明

(1) 托运人(SHIPPER)

此项一般填写信用证中的受益人，托收方式下以托收的委托人为托运人。如果开证人为了贸易上的需要，要求做第三者提单(THIRD PARTY B/L)，也可照办。

(2) 收货人(CONSIGNEE)

如要求记名提单，则可填上具体的收货公司或收货人名称；如属指示提单，则填为“指示”(ORDER)或“凭指示”(TO ORDER)；如需在提单上列明指示人，则可根据不同要求，做成“凭托运人指示”(TO ORDER OF SHIPPER)，“凭收货人指示”(TO ORDER OF CONSIGNEE)或“凭银行指示”(TO ORDER OF ×× BANK)。

实际业务中，L/C项下提单多使用指示式，托收方式也普遍使用不记名指示式。若做成代收行指示式，事先要征得代收行同意。因为根据《托收统一规则》(URC522)中第10条a项规定，除非先征得银行同意，货物不应直接运交银行，亦必应以银行或银行的指定人为收货人。若未经银行事先同意，货物直接运交银行，或以银行的指定人为收货人，然后由银行付款或承兑后将货物交给付款人，则该银行并无义务提取货物，货物的风险和责任由发货人承担。

(3) 被通知人(NOTIFY PARTY)

这是船公司在货物到达目的港时发送到货通知的收件人，一般是收货人的代理人或提货人，有时即为进口人。托收方式下，被通知人一般填写托收的付款人。提单的被通知人一定要有详细的名称和地址，供承运人到目的港时及时通知提货。在L/C项下的提单，如信用证上对提单被通知人有具体规定时，则必须严格按信用证要求填写。若L/C未规定明确地址，为保持单证一致，可在正本提单中不列明，但要在副本提单上写明被通知人的详细地址。如果是记名提单或收货人指示提单，且收货人又有详细地址的，则此栏可以不填。如果是空白指示提单或托运人指示提单则此栏必须填列被通知人名称及详细地址，否则船方就无法与收货人联系，收货人也不能及时报关提货，甚至会因超过海关规定申报时间被没收。

(4) 提单号码(B/L NO)

此项一般列在提单右上角，以便于工作联系和查核。发货人向收货人发送装船通知(SHIPMENT ADVICE)时，也要列明船名和提单号码。

(5) 船名(OCEAN VESSEL)

此项应填列货物所装的船名及航次。

(6) 装货港(PORT OF LOADING)

此项应填列实际装船港口的具体名称。L/C项下一定要符合L/C的规定和要求。如果L/C规定为“中国港口”(CHINESE PORT)，此时不能照抄，而要按实际装运的我国某一港口名称填写。

(7) 卸货港(PORT OF DISCHARGE)

此项填列货物实际卸下的港口名称。如属转船,第一程提单上的卸货港填转船港,收货人填二程船公司;第二程提单装货港填上述转船港,卸货港填最后目的港。如由第一程船公司出联运提单(THROUGH B/L),则卸货港即可填最后目的港,提单上列明第一和第二程船名。如经某港转运,要显示"VIA ××"字样。在运用集装箱运输方式时,目前使用"联合运输提单"(COMBINED TRANSPORT B/L),提单上除列明装货港,卸货港外,还要列明"收货地"(PLACE OF RECEIPT),"交货地"(PLACE OF DELIVERY)以及"第一程运输工具"(PRE-CARRIAGE BY),"海运船名和航次"(OCEAN VESSEL, VOY NO.)。填写卸货港时,还要注意同名港口问题,如属选择港提单,就要在这栏中注明。

(8) 唛头(SHIPPING MARKS)

信用证有规定的,必须按规定填列;否则可按发票上的唛头填列,并注意做到单单一致。

(9) 件数和包装种类(NUMBER AND KIND OF PACKAGES)

此项要按货物实际包装情况填列。一般对于散装货物,该栏只填"IN BULK",大写件数栏可留空不填。单位件数与包装都要与实际货物相符,并在大写合计数内填写英文大写文字数目。如总件数为 320 CARTONS 填写在该栏项下,然后在总件数大写栏(TOTAL NUMBERS OF PACKAGES IN WORDS)填写:THREE HUNDRED AND TWENTY CARTONS ONLY。

如果货物包括二种以上不同包装单位(如纸箱、铁桶),应分别填列不同包装单位的数量,然后再表示件数,如:300 Cartons

400 Iron drums

700 Packages

然后在总件数大写栏填写:SAY TOTAL THREE HUNDRED CARTONS, FOUR HUNDRED IRON DRUMS AND SEVEN HUNDREND PACKAGES ONLY。

(10) 货名(DISCRIPTION OF GOODS)

原则上提单上的商品描述应按信用证规定填写,并与发票等其他单据相一致。但若信用证上货物的品名较多,则提单上允许使用类别总称来表示商品名称。如出口货物有餐刀、水果刀、餐叉、餐匙等,信用证上分别列明了各种商品名称、规格和数量,但包装都用纸箱,提单上就可以笼统写:餐具×××Cartons。

(11) 毛重,尺码(GROSS WEIGHT, MEASUREMENT)

除信用证另有规定者外,提单上一般只填货物的总毛重和总体积,而不表明净重和单位体积,因为单证当中有专门的装箱单会列明具体每一项。一般重量均以千克表示,体积用立方米表示。

(12) 运费和费用(FREIGHT AND CHARGES)

此项一般为预付(FREIGHT PREPAID)或到付(FREIGHT COLLECT)。如 CIF 或 CFR 出口,一般均填上运费预付字样,千万不可漏列,否则收货人会因运费问题提不到货,虽可查清情况,但拖延提货时间,也将造成损失。如为 FOB 出口,则运费可制作"运费到付"字样,即"FREIGHT COLLECT"或"FREIGHT PAYABLE AT DESTINATION",除非收货人委托发货人垫付运费。

若租船契约提单,有时要求填写"FREIGHT PAYABLE AS PER CHARTER

PARTY”。有时信用证还要求注明运费的金额，按实际运费支付额填写即可。

(13) 提单的签发地点、日期和份数

提单必须由承运人或船长或他们的代理签发，并应明确表明签发人身份。一般表示方法有 CARRIER，CAPTAIN 或“AS AGENT FOR THE CARRIER：×××”等。若信用证要求手签的也要照办。

提单的签发地点一般在货物运港所在地，日期则按信用证的装运期要求，一般要早于或与装运期为同一天。如果卖方估计货物无法在信用证装运期前装上船，应尽早通知买方，要求修改信用证，而不应利用倒签提单、预借提单等欺诈行为取得货款。

提单份数一般按信用证要求出具，如“FULL SET OF”一般理解成三份正本若干份副本。等其中一份正本完成提货任务后，其余各份失效。若在提单条款上未规定份数，而是在其他地方指明“AVAILABLE BY BENEFICIARY'S DRAFT AT SIGHT DRAWN ON US AND ACCOMPANIED BY THE FOLLOWING DOCUMENTS IN DUPLICATE”，表明信用证所要求提交的单据，当然包括提单，全都是一式两份。

(14) 已装船批注、装船日期、发运日期(ON BOARD NOTATION, ON BOARD DATE, SHIPMENT DATE)

如果提单上预先印就“已装船”文字或相同意思，这种提单通常被认为是“已装船提单”，不必另行加注“已装船”批注，提单的出具日期就是发运日期，除非提单载有表明发运日期的已装船批注，此时已装船批注中显示的日期将被视为发运日期。

4. 装船通知填写的注意事项

装船通知是出口商向进口商发出货物已于某月某日或将于某月某日装运某船的通知。装运通知的作用在方便买方购买保险或准备提货手续或转售，其内容通常包括所发运货物的合同号或信用证号、货名、装运数量、金额、船名、装船日期、启运地、目的地、提单号、运输标志、ETD 时间、ETA 时间等。如果信用证提出具体通知内容要求，应严格按规定出单。

装船通知大多以传真、电报或电传方式发送，也有用航邮方式发送的。议付时，须提供该传真、电报等予以证明。出口商作此项通知时，有时会附上或另行寄上货运单据副本，以便进口商明了装货内容，以防货运单据正本迟到时，可及时办理担保提货(delivery against letter of guarantee)。为简化投保手续，当国外进口商办理预约保险后，出口商可直接发出装船通知给进口商及其保险公司，以办理投保。此时，装船通知也是保险声明书。

装运通知填写的注意事项如下：

① 通知对象。填列通知对象，应按信用证规定填写，可以是开证申请人、申请人的指定人或保险公司等。若抬头为买方指定的保险公司，则应同时注明预约保险单号码。

② 通知内容。通知内容的填写必须与发票、提单等相关单据内容保持一致。

③ 特殊要求。如果信用证要求加具一些特殊说明，如信用证要求在装船通知中要显示信用证号码、开证日期和开证行名称等，则应显示出来；又如，信用证要求将装运通知发给保险公司和开证申请人，装船通知上须指明保单号码和运输详情，则信用证受益人要照办。

④ 制作和发出时间。日期不能超过信用证约定的时间，常见的有以小时为准(within 24/48 hours)和以天为准(within 2 days after shipment date)两种情形。若信用证未对装船通知的出单日期做出明确规定，或要求装船后立即通知(immediately after shipment)，一般要求出口商在货物离开启运地后 3 个工作日内向进口商发出装船通知，即提单日后 3 个工

作日内。装运通知一般可以不签署,但如果信用证要求"CERTIFIED COPY OF SHIPPING ADVICE",则受益人必须在该装船通知上进行签字盖章。

9.5 能力实训

实训1 请根据信用证相关内容确认提单,提单若有误请予以改正。

1. 信用证相关内容

L/C No.: 894010151719

PLACE AND DATE OF ISSUE: HONG KONG MAR 04, 2004

APPLICANT: BERNARD & COMPANY LIMITED
UNIT 1001 - 3 10/F YUE XIU BLDG
160 - 174 LOCKHART ROAD
WANCHAI HONG KONG

BENEFICIARY: NANJING CANTI IMPORT AND EXPORT CORP.
120 MX STREET, NANJING, CHINA

SHIPMENT: FROM SHANGHAI, CHINA TO SYDNEY, AUSTRALIA BEFORE APR. 04, 2004

TRANSHIPMENT: ALLOWED

PARTIAL SHIPMENT: NOT ALLOWED

DOCUMENTS REQUIRED:

-FULL SET OF CLEAN ON BOARD FREIGHT COLLECT OCEAN BILL OF LADING, MADE OUT TO ORDER OF SHIPPER AND BLANK ENDORSED, MARKED "NOTIFY ID COM CO., 79 - 81 WALES RD, NSW, AUSTRALIA" AND THE L/C NO.

-INVOICE IN TRIPLICATE

-PACKING LIST IN TRIPLICATE

DESCRIPTION OF GOODS: LUGGAGE SET OF 8 PCS

2. 提单内容

SHIPPER: NANJING CANTI IMPORT AND EXPORT LTD. 120 MX STREET, NANJING, CHINA	B/L NO.:
CONSIGNEE: TO ORDER	COSCO
NOTIFY: BERNARD & COMPANY LIMITED UNIT 1001 - 3 10/F YUE XIU BLDG, 160 - 174 LOCKHART ROAD WANCHAI HONG KONG	*OCEAN BILL OF LADING*

PRE CARRIAGE BY	PORT OF LOADING SHANGHAI, CHINA	PORT OF RECEIPT SHANGHAI, CHINA
OCEAN VESSEL/VOYAGE NO. BERLIN EXPRESS V. 06W01	PORT OF DISCHARGE SYDNEY, AUSTRIA	PLACE OF DELIVERY SYDNEY, AUSTRIA

MKS& NOS. CONTAINER NO. SEAL NUMBER	NOS AND KIND OF PKGS	DESCRIPTION OF GOODS	GROSS WEIGHT	MEASURE-MENT
ID COM PART OF 1×40′GP MLCU4578618/C423776 FREIGHT PREPAID COLLECT	372CNTS	SAID TO CONTAIN: LUGGAGE SET OF 5PCS	8 484.00 KGS	47.768 CBM

TOTAL NO. OF CONTAINERS OR PACKAGES (IN WORDS): SAY THREE HUNDRED AND SEVENTY (TWO) CARTONNS ONLY

OVERSEA OFFICE OR DESTINATION PORT AGENT	NO. OF ORIGINAL B/Ls THREE(3)	FREIGHT PAYBALE AT DESTINATION
	ON BOARD DATE 2003 - 04 - 08	PLACE & DATE OF ISSUE SHANGHAI, 03 - 04 - 08
	SIGNED BY: 签名 AS AGENT FOR THE CARRIER	

实训 2　根据下列所给的内容缮制装船通知，注意唛头由卖方自行设计。

BUYER: WEILI INT'L TRADING CORP.

SELLER: SUNSHINE TOY CORP. 221/18 SUNSHINE BUILDING, SHANGHAI, CHINA

DESCRIPTION:

ORDER NO.	GOODS	QUANTITY/PACKAGES	COLOUR
A220	BAGS	3 200PCS/100CTNS	GREY
A320	BAGS	4 000PCS/200CTNS	WHITE
C153	BAGS	4 000PCS/200CTNS	WHITE

SHIPMENT: MAR. 22, 2004 FROM SHANGHAI TO HAMBURG

CONTAINER NO. & SEAL NO.: 1×40′GP MLCU4578610/C423775

VOYAGE NAME & NO.: CMA CGM NEPTUNE V.485W

B/L NO.: CGLSHA0303088NA

INVOICE NO. & AMOUNT: SUNJA20040322 TOTAL USD22 000.00

实训 3　根据下列信用证和相关资料自行设计和制作装船通知

Form of Doc. Credit	*40 A: IRREVOCABLE
Doc. Credit Number	*20: LC-2008-1098
Date of Issue	31C: 081010
Expiry	*31D: Date 081230 Place CHINA
Applicant	*50: AL-HADON TRADING COMPANY P.O. BOX NO. 1198, DUBAI U.A.E
Beneficiary	* 59: NANJING GARMENTS IMP. AND EXP. CO., LTD. NO. 301 ZHEN AN TONG ROAD, NANJING, CHINA
Amount	*32B: Currency USD Amount 40,750.00
Pos./Neg. Tol. (%)	39A: 5/5
Available with/by	*41D: ANY BANK BY NEGOTIATION
Draft at ...	42C: DRAFTS AT 60 DAYS AFTER SIGHT FOR FULL INVOICE VALUE
Drawee	42A: * HABIB BANK LTD., DUBAI * TRADING SERVICES, POX 1106, DUBAI U.A.E.
Partial Shipments	43P: ALLOWED
Transshipment	43T: ALLOWED
Port of loading	44E: NANJING CHINA
Port of discharge	44F: DUBAI U A E
Latest Date of Ship.	44C: 081215
Descript. of Goods	45A:

MEN'S UNDERWEAR 2 PCS SET CFR DUBAI

ART NO. 3124A, U. PRICE USD52.50/DOZ, 300DOZ

ART NO. 3125A, U. PRICE USD50.00/DOZ, 500DOZ

ALL OTHER DETAILS AS PER PROFORMA INVOICE NO. HT-2578

Documents required　46A:

+FULL SET OF CLEAN ON BOARD BILLS OF LADING MADE OUT TO ORDER OF SHIPPER AND BLANK ENDORSED AND MARKED FREIGHT PREPAID, NOTIFY M/S HALLSON TRADING, P. O. BOX NO. 2512 DUBAI U A E AND ALSO SHOWING THE NAME, ADDRESS, TEL. NO. OR FAX NO. OF THE CARRYING VESSEL'S AGENT AT PORT OF DISCHARGE

+ SHIPPING ADVICE MUST BE SENT TO THE DUBAI INSURANCE COMPANY ON FAX NO. 82354322 SHOWING THE SHIPPING DETAILS

Additional Conditions　47A: ALL DOCUMENTS MUST SHOW OUR L/C NUMBER AND DATE

Details of Charges　71B: ALL BANKING CHARGES OUTSIDE DUBAI ARE FOR A/C OF BENEFICIARY

Presentation Period 48: DOCUMENTS TO BE PRESENTED WITHIN 15 DAYS AFTER THE DATE OF SHIPMENT, BUT WITHIN THE VALIDITY OF THE CREDIT

相关资料：

发票号码：20141500　　发票日期：2014年1月30日

提单号码：HSKK50088　　提单日期：2014年12月10日

船名：CMA CROWN V.987　　集装箱：1×20′LCL CFS/CFS

集装箱号：TRIU287756　　封号：80709

合同号：NG14-2578　　预约保单号：14-236147

唛头：HALLSON/HT-2578/DUBAI/NO. 1-200

项目 10　制作附属单据

10.1　学习目标

知识目标:了解附属单据的作用;掌握附属单据填制的规范。

能力目标:能够根据外贸合同或信用证等信息准确制作受益人证明、船公司证明等附属单据。

10.2　工作任务

无锡蓝天进出口公司向加拿大出口女童连衣裙。根据信用证的规定,BENEFICIARY'S CERTIFICATE CERTIFYING THAT ONE SET OF COPIES OF SHIPPING DOCUMENTS HAS BEEN SENT TO APPLICANT WITHIN 7 DAYS AFTER SHIPMENT; CERTIFICATE TO EVDIENT TO EVIDENCE THE SHIP IS NOT OVER 15 YEARS OLD。该要求需要出口商提供一份受益人证明作为议付单据和一份船公司证明。郭晓芳应依据相关资料及信用证的要求缮制受益人证明和船公司证明。

10.3　操作范例

1. 受益人证明

BENEFICIARY'S CERTIFICATE

TO: WHOM IT MAY CONCERN　　DATE: JUL. 18, 2015

INVOICE NO. ZYIE1502

RE: L/C NO. 123456

WE HEREBY CERTIFY THAT ONE SET OF COPIES OF SHIPPING DOCUMENTS HAS BEEN SENT TO APPLICANT WITHIN 7 DAYS AFTER SHIPMENT.

DOCUMENTARY CREDIT NO.: 123456
DATE OF ISSUE: 150520
NAME OF ISSUING BANK: HSBC BANK PLC, MONTREAL, CANADA

WUXI BLUE SKY IMP&EXP. Co., LTD.
郭晓芳

2. 船公司证明

CERTIFICATE

TO: WHOM IT MAY CONCERN　　　　DATE: JUL.16,2015

INVOICE NO. K123

RE: L/C NO.123456

THIS IS TO CERTIFY THAT THE S. S. DONDFANG V. 009J WAS BULIT IN 2001, AND HAS THEREFORE NOT BEEN IN OPERATION FOR MORE THAN 15 YEARS AT TIME OF CARGO LOADING.

DOCUMENTARY CREDIT NO.: 123456

DATE OF ISSUE: 150620

NAME OF ISSUING BANK: HSBC BANK PLC, MONTREAL, CANADA

COSCO CONTAINER LINES

×××

10.4 知识链接

(一) 受益人证明填制规范

具体内容	填写内容	要点提示
(1) 单据名称 Name of Doc	Certificate	单据名称应与信用证一致
(2) 日期 Date	证明日期	应符合信用证规定
(3) 发票号 Invoice No.	发票号码	
(4) 抬头人 To	To whom it may concern	不填实际当事人
(5) 证明文句	需证明的内容	应符合信用证的规定,注意人称、时态、语态的变化
(6) 签署 Signature	受益人签章	证明函必须签署

(二) 船公司证明填制规范

具体内容	填写内容	要点提示
(1) 单据名称 Name of Doc	Certificate	应与信用证要求的单据名称一致
(2) 日期 Date	证明的日期	一般与提单日期相同
(3) 抬头人 Contents	To whom it may concern	不填实际当事人
(4) 证明文句 Statement	需证明的内容	按信用证要求并结合实际情况做出证明
(5) 签署 Signature	船公司	应该与提单签单人一致

受益人证明

受益人证明(Beneficiary' Certificate)是根据信用证条款,由出口商签发的用来证实有关内容的书面证明。证明的内容包括:寄出有关的副本单据、船样、样卡、码样、包装标签;商品已经检验;已发出装船通知等。受益人证明一般无固定格式,内容多种多样,以英文制作,通常签发一份。

如来证要求:"one copy of invoice and packing list to be sent directly to applicant immediately after shipment, and beneficiary's certificate to be effect is required."按此条款,受益人应提供受益人证明。

出口方能否制作该证明

出口方收到的信用证上有如下条款:DOCUMENTS REQUIRED:BENEFICIARY'S CERTIFICATE CERTIFYING 1/3 ORIGINAL B/L HAS BEEN SENT DIRECTLY TO THE APPLICANT WITHIN 2 DAYS AFTER DATE OF SHIPMENT(单据要求,受益人证明证实 1/3 正本提单已在装运日后 2 日内直寄给开证申请人)。那么出口方能否接受该条款,并制作受益人证明?

船公司证明

船公司证明(Shipping Company'S Certificate)系信用证受益人应开证申请人的要求,请船公司出具的不同认定内容的证明。常见的船公司证明有:

1. 集装箱船只证明(Certificate of Container Vessel)。进口商或银行在合同/信用证中规定货物须装集装箱船并出具相应证明的,可由受益人自行制作并加盖有关签发人的图章,也可在运输单据上加以注明。如条款做如下规定:"SHIPMENT TO BE MADE BY CONTAINER VESSEL AND BENEFICIARY TO CERTIFY TO THIS EFFECT",则须提供证明。

2. 船龄证明。有些国家/地区来证规定装载货物的船舶的船龄不得超过 15 年,受益人必须要求船代或船公司出具载货船只的船龄证明书(Certificate to evidence the ship is not over 15 years old 或 is under 15 years of age),这样的要求主要目的在于禁止使用老龄船,保护货物运输安全。

3. 船籍证明(Certificate of Registry)用于证明船舶所属国籍。

4. 船级证明(Confirmation of Class)。有的信用证规定提供英国劳合社船级证明,如"Class certificate certifying that the shipment is made by a seaworthy vessel which are classified 100 A1 issued by Lloyds or equivalent classification society",劳合社的船级符号为 LR,标志 100A1,100A 表示该船的船体和机器设备是根据劳氏规范和规定建造的,I 表

示船舶的装备如船锚、锚链和绳索等处于良好和有效的状态，对这样的要求我们通常应予以满足。国际上著名的船级社有英国劳合社 、德国船级社(GL)、挪威船级社(DNV)、法国船级社(BV)、日本海事协会(NK)、美国船级社(ABS)等。船级证明如下：

CONGIRMATION OF CLASS

TO WHOM IT MAY CONCEN:

THIS IS TO CERTIFY THAT ACCORDING TO CURRENT INFORMATION AVAILABLE IN THIS OFFICE THE CLASS STATUS OF THE UNDER MENTIONED SHI/UNIT IS AS FOLLOWS:

L. R. Number 129034

Name of Ship/Unit ADRIAN MAERSK

Gross Tonnage 21100

Date of Build 1976 - 7

Class Status The above ship maintains the Class+100AL and+LMC

The above ship has the notation UMS(Unattended Machinery Space)

Issuing office

Hongkong

×××××

5. 航程证明(Certificate of Itinerary)。主要说明航程中船舶停靠的港口，一些阿拉伯国家开来的信用证中，往往要求在提单上随附声明一份，明确船籍、船名、船东及途中所经港口顺序，出口方须按要求签发此类证明并按证明中所述行驶、操作船舶。

6. 转船证明书(Certificate of Transshipment)。出口方出具转船证明书，说明出口货物将在中途转船且已联系妥当，并由托运人负责将有关转船事项通知收货人。

7. 货装具名船舶证明。如信用证要求："A certificate from the shipping company or its agent stating that goods are shipped by APL"(意思是要求出口方提供由船公司或其代理出具的货装美国总统轮船公司的证明)。

8. 船长收据(Captain's Receipt)。有的信用证规定，样品或单据副本交载货船只的船长带交进口商，并提供船长收据，如委托船长带去而未取得船长收据将影响出口商收汇，常见于近洋运输。

超链接

寄单证明、寄样证明

有些信用证经常规定受益人在货物装运后，应立即邮寄某些给收货人或其指定的人，并出具有关证明即寄单证明作为议付单证之一，以证明其已按信用证的规定办事。寄单证明通常由出口公司或受益人出具，此时，寄单证明也可以称作受益人证明，其格式一般与受益人证明的要求基本一致，通常包括所寄单证的份数、寄出时间、寄送方式、寄送对象等，寄单证明可按如下格式出具。

CERTIFICATE

DATE: 20 JUL. 2016
INV. NO. : 3478
L/C NO. : 98234

TO WHOM IT MAY CONCEN:

RE: SHIPPING DOCUMENTS UNDER L/CNO. ××

WE HEREBY CERTIFY THAT WE HAVE SENT THE FOLLOWING DOCUMENTS TO MESSERS CO. LTD. BY REGISTERED AIRMAIL:

1) TO COPIES OF ××.

2) TO COPIES OF ××.

CHINA TEXTILE I/E COMPANY
(SIGNATURE)

与寄样证明类似的还有寄样证明，由受益人根据信用证的规定，签发寄出船样、样卡、码样等情况的证明。

CERTIFICATE

DATE: 20 JUL. 2016
INV. NO. : 3478
L/C NO. : 98234

TO WHOM IT MAY CONCEN:

RE:SHIPPING DOCUMENTS UNDER L/CNO. ××

WE HEREBY CERTIFY THAT IN COMPLIANCE WITH THE TERM OF THE RELATIVE LETTER OF CREDIT, WE HAVE SENT FOUR PIECES OF SHIPMENT SAMPLES TO THE NOMINEES BY DHL SERVICES BEFORE SHIPMENT.

CHINA TEXTILE I/E COMPANY
(SIGNATURE)

证明类单据的签署

(1) 证明类单据一定要签署吗?

(2) 一装箱单无签署，现按信用证要求加入证明语句:“we hereby certify that the packing areseaworthy”那么该装箱单还需签署吗?

10.5　能力实训

实训 1　根据以下资料请缮制受益人证明和船舶证明

L/C NO.　　20: CBCL123
DATE OF ISSUE　　31C: NOV.18, 2012
EXPIRY DATE　　31D: JAN.18, 2012, PLACE: CHINA
APPLLCANT　　50: RAIN DREANS I/E CORP
NO.80. MOSQUE ROAD, GORAKANA, MORATUWA
SRI LANKA
BENEFICIARY　　59: GUANGDONG TRADING CO., LTD
123TLANHE ROAD, GUANGZHOU P.R.CHINA
LATEST DATE　　44C: JAN 3.2012
DOCUMENTS REQUIRED: 46A

...

+ONE SET OF COPIES OFSHIPPING DOCUMENTS MUST BE SENT DIRDCTLY TO THE APPLICANT IN 3 DAYS AFTER SHIPMENT. BENEFICIARY'S CERTIFICATE TO THIS EFFECT IS REQUIRED

+A CERTIFICATE OF TRANSSIPMENT FROMTHE SHIPPING COMPANY OR ITS AGENT STATING THAT GOODS ARE SHIPPED BY APL.

1. 受益人证明

广东进出口贸易公司
GUANGDONG FOREIGN TRADE IMP &EXP CORPORATION
123TLANHE ROAD, GUANGZHOU P.R.CHINA
BENEFICIARY'S　CERTIFICATE

TO:　　DATE:
INVOICE NO.123

2. 船舶证明

CERTIFICATE

TO: WHOM IT MAY CONCERN DATE:

INVOICE NO. 123

AMERICAN PRESIDENT LINES

×××

实训 2 根据项目二任务二训练 2 的信用证和相关资料，以及信用证如下要求，自行设计和制作证明类单据。

(1) A SEPARATE CERTIFICATE FROM THE SHIPPING CO. OR ITS AGENT CERTIFYING THAT THE CARRYING VESSEL IS ALLOWED BY ARAB AUTHORITIES TO CALL AT ARABIAN PORTS AND IS NOT SCHEDULED TO CALL AT ANY ISRAELI PORTS DURING ITS TRIP TO ARABIAN COUNTRIES.

(2) ONE SET OF NON-NEGOTIABLE SHIPPING DOCUMENTS AND SHIPMENT SAMPLES SHOULD BE SENT DIRECTLY TO THE OPENERS AND A CERTIFICATE AND RELATIVE POST RECEIPT FOR THIS EFFECT IS REQUIRED.

项目 11　制作汇票

11.1　学习目标

知识目标:掌握汇票填制的规范

能力目标:根据外贸合同或信用证等信息准确填制汇票

11.2　工作任务

无锡蓝天进出口公司外贸单证员郭晓芳制作好附属单据后,准备在信用证交单期限要求交单之前,根据以信用证和商业发票制作汇票。

1. 信用证

MT 700	ISSUE OF A DOCUMENTARY CREDIT
SENDER	HSBC BANK PLC, MONTREAL, CANADA
RECEIVER	BANK OF CHINA, WUXI BRANCH, CHINA
SEQUENCE OF TOTAL	27: 1/1
FORM OF DOC. CREDIT	40A: IRREVOCABLE
DOC. CREDIT NUMBER	20: 123456
DATE OF ISSUE	31C: 150520
APPLICABLE RULES	40E: UCP LATEST VERSION
DATE AND PLACE OF EXPIRY	31D: 150815 IN CHINA
APPLICANT	50: KU TEXTILE CORPORATION 430 VTRA MONTREAL CANADA
BENEFICIARY	59: WUXI BLUE SKY IMP&EXP. Co., LTD NO.53 ZHONGSHAN ROAD, WUXI, CHINA
AMOUNT	32B: USD 65300.00
PERCENTAGE CREDIT AMOUNT TOLERANCE	39A: 5/5
AVAILABLE WITH/BY	41D: ANY BANK IN CHINA, BY NEGOTIATION
DRAFTS AT ...	42C: AT 30 DAYS AFTER SIGHT
DRAWEE	42A: HSBC BANK PLC, MONTREAL, CANADA
PARTIAL SHIPMENT	43P: ALLOWED
TRANSSHIPMENT	43T: ALLOWED
PORT OF LOADING/ AIRPORT OF DEPARTURE	44E: CHINESE MAIN PORT

PORT OF DISCHARGE 44F: MONTREAL, CANADA
LATEST DATE OF SHIPMENT 44C: 150731
DESCRIPTION OF GOODS AND/OR SERVICES. 45A:

9400 PIECES GIRL DRESS 100% COTTON

AS PER S/C NO. 123

STYLE NO.	QUANTITY	UNIT PRICE	AMOUNT
11754	2400PCS	USD6.50/PC	USD15600.00
11575	3000PCS	USD5.50/PC	USD16500.00
11576	2400PCS	USD8.50/PC	USD20400.00
11577	1600PCS	USD8.00/PC	USD12800.00

AT CIF MONTREAL, CANADA

DOCUMENTS REQUIRED 46A:

+ SIGNED COMMERCIAL INVOICE IN DUPLICATE CERTIFYING GOODS OF CHINA ORIGIN.

+PACKING LIST IN THREE FOLDS SHOWING G. W. , N. W., AND MEAS. OF EACH PACKGE.

+ CERTIFICATE OF CHINESE ORIGIN CERTIFIED BY CHAMBER OF COMMERCE OR CCPIT.

+ G. S. P. CERTIFICATE OF ORIGIN FORM A IN DUPLICATE BY CIQ.

+ FULL SET OF CLEAN ' ON BOARD ' OCEAN BILLS OF LADING MADE OUT TOORDER AND BLANK ENDORSED MARKED FREIGHT PREPAID AND NOTIFY APPLICANT.

+ INSURANCE POLICY OR CERTIFICATE ENDORSED IN BLANK FOR 110 PCT OF CIF VALUE, COVERING ALL RISKS AND WAR RISK SUBJECT TO THE RELEVANT OCEAN MARINE CLAUSE OF THE PEOPLE'S INSURANCE COMPANY OF CHINA, DATED 1/1/1981.

+ SHIPPING ADVICE SHOWINGB/L NO., GOODS NAME, QUANTITY AND AMOUNT OF GOODS, NUMBER OF PACKAGES, NAME OF VESSEL AND VOYAGE NO., AND DATE OF SHIPMENT TO APPLICANT WITHIN 3 DAYS AFTER THE DATE OF BILL OF LADING.

+BENEFICIARY'S CERTIFICATE CERTIFYING THAT ONE SET OF COPIES OF SHIPPING DOCUMENTS HAS BEEN SENT TO APPLICANT WITHIN 7 DAYS AFTER SHIPMENT

+ CERTIFICATE TO EVDIENT TO EVIDENCE THE SHIP IS NOT OVER 15 YEARS OLD.

ADDITIONAL CONDITION 47A:

+ DOCUMENTS DATED PRIOR TO THE DATE OF THIS CREDIT ARE NOT ACCEPTABLE.

+ THE NUMBER AND THE DATE OF THIS CREDIT AND THE NAME OF ISSUING BANK MUST BE QUOTED ON ALL DOCUMENTS.
+ TRANSSHIPMENT ALLOWED AT HONGKONG ONLY.
+ SHORT FORM/CHARTER PARTY/THIRD PARTY BILL OF LADING ARE NOT ACCEPTABLE.
+ SHIPMENT MUST BE EFFECTED BY40' FULL CONTAINER LOAD. B/L TO SHOW EVIDENCE OF THIS EFFECT IS REQUIRED.
+ ALL PRESENTATIONS CONTAINING DISCREPANCIES WILL ATTRACT A DISCREPANCY FEE OF USD50.00 PLUS TELEX COSTS OR OTHER CURRENCY EQUIVALENT. THIS CHARGE WILL BE DEDUCTED FROM THE BILL AMOUNT WHETHER OR NOT WE ELECT TO CONSULT THE APPLICANT FOR A WAIVER.
CHARGES 71B: ALL CHARGES AND COMMISSIONS OUTSIDE CANADA ARE FOR BENEFICIARY'S ACCOUNT.
PERIOD FOR PRESENTATION 48: WITHIN 15 DAYS AFTER THE DATE OF SHIPMENT, BUT WITHIN THE VALIDITY OF THIS CREDIT.
CONFIRMATION INSTRUCTION 49: WITHOUT
INFORMATION TO PRESENTING BANK 78:
ALL DOCUMENTS ARE TO BE REMITTED IN ONE LOT BY COURIER TO HSBC BANK
PLC, TRADE SERVICES, MONTREAL BRANCH, P O BOX 66, HSBC BANK BUILDING
312/45 Al SUQARE ROAD, MONTREAL, CANADA

2. 商业发票

COMMERCIAL INVOICE

<table>
<tr><td rowspan="3">1) SELLER
WUXIBLUE SKY IMP&EXP. Co., LTD.
NO. 53 ZHIGONG STREET, WUXI, P. R. CHINA</td><td>3) INVOICE NO.
ZYIE1502</td><td>4) INVOICE DATE
MAY20, 2015</td></tr>
<tr><td>5) L/C NO.
123456</td><td>6) DATE
MAY20, 2015</td></tr>
<tr><td colspan="2">7) ISSUED BY
HSBC BANK PLC, MONTREAL, CANADA</td></tr>
<tr><td rowspan="3">2) BUYER
KU TEXTILE CORPORATION
430 VTRA MONTREAL CANADA</td><td>8) CONTRACT NO.
K123</td><td>9)DATE
APR.9, 2015</td></tr>
<tr><td>10) FROM
SHANGHAI</td><td>11) TO
MONTREAL</td></tr>
<tr><td>12) SHIPPED BY
DONG FANG V.25</td><td>13) PRICE TERM
CIF MONTREAL</td></tr>
</table>

14) MARKS&NOS.	15) DESCRIPTIONS OF GOODS	16) QTY	17) UNIT PRICE	18) AMOUNT

GIRL DRESS 100%COTTON AS PER SALES COMTRACT NO. K123 DATED APR. 9, 2015

KU	11574	2400PCS	US$6.50	US$15600.00
K123	11575	3000PCS	US$5.50	US$16500.00
MONTREAL	11576	2400PCS	US$8.50	US$20400.00
C/NO.1-235	11577	1600PCS	US$8.00	US$12800.00
		TOTAL 9400PC		US$65300.00

TOTAL AMOUNT IN WORDS: SAY US DOLLARS SIXTY FIVE THOUSAND AND THREE HUNDRED ONLY

SAY US DOLLARSTWO THOUSAND THREE HUNDRED ONLY.

WE HEREBY CERTIFY THAT GOODS ARE OF CHINA ORIGIN.

19) ISSUEDY BY

WUXIBLUE SKY IMP&EXP. Co., LTD.

郭晓芳

11.3 操作范例

BILL OF EXCHANGE

NO. ZYIE1502　　Date: JUL. 21, 2015

FOR USD65,300.00

At 30 DAYS AFTER Sight of THIS SECOND BILL of EXCHANGE

(First of the tenor and date being unpaid) BANK OF CHINA, ZHEJIANG BRANCH.

Pay to

SAY US DOLLARS SIXTY FIVE THOUSAND THREE HUNDRED ONLY

Drawn under HSBC BANK PLC, MONTREAL, CANADA

L/C NO. 123456　　Dated MAY20, 2015

TO.

HSBC BANK PLC, MONTREAL, CANADA

WUXI BLUE SKY IMP&EXP. Co., LTD

签章

缮制汇票的注意事项

① 票面必须整洁、干净、清楚，金额不得涂改，不得加注与汇票无关的内容。

② 为防备单据在邮寄途中遗失，一般远洋单据都分两次邮寄，所以，汇票都应该制成一式两联，“付一不付二”或“付二不付一”，两联具有同等效力。

③ 一般情况下，汇票的金额与发票的金额一致，除非信用证另有规定。

④ 汇票必须由受益人或卖方出具。

汇票的主要当事人见表 11-1。

表 11-1 汇票的主要当事人

项 目	内 容	涉外商业汇票	涉外银行汇票
出票人	即签发汇票的人	通常为出口商	通常为进口地银行
付款人	受票人，支付汇票款项的人	信用证：通常为银行（开证行或指定受票银行） 托收：通常为进口商	通常为出口地银行
收款人	抬头人 (1) 记名抬头：××（确定的人） (2) 不记名抬头：空白 (3) 指示抬头：Pay to order of ××（即付款给×××指定的人）	实务中通常做成指示抬头，以便背书转让。 常做成：pay to order of XXCO. XXBANK（出口商银行）	通常为出口商

11.4 知识链接

汇票的填制规范如表 11-2 所示。

表 11-2 汇票的填制规范

汇票的具体内容	填写内容	要点提示
(1) 单据名称 Name of Doc	Bill of Exchange	一般已印妥
(2) 汇票号码 No.	填此笔业务发票的日期	
(3)日期和地点	汇票的出票日期和地点	出票地点一般为出票人所在地； 出票日期应信用证向银行交单时段内

（续表）

汇票具体内容	填写内容	要点提示
(4) 小写金额	币种金额	根据合同或信用证填写；
(5) 付款期限	1. 即期付款，在 AT 和 SIGHT 之间填写---、*** 2. 远期付款，在 AT 和 SIGHT 之间填写具体期限	远期付款的几种表示方法： 见票后×××天付款 出票后×××天付款 提单日后×××天付款 指定日付款
(6) 收款人	限制性抬头 来人抬头 指示性抬头	Pay to ×××. only. Pay to the bearer. Pay to the order of ×××
(7) 大写金额	与前面小写金额一致	习惯上，在货币名称前加“SAY”，在大写金额后加“ONLY”字样
(8) 出票依据	信用证项下，填写开证行名称、信用证号码和开证日期 托收项下，填写 FOR COLLECTION	信用证有规定的文具照抄即可
(9) 付款人	信用证项下，一般为开证行或信用证指定的付款银行 托收项下，填写进口商	信用证有规定的文具照抄即可
(10) 出票人	受益人或合同中出口商	加盖收益人签章； 如果要求手签，则必须亲笔签名

汇　票

1. 汇票的定义

《中华人民共和国票据法》对汇票(BILL OF EXCHANGE, DRAFT)的定义为：“汇票是出票人签发的，委托付款人在见票时或在指定日期无条件支付确定的金额给收款人或其指定人或持票人的票据。”

《英国票据法》对汇票的定义为：“汇票是由一人签发给另一人的无条件书面命令，要求受票人见票时或于未来某一规定的或可以确定的时间，将一定金额的款项支付给某一特定的人或其指定人或持票人”。

汇票是国际结算中广为使用的一种单据，在托收/信用证结算方式下，出口商通常都要制作汇票，通过自己的往来银行向进口商/出口商的银行索要货款。汇票制作得正确与否，会在一定程度上影响出口商按时收汇，虽然部分一行代客户制作汇票，作为单证员还是要制作出正确的汇票供银行参考。

2. 汇票的种类

汇票的分类

分类标准	分 类	特 征
是否附有单据	跟单汇票 (Documentary Bill)	附有货运单据的汇票,使用较多
	光票 (Clean Bill)	不附带货运单据的汇票。常用于收取小额款项(贸易从属费用、货款尾数、佣金等)使用较少
付款期限不同	即期汇票 (SIGHT DRAFT)	即期付款,付款人见票即付
	远期汇票 (USANCE BILL)	远期付款,付款人到期付款
出票人不同	银行汇票 (BANKER'S DARFT)	出票人和付款人都是银行,常用于汇付(票汇)
	商业汇票 (COMMERCIAL DARFT)	出票人不是银行,付款人不限,常用于信用证和托收
承兑人不同	商业承兑汇票 (COMMERCIAL ACCEPTANCE BILL)	由银行承兑,易贴现
	银行承兑汇票 (BANKER'S ACCEPTANCE BILL)	不由银行承兑,不易贴现

3. 汇票的使用

汇票的使用随汇票是即期还是远期而有所不同。

即期汇票只需经过出票、提示和付款。

远期汇票须经过承兑手续。如需流通转让,通常要经过背书。汇票遭到拒付时,还要涉及做成拒绝证明,依法行使追索权等法律问题。

(1) 出票(ISSUE)

出票是指出票人签发票据并将其交付给收款人的票据行为。出票由两个动作组成,一是由出票人写成汇票,并在汇票上签字;二是由出票人将汇票交付给收款人。由于出票是设立债权债务的行为,所以,只有经过交付汇票才开始生效。

(2) 提示(PRESENTATIONO)

提示是指收款人或持票人将汇票提交付款人要求付款或承兑的行为。提示可分为提示承兑和提示付款。提示承兑是指远期汇票持票人向付款人出示汇票,并要求付款人承诺付款的行为。提示付款是指汇票的持票人向付款人(或远期汇票的承兑人)出示汇票要求付款人(或承兑人)付款的行为。

(3) 承兑(ACCEPTANCE)

承兑是指汇票付款人承诺在汇票到期日支付汇票金额的票据行为。汇票一经承兑,付款人就成为汇票的承兑人,并成为汇票的主债务人,而出票人便成为汇票的次债务人。

(4) 付款(PAYMENT)

付款是指付款人向持票人支付汇票金额的行为。即期汇票在付款人见票时照付;远期汇票于到期日在持票人作提示付款时由付款人付款。汇票一经付款，汇票上的一切债权债务即告结束。

(5) 背书(ENDORSEMENT)

背书是一种以转让票据权利为目的的行为。背书通常由持票人在汇票的背面或粘单上签上自己的名字，或者再加上受让人即被背书人的名称，并把汇票交给受让人。汇票经过背书后，收款的权利就转让给了被背书人。

背书方式的表示见表11-3。

表11-3 背书方式的表示

制作方式	常见格式	要点提示
(1) 限定性背书	背书人:签章 被背书人:Pay to ××× ONLY,或者to ××× NOT NEGOTIABLE(付给×××,不得转让)	不得继续转让(或背书人对被背书人的"后手"免责),使用较少
(2) 特别背书	背书人:签章 被背书人:Pay tothe order of ×××(付给××的×指定人)	又称记名背书、完全背书。背书即可继续转让
(3) 空白背书	背书人:签章 被背书人空白	又称不记名背书。无须背书即可继续转让,使用最多

(6) 拒付(DISHONOUR)与追索(RECOURSE)

拒付包括拒绝付款和拒绝承兑两个内容。汇票被拒付，持票人除可向承兑人追索外，还有权向其前手，包括所有的背书人和出票人行使追索权。持票人进行追索时，应将拒付事实书面通知其前手，并提供被拒绝承兑或被拒绝付款的证明或退票理由。持票人不能出示拒绝证明、退票理由书的，丧失对其前手的追索权。追索的金额包括被拒付的汇票金额和自到期日或提示付款日起至清偿日至的利息，以及取得拒绝证书和向前手发出被拒绝通知的费用。

无锡福光服装有限公司与BRUCE公司交易中，在信用证方式下出票人、付款人、收款人分别是谁？汇票如何操作？若是远期汇票，应如何操作？若是托收，出票人、付款人、收款人分别是谁？汇票如何操作？

16. L/C与托收项下汇票缮制的区别

11.5　能力实训

实训 1　根据所给的托收汇票回答问题

BILL OF EXCHANGE

号码　　　　　　　　汇票金额　　　　　　　　上海
No. **HLK356**　Exchange for　**USD 56,000.00**　Shanghai, Sep. 20, 2010
见票　　　　　　　　日后(本汇票之副本未付)付交
D/P At **90 DAYS AFTER** sight of this FIRST of Exchange (Second of Exchange being unpaid)
pay to the order of **BANK OF CHINA, SHANGHAI BRANCH**
金额
the sum of　SAY US DOLLARS FIFTY SIX THOUSAND ONLY
此致
To MITSUBISHI TRUST & BANKING
CO. LTD.,
INTERNATIONAL　DEPARTMENT,
4—5
MARUNOUCHI 1—CHOME
CHIYODA-KU, TOKYO 100, JAPAN

CHINA NATIONAL ANIMAL BYPRODUCTS
IMP. & EXP. CORP. TIANJIN BRANCH
66 YANTAI STREET
TIANJIN CHINA
×××

1. 汇票的出票人、付款人分别是谁?
2. 汇票是即期还是远期? 有几份汇票?
3. 该笔托收业务的托收行是谁?

实训 2　根据所给的信用证及相关资料填制汇票

DATE OF ISSUE	31 C:150808
DATE AND PLACE OF EXPIRY	*31 D:151003　CHINA
APPLICANT	*50:SEMPREVIVO SRL IMPORT EXPORT VIA GINO FUNAIOLI I/B 90123　PALERMO
BENEFICIARY	*59:SHANGHAI ZHEN YUAN IMP. AND EXP. CO. LTD RM 302－305, 700 JIAN GUO DONG RD. SHANGHAI, CHINA
AMOUNT	*32 B:US DOLLARS 24284,00

AVAILABLE WITH/BY 41A: ANY BANK BY NEGOTIATION
DRAFTS AT ... 42C: 30 DAYS AFTER SIGHT
DRAWEE 42D: ISTITUTO BANCARIO SAN PAOLO DI
TORINO S. P. A.
PALERMO
LATEST DATE OF SHIPMENT 44 C: 150918
DESCRIPT OF GOODS AND / OR SERVICKS 45 A:
SPORTS MUG AS PER SALES COMTRACT NO. 15SH01 DATED 10-JUL-15CIF PALERMO
ADDITIONAL CONDITIONS 47A: DOCUMENTARY CREDIT NO. AND NAME OF ISSUING BANK MUST BE QUOTED ON ALL DOCUMENTS.
PERIOD FOR PRESENTATION 48: DOCUMENTS HAVE TO BE PRESENTED WITHIN
15DAYS AFTER DATE OF SHIPMENT BUT WITHIN VALIDITY DATE.

BILL OF EXCHANGE

No. 15 - 123 ____________________

For ____________________ ____________________

(amount in figure) (place and date of issue)

At ____________________ sight of this FIRST Bill of exchange (SECOND being unpaid)

pay to ____ or order the sum of

____

(amount in words)

Value received for 350 CARTONS of

____________________ ____________________

(quantity) (name of commodity)

Drawn under ____

L/C No. ____________________ dated ____________________

To: For and on behalf of

____

(Signature)

实训 3 根据所给的合同及相关资料填制汇票

SALES CONTRACT

SELLER:	DESUNSOFT CO., LTD. Room 2901, HuaRong Mansion, GuanJiaQiao 85#, Nanjing 210005, P.R.China TEL: 025－4711363 FAX: 025－4691619	NO.: DATE: **SIGNED IN:**	DS2014SC205 Mar. 23, 2014 NANJING, CHINA
BUYER:	SAMAN AL-ABDUL KARIM AND PARTNERS CO. POB 13552, RIYADH 44166, KSA TEL: 4577301/4577312/4577313 FAX:4577461		

买、卖双方同意以下条款将达成交易：

This contract Is made by and agreed between the BUYER and SELLER, in accordance with the terms and conditions stipulated below.

1. 品名及规格 **Commodity & Specification**	2. 数量 **Quantity**	3. 单价及价格条款 **Unit Price & Trade Terms**	4. 金额 **Amount**
		CFR DAMMAM PORT, SAUDI ARABIA	
CANNED APPLE JAM 24 TINS X 340 GMS	2200CARTONS	USD6.80	USD14960.00
CANNED STRAWBERRY JAM 24 TINS X 340 GMS	2200CARTONS	USD6.80	USD14960.00
Total:	**4400CARTONS**		**USD29920.00**

允许 With 10% 溢短装，由卖方决定 More or less of shipment allowed at the sellers' option

5. 总值 Total Value: U. S. DOLLAR TWENTY NINE THOUSAND NINE HUNDRED AND TWENTY ONLY.
6. 包装 Packing: EXPORT CARTONS
7. 唛头 Shipping Marks: N/M
8. 装运期及运输方式 Time of Shipment & means of Transportation: Not Later Then Jun. 05, 2014 BY VESSEL

9. 装运港及目的地 Port of Loading & Destination	From：TIANJIN PORT，P. R. CHINA To：DAMMAM PORT，SAUDI ARABIA
10. 保险 Insurance	TO BE COVERED BY THE BUYER.
11. 付款方式 Terms of Payment	20% T/T IN ADVANCE，THE OTHER 80% D/P AT SIGHT
12. 备注 Remarks	1）Transshipment allowed，Partial shipment not allowed. 2）Shipment terms will be fulfilled according to the L/C finally.

The Buyer	**The Seller**
SAMAN AL-ABDUL KARIM AND PARTNERS CO.	DESUNSOFT CO. ,LTD.

其他补充资料：

（1）发票号码:XY1116

（2）发票日期:2014 年 3 月 31 日

（3）托收项下汇票的日期:2014 年 6 月 6 日

BILL OF EXCHANGE

凭 Drawn Under		不可撤销信用证 Irrevocable	L/C No.
日期 Date	支取	Payable With interest @ %	按 息 付款
号码 No.	汇票金额 Exchange for		南京 Nanjing
	见票 at	日后(本汇票之副本未付)付交 sight of this FIRST of Exchange (Second of Exchange Being unpaid) Pay to the order of	
金额 the sum of			
此致 To			

项目 12 综合业务实训

12.1 电汇方式下的单据制作

12.1.1 实训目标

能够灵活运用电汇付款方式;掌握电汇方式下各种出口单据的操作。

12.1.2 工作任务

阅读资料,完成电汇方式下各种单据的制作。

12.1.3 能力实训

根据销售合同及相关信息制单。

(一) 销售合同书

WUXI SKY TOOL MANUFACTURE CO., LTD

NO 258, ZHONGSHAN ROAD, CHONGAN DISTRICT, WUXI, JIANGSU, CHINA

TEL: 0086-510-82265943　　P/I NO.: 20150326

FAX: 0086-510-82265945　　S/C NO.:20150528

DATE: JUNE 12, 2015

SALES CONTRACT

TO: PY. HJOY LANGGENG.

NO 310 RA SEMARANG INDONESIA.

DEAR SIRS,

WE HEREBY CONFIRM HAVING SOLD TO YOU THE FOLLOWING GOODS ON TERMS AND CONDITIONS AS SPECIFIED BELOWS:

SHIPPING MARKS	DESCRIPTIONS OF GOODS	QTY (PCS)	UNIT PRICE (USD)	AMOUNT (USD)
N/M	TOOLS DOUBLE OPEN END SPANNER 8X12 MM (MTM) 12X14 MM(MTM)	 60 000 80 000	CFR SEMARANG, INDONESIA 0.50 0.40	 30 000.00 32 000.00
TOTAL:		140 000		62 000.00

TOTAL AMOUNT:SAY U.S DOLLAR SIXTY TWO THOUSAND ONLY.

1) PRODUCT FINISHED TIME: JUNE 20, 2015

2) TERMS OF PAYMENT: 30% T/T IN ADVANCE, THE OTHER 70% T/T BEFORE SHIPMENT.

3) PORT OF LOADING: SHANGHAI, CHINA .

4) PORT OF DISCHARGE: SEMRANG, INDONESIA.

5) LATEST DATE OF SHIPMENT: JULY 10, 2015

OUR BANK INFORMATION IS AS FOLLOWS:

BENEFICIARY ADDRESS: NO 258, ZHONGSHAN ROAD, CHONGAN DISTRICT, WUXI, JIANGSU, CHINA

BANK NAME: BANK OF CHINA, WUXI CHONGAN BRANCH.

ACCOUNT NO.: RMB7986624

BANK ADDRESS: NO. 3188 ZHONGSHAN ROAD, CHONGAN DISTRICT, WUXI, JIANGSU, CHINA .

THE BUYER: THE SELLER:

PY. HJOY LANGGENG. WUXI SKY TOOL MANUFACTURE CO., LTD

BOB *LIU YANG*

附加资料:

1) INV NO: TKY068. DATE:JUNE 20.2015

2) PACKING G.W N.W MEAS

DOUBLE OPEN END SPANNER

8X12 MM (MTM) 2KGS/CTN 1.8KGS/CTN 0.02M3/ CTN

PACKED IN 1 CARTON OF 100PCS EACH

12X14 MM(MTM) 2.5KGS/CTN 2.2KGS/CTN 0.01M3/CTN

PACKED IN 1 CARTON OF 100PCS EACH

PACKED IN ONE 20' CONTAINER NO: TEX312214

3) HS CODE: 8204110000

4) CERTIFICATE NO: 500511266

5) FREIGHT: USD 2400.00

6) BILL OF LADING NO: COSCO76598468

7) SHIPMENT DATE: JULY 02, 2015

8) 报检单位登记号:13677688452

9) 报检单编号:T006688563

10) 生产单位注册号:TY1896451

11) 申请单位注册号:SK68114689

12) 发货人账号:046568

13) 外币账号:SMY789124566,

14) 海关编码:8328866457

15) 境内货源地: 无锡

16) 生产厂家:无锡天空玩具制造有限公司(3105226441)

17) 代理报关公司:上海林木报关公司(3122668874)

地址:上海,浦东开发大道,浦前路 66 号,

电话:021 - 62956879

报关员:张华

18) 随附单据:出口通关单(B5461786256)

19) VESSEL NO: COSCO V. 320

请根据以上资料填写下列单据:

COMMERCIAL INVOICE

WUXI SKY TOOL MANUFACTURE CO., LTD

NO 258, ZHONGSHAN ROAD, CHONGAN DISTRICT, WUXI, JIANGSU, CHINA

TO: ______________________

P/I NO: __________

______________________________ INV NO: __________

DATE __________

FROM ______ VIA ______ TO ______ BY ______

MARKS	DESCRIPTION OF GOODS	QUANTITY (SETS)	UNITE PRICE (USD)	AMOUNT (USD)
TOTAL:				
TOTAL AMOUNT: ______________________________				

REMARKS:

1: TERMS OF PAYMENT: ______________

2: TERMS OF TRADE: ______________

WUXI SKY TOOL MANUFACTURE CO., LTD

LIU YANG (STAMP & SIGNATURE)

<table>
<tr><td colspan="2">ISSUER</td><td colspan="5" rowspan="2">装箱单
PACKING LIST</td></tr>
<tr><td colspan="2">TO</td></tr>
<tr><td colspan="2"></td><td colspan="3">INVOICE NO.</td><td colspan="2">DATE</td></tr>
<tr><th>Marks and Numbers</th><th>Number and kind of package Description of goods</th><th>Quantity</th><th>Package</th><th>G.W</th><th>N.W</th><th>Meas.</th></tr>
<tr><td></td><td></td><td></td><td></td><td></td><td></td><td></td></tr>
<tr><td colspan="7">SAY TOTAL:

签章</td></tr>
</table>

出口货物订舱委托书

<table>
<tr><td colspan="3" rowspan="4">托运人 SHIPPER：</td><td colspan="2">合同号：</td></tr>
<tr><td colspan="2">发票号：</td></tr>
<tr><td colspan="2">信用证号：</td></tr>
<tr><td colspan="2">运输方式：</td></tr>
<tr><td colspan="3" rowspan="4">收货人 CONSIGNEE：</td><td colspan="2">启运港：</td></tr>
<tr><td colspan="2">目的港：</td></tr>
<tr><td colspan="2">装运期：</td></tr>
<tr><td colspan="2">可否转运：</td></tr>
<tr><td colspan="3" rowspan="3">通知方 NOTIFY PARTY</td><td colspan="2">可否分批：</td></tr>
<tr><td colspan="2">运费支付方式：</td></tr>
<tr><td colspan="2">正本提单份数：</td></tr>
<tr><td>唛头</td><td>件数</td><td>货名</td><td>毛重 KGS</td><td>体积 CBM</td></tr>
<tr><td></td><td></td><td></td><td></td><td></td></tr>
<tr><td colspan="5">注意事项：</td></tr>
<tr><td colspan="2">受托人：
电话：　　　　传真：
签字盖章：</td><td colspan="3">委托人：
电话：　　　　传真：
签字盖章：</td></tr>
</table>

ORIGINAL

<table>
<tr><td colspan="2">1. Exporter</td><td colspan="3" rowspan="2">Certificate No. 041898699

CERTIFICATE OF ORIGIN
OF
THE PEOPLE'S REPUBLIC OF CHINA</td></tr>
<tr><td colspan="2">2. Consignee</td></tr>
<tr><td colspan="2">3. Means of transport and route</td><td colspan="3" rowspan="2">5. For certifying authority use only</td></tr>
<tr><td colspan="2">4. Country / region of destination</td></tr>
<tr><td>6. Marks and numbers</td><td>7. Number and kind of packages; description of goods</td><td>8. H.S. Code</td><td>9. Quantity</td><td>10. Number and date of invoices</td></tr>
<tr><td colspan="2">11. Declaration by the exporter
The undersigned hereby declares that the above details and statements are correct, that all the goods were produced in China and that they comply with the Rules of Origin of the People's Republic of China.
- - - - - - - - - -
Place and date, signature and stamp of authorized signatory</td><td colspan="3">12. Certification
It is hereby certified that the declaration by the exporter is correct.
- - - - - - - - - -
Place and date, signature and stamp of certifying authority</td></tr>
</table>

报检委托书

检验检疫局：

本委托人郑重声明：保证遵守《中华人民共和国进出口商品检验法》《中华人民共和国进出境动植特检疫法》《中华人民共和国国境卫生检疫法》等有关法律、法规的规定和检验检疫机构制定的各项规章制度。如有违法行为，自愿接受检验检疫机构的处罚并负法律责任。

本委托人所委托受委托人向检验检疫机构提交的“报检申请单”和随附各种单据所列内容是真实无讹的。具体委托情况如下：

本单位将于　　　年　　月间进境/出境如下货物(物品)：

品　　名：　　　　　　　　　　合同号：

数(重)量：　　　　　　　　　　信用证号：

特委托　　　　　　　　　　　　代表本单位办理所有报检事宜，其间发生的一切相关的法律责任由本单位承担。请贵局按有关法律规定予以办理。

委托方名称：　　　　　　　　　被委托方名称

单位地址：　　　　　　　　　　单位地址：

联系人：　　　　　　　　　　　联系人：

联系电话：　　　　　　　　　　联系电话：

(签章)　　　　　　　　　　　　(签章)

年　月　日　　　　　　　　　　年　月　日

注：1. 本委托书仅适用于代理报检。

2. 经双方盖章方为有效。有效期至　　年　月　　日止。

中华人民共和国出入境检验检疫

出境货物报检单

报检单位（加盖公章）：　　　　　　　　　　　　　　　　＊编　　号＿＿＿＿＿＿＿＿

报检单位登记号：　　　联系人：　　　电话：　　　报检日期：　　年　月　日

<table>
<tr><td rowspan="2">发货人</td><td colspan="7">（中文）</td></tr>
<tr><td colspan="7">（外文）</td></tr>
<tr><td rowspan="2">收货人</td><td colspan="7">（中文）</td></tr>
<tr><td colspan="7">（外文）</td></tr>
<tr><td colspan="8">货物名称（中/外文）　H. S. 编码　产地　数/重量　货物总值　包装种类及</td></tr>
<tr><td colspan="8"></td></tr>
<tr><td>运输工具名称号码</td><td colspan="2"></td><td>贸易方式</td><td></td><td>货物存放地点</td><td colspan="2"></td></tr>
<tr><td>合同号</td><td colspan="2"></td><td>信用证号</td><td></td><td>用途</td><td colspan="2"></td></tr>
<tr><td>发货日期</td><td></td><td>输往国家（地区）</td><td></td><td>许可证/审批号</td><td colspan="3"></td></tr>
<tr><td>启运地</td><td></td><td>到达口岸</td><td></td><td>生产单位注册号</td><td colspan="3"></td></tr>
<tr><td>集装箱规格、数量及号码</td><td colspan="7"></td></tr>
<tr><td colspan="2">合同、信用证订立的检验检疫条款或特殊要求</td><td colspan="3">标记及号码</td><td colspan="3">随附单据（划“✓”或补填）</td></tr>
<tr><td colspan="2"></td><td colspan="3"></td><td colspan="2">□合同
□信用证
□发票
□换证凭单
□装箱单
□厂检单</td><td>□包装性能结果单
□许可/审批文件</td></tr>
</table>

<table>
<tr><td colspan="2">需要证单名称（划“✓”或补填）</td><td colspan="2">＊检验检疫费</td></tr>
<tr><td rowspan="3">□品质证书　＿正＿副
□重量证书　＿正＿副
□数量证书　＿正＿副
□兽医卫生证书　＿正＿副
□健康证书　＿正＿副
□卫生证书　＿正＿副
□动物卫生证书　＿正＿副</td><td rowspan="3">□植物检疫证书　＿正＿副
□熏蒸/消毒证书　＿正＿副
□出境货物换证凭单　＿正＿副
□
□
□
□</td><td>总金额
（人民币元）</td><td></td></tr>
<tr><td>计费人</td><td></td></tr>
<tr><td>收费人</td><td></td></tr>
</table>

<table>
<tr><td rowspan="3">报检人郑重声明：
1. 本人被授权报检。
2. 上列填写内容正确属实，货物无伪造或冒用他人的厂名、标志、认证标志，并承担货物质量责任。
签名：＿＿＿＿＿＿</td><td colspan="2">领取证单</td></tr>
<tr><td>日期</td><td></td></tr>
<tr><td>签名</td><td></td></tr>
</table>

注：有“＊”号栏由出入境检验检疫机关填写　　　　　　◆国家出入境检验检疫局制

中华人民共和国海关出口货物报关单

预录入编号：　　　　　　　　海关编号

收发货人	出口口岸	出口日期	申报日期	
生产销售单位	运输方式 江海运输	运输工具名称	提运单号	
申报单位	监管方式	征免性质	备案号	
贸易国(地区)	运抵国(地区)	指运港	境内货源地	
许可证号	成交方式	运费	保费	杂费
合同协议号	件数	包装种类	毛重(公斤)	净重(公斤)
集装箱号	随附单证			
标记唛码及备注				

项号　商品编号　商品名称、规格型号　数量及单位　最终目的国(地区)　单价　总价　币制　征免

特殊关系确认:是　　　　价格影响确认:否　　　　支付特许权使用费确认: 是

录入员　　　录入单位	兹申明对以上内容承担如实申报、依法纳税之法律责任	海关批注及签章
报关人员	申报单位(签章)	

12.2　托收方式下的单据制作

12.2.1　实训目标

能够灵活运用托收付款方式;掌握托收方式下各种出口单据的操作。

12.2.2　工作任务

阅读资料,完成托收方式下各种单据的制作。

12.2.3　能力实训

2015年3月15日,石家庄华燕进出口有限公司与英国的SKY贸易有限公司签订了一份全棉女式夹克出口的销售合同。本次采用托收方式收款。合同内容如下:

SALES CONTRACT

NO.: SJZHY0739　　　　DATE: MAR. 15, 2015

THE SELLER: SHIJIAZHUANG HUAYAN IMPORT & EXPORT CO., LTD.
18 ZHONGHUA STREET, SHIJIAZHUANG, CHINA
THE BUYER: SKY TRADING CO., LTD.
16 JOHNSON STREET, U.K

This Contract is made by and between the Buyer and Seller, whereby the Buyer agree to buy and the Seller agree to sell the under-mentioned commodity according to the terms and conditions stipulated below:

Commodity & specification	Quantity	Unit price	Amount
Ladies Jacket (6204320090) 100% COTTON, As per the confirmed sample of FEB. 10, 2015 and Order no. SKY888	4500pcs	CIF LONDON USD15.00/pc	USD67500.00
TOTAL	4500pcs		USD67500.00
TOTAL CONTRACT VALUE: SAY U. S. DOLLARS SIXTY SEVEN THOUSAND FIVE HUNDRED ONLY.			

Size/color assortment **Unit: piece**

Size	S	M	L	XL	Total
White	250	500	1 000	500	2 250
Red	250 ·	500	1 000	500	2 250
Total	500	1 000	2 000	1 000	4 500

More or less 5% of the quantity and the amount are allowed.

PACKING: 10 pieces of ladies jackets are packed in one export standard carton, solid color and solid size in the same carton. .

MARKS:

Shipping mark includes SKY, S/C no., style no., port of destination and carton no.

Side mark must show the color, the size of carton and pieces per carton.

TIME OF SHIPMENT:

Within 60 days after this Contract.

PORT OF LOADING AND DESTINATION:

From Tianjin, China to London, U.K.

Transshipment is allowed. and partial shipment is prohibited.

INSURANCE: To be effected by the seller for 110% of invoice value covering All Risks as per CIC of PICC dated 01/01/1981.

TERMS OF PAYMENT: By D/P after 30 days sight.

DOCUMENTS:

+ Signed Commercial Invoice in triplicate.
+ Full set of clean on board ocean Bill of Lading marked "freight prepaid" made out to order of shipper blank endorsed notifying the applicant.
+ Insurance Policy in duplicate endorsed in blank.
+ Packing List in triplicate.
+ Certificate of Origin certified by Chamber of Commerce or CCPIT.

INSPECTION:

The certificate of Quality issued by the China Entry-Exit Inspection and Quarantine Bureau shall be taken as the basis of delivery.

CLAIMS:

In case discrepancy on the quality or quantity (weight) of the goods is found by the buyer, after arrival of the goods at the port of destination, the buyer may, within 30 days and 15 days respectively after arrival of the goods at the port of destination, lodge with the seller a claim which should be supported by an Inspection Certificate issued by a public surveyor approved by the seller. The seller shall, on the merits of the claim, either make good the loss sustained by the buyer or reject their claim, it being agreed that the seller shall not be held responsible for any loss or losses due to natural cause failing within the responsibility of Ship-owners of the Underwriters. The seller shall reply to the buyer within 30 days after receipt of the claim.

LATE DELIVERY AND PENALTY:

In case of late delivery, the Buyer shall have the right to cancel this contract, reject the goods and lodge a claim against the Seller. Except for Force Majeure, if late delivery occurs, the Seller must pay a penalty, and the Buyer shall have the right to lodge a claim against the Seller. The rate of penalty is charged at 0.5% for every 7 days, odd days less than 7 days should be counted as 7 days. The total penalty amount will not exceed 5% of the shipment value. The penalty shall be deducted by the paying bank or thc Buycr from the payment.

FORCE MAJEURE:

The seller shall not held responsible if they, owing to Force Majeure cause or causes, fail to make delivery within the time stipulated in the Contract or cannot deliver the goods. However, in such a case, the seller shall inform the buyer immediately by cable and if it is requested by the buyer, the seller shall also deliver to buyer by registered letter, a certificate attesting the existence of such a cause or causes.

ARBITRATION:

All disputes in connection with this contract or the execution thereof shall be settled amicably by negotiation. In case no settlement can be reached, the case shall then be submitted to the China International Economic Trade Arbitration Commission for settlement by arbitration in accordance with the Commission's arbitration rules. The award rendered by the commission shall be final and binding on both parties. The fees for arbitration shall be borne by the losing party unless otherwise awarded.

This contract is made in two original copies and becomes valid after signature, one copy to be held by each party.

Signed by:

THE SELLER:	**THE BUYER:**
SHIJIAZHUANG HUAYAN IMPORT & EXPORT CO., LTD.	SKY TRADING CO., LTD
李红	Johnson Black

请根据以上合同资料制作下列单据：

SHIJIAZHUANG HUAYAN IMPORT AND EXPORT CO., LTD.
18 ZHONGHUA STREET, SHIJIAZHUANG, CHINA
TEL: 0086-311-85876612 FAX: 0086-311-85876612
COMMERCIAL INVOICE

To:		**Invoice No.:**	
		Invoice Date:	
		S/C No.:	
		S/C Date:	

From:		**To:**		
Letter of Credit No.:		**Issued By:**		
Date of Issue:				
Marks and Numbers	**Number and kind of package Description of goods**	**Quantity**	**Unit Price**	**Amount**
	TOTAL:			
SAY TOTAL:				

<table>
<tr><td colspan="8">SHIJIAZHUANG HUAYAN IMPORT AND EXPORT CO., LTD.
18 ZHONGHUA STREET, SHIJIAZHUANG, CHINA
TEL: 0086 - 311 - 85876612　　FAX: 0086 - 311 - 85876612</td></tr>
<tr><td colspan="8">PACKING LIST</td></tr>
<tr><td>To:</td><td colspan="3"></td><td colspan="2">Invoice No.:</td><td colspan="2"></td></tr>
<tr><td></td><td colspan="3"></td><td colspan="2">Invoice Date:</td><td colspan="2"></td></tr>
<tr><td></td><td colspan="3"></td><td colspan="2">S/C No.:</td><td colspan="2"></td></tr>
<tr><td></td><td colspan="3"></td><td colspan="2">S/C Date:</td><td colspan="2"></td></tr>
<tr><td>From:</td><td colspan="3"></td><td colspan="2">To:</td><td colspan="2"></td></tr>
<tr><td>Letter of Credit No.:</td><td></td><td colspan="2">Issued By:</td><td colspan="4"></td></tr>
<tr><td>Date of Issue:</td><td></td><td colspan="2"></td><td colspan="4"></td></tr>
<tr><td>Marks and Numbers</td><td>Number and kind of package
Description of goods</td><td>Quantity</td><td>Package</td><td>G.W</td><td>N.W</td><td colspan="2">Meas.</td></tr>
<tr><td></td><td></td><td></td><td></td><td></td><td></td><td colspan="2"></td></tr>
<tr><td colspan="2">TOTAL:</td><td></td><td></td><td></td><td></td><td colspan="2"></td></tr>
<tr><td>SAY TOTAL:</td><td colspan="7"></td></tr>
<tr><td></td><td colspan="7"></td></tr>
<tr><td></td><td colspan="7"></td></tr>
</table>

出口货物订舱委托书

托运人 SHIPPER:	合同号：
	发票号：
	信用证号：
	运输方式：
收货人 CONSIGNEE:	启运港：
	目的港：
	装运期：
	可否转运：
通知方 NOTIFY PARTY	可否分批：
	运费支付方式：
	正本提单份数：

唛头	件数	货名	毛重 KGS	体积 CBM

注意事项：	
受托人： 电话：　　　　传真： 签字盖章：	委托人： 电话：　　　　传真： 签字盖章：

报检委托书

检验检疫局：

本委托人郑重声明：保证遵守《中华人民共和国进出口商品检验法》《中华人民共和国进出境动植特检疫法》《中华人民共和国国境卫生检疫法》等有关法律、法规的规定和检验检疫机构制定的各项规章制度。如有违法行为，自愿接受检验检疫机构的处罚并负法律责任。

本委托人所委托受委托人向检验检疫机构提交的“报检申请单”和随附各种单据所列内容是真实无讹的。具体委托情况如下：

本单位将于　　　年　　月间进境/出境如下货物(物品)：

品　　名：　　　　　　　　　　　　合同号：

数(重)量：　　　　　　　　　　　　信用证号：

特委托　　　　　　　　　　　　　　代表本单位办理所有报检事宜，其间发生的一切相关的法律责任由本单位承担。请贵局按有关法律规定予以办理。

委托方名称：　　　　　　　　　　　被委托方名称

单位地址：　　　　　　　　　　　　单位地址：

联系人：　　　　　　　　　　　　　联系人：

联系电话：　　　　　　　　　　　　联系电话：

(签章)　　　　　　　　　　　　　　(签章)

年　月　日　　　　　　　　　　　　年　月　日

注：1. 本委托书仅适用于代理报检。

2. 经双方盖章方为有效。有效期至　　年　月　　日止。

中华人民共和国出入境检验检疫

出境货物报检单

报检单位（加盖公章）： ＊编　　号＿＿＿＿＿

报检单位登记号：　联系人：　电话：　报检日期：　年　月　日

发货人	（中文）
	（外文）
收货人	（中文）
	（外文）

货物名称（中/外文）	H. S. 编码	产地	数/重量	货物总值	包装种类及

运输工具名称号码		贸易方式		货物存放地点	
合同号		信用证号		用途	
发货日期		输往国家（地区）		许可证/审批号	
启运地		到达口岸		生产单位注册号	
集装箱规格、数量及号码					

合同、信用证订立的检验检疫条款或特殊要求	标记及号码	随附单据（划“✓”或补填）	
		□合同 □信用证 □发票 □换证凭单 □装箱单 □厂检单	□包装性能结果单 □许可/审批文件

需要证单名称（划“✓”或补填）		＊检验检疫费	
□品质证书　＿正＿副 □重量证书　＿正＿副 □数量证书　＿正＿副 □兽医卫生证书　＿正＿副 □健康证书　＿正＿副 □卫生证书　＿正＿副 □动物卫生证书　＿正＿副	□植物检疫证书　＿正＿副 □熏蒸/消毒证书　＿正＿副 □出境货物换证凭单　＿正＿副 □ □ □ □	总金额 （人民币元）	
		计费人	
		收费人	

报检人郑重声明：	领取证单	
1. 本人被授权报检。 2. 上列填写内容正确属实，货物无伪造或冒用他人的厂名、标志、认证标志，并承担货物质量责任。 签名：＿＿＿＿＿	日期	
	签名	

注：有“＊”号栏由出入境检验检疫机关填写　　◆国家出入境检验检疫局制

<table>
<tr><td colspan="2">1. Exporter</td><td colspan="3" rowspan="2">Certificate No.

CERTIFICATE OF ORIGIN
OF
THE PEOPLE'S REPUBLIC OF CHINA</td></tr>
<tr><td colspan="2">2. Consignee</td></tr>
<tr><td colspan="2">3. Means of transport and route</td><td colspan="3" rowspan="2">5. For certifying authority use only</td></tr>
<tr><td colspan="2">4. Country/region of destination</td></tr>
<tr><td>6. Marks and numbers</td><td>7. Number and kind of packages; description of goods</td><td>8. H.S. Code</td><td>9. Quantity</td><td>10. Number and date of invoices</td></tr>
<tr><td colspan="2">11. Declaration by the exporter
The unsersingned hereby declares that the abore details and statements
Are correct, that all the goods were produced in china and that they comply
With the rules of Origin of the People's Republic of china.</td><td colspan="3">12. Certification
It is hereby certified that the declaration by the exporter is correct</td></tr>
<tr><td colspan="2">Place and date, signature and stamp of authorized signatory</td><td colspan="3">Place and date, signature and stamp of certifying authority</td></tr>
</table>

我单位保证遵守《海关法》和国家有关法规，保证所提供的情况真实、完整、单货相符。否则，愿承担相关法律责任。

本委托书自签字之日起至　年　月　日止。

委托方（盖章）：

法定代表人或其授权签署《代理报关委托书》的人（签字）

年　月　日

委托报关协议

为明确委托报关具体事项和各自责任，双方经平等协商签订协议如下：

委托方		被委托方		
主要货物名称		＊报关单编码	No.	
HS 编码		收到单证日期	年　月　日	
货物总价		收到单证情况	合同□	发票□
进出口日期	年　月　日		加工贸易手册□	许可证件□
提单号			其他	
贸易方式		报关收费	人民币：________元	
原产地/货源地				
其他要求：		承诺说明：		
背面所列通用条款是本协议不可分割的一部分，对本协议的签署构成了对背面通用条款的同意。		背面所列通用条款是本协议不可分割的一部分，对本协议的签署构成了对背面通用条款的同意。		
委托方业务签章： 经办人签章： 联系电话： 年　月　日		被委托方业务签章： 经办报关员签章： 联系电话： 年　月　日		

CCB/L　　（白联：海关留存、黄联：被委托方留存、红联：委托方留存）

中国报关协会监制

中华人民共和国海关出口货物报关单

预录入编号：　　　　　　　　　　　　海关编号：

<table>
<tr><td colspan="2">收发货人</td><td colspan="2">出口口岸</td><td>出口日期</td><td>申报日期</td></tr>
<tr><td colspan="2">生产销售单位</td><td colspan="2">运输方式</td><td>运输工具名称</td><td>提运单号</td></tr>
<tr><td colspan="2">申报单位</td><td colspan="2">监管方式</td><td>征免性质</td><td>备案号</td></tr>
<tr><td>贸易国(地区)</td><td colspan="2">运抵国(地区)</td><td>指运港</td><td colspan="2">境内货源地</td></tr>
<tr><td>许可证号</td><td>成交方式</td><td>运费</td><td>保费</td><td colspan="2">杂费</td></tr>
<tr><td>合同协议号</td><td>件数</td><td>包装种类</td><td>毛重(公斤)</td><td colspan="2">净重(公斤)</td></tr>
<tr><td>集装箱号</td><td colspan="5">随附单证</td></tr>
<tr><td colspan="6">标记唛码及备注</td></tr>
<tr><td colspan="6">项号　商品编号　商品名称、规格型号　数量及单位　最终目的国(地区)　单价　总价　币制　征免</td></tr>
<tr><td colspan="6">1.</td></tr>
<tr><td colspan="6">2.</td></tr>
<tr><td colspan="6">3.</td></tr>
<tr><td colspan="6">4.</td></tr>
<tr><td colspan="6">5.</td></tr>
<tr><td colspan="6">6.</td></tr>
<tr><td colspan="6">7.</td></tr>
<tr><td colspan="6">8.</td></tr>
<tr><td colspan="6">特殊关系确认：　　　　价格影响确认：　　　　支付特许权使用费确认：</td></tr>
<tr><td colspan="2">录入员　　　　录入单位</td><td colspan="2">兹申明对以上内容承担如实申报、依法纳税之法律责任</td><td colspan="2">海关批注及签章</td></tr>
<tr><td colspan="6">报关人员　　　　　　申报单位(签章)
北京××××货运代理有限公司</td></tr>
</table>

石家庄华燕进出口有限公司

SHIJIAZHUANG HUAYAN IMPORT & EXPORT CO., LTD.
18 ZHONGHUA STREET, SHIJIAZHUANG, CHINA

SHIPPING ADVICE

TO: ISSUE DATE: ____________

Dear Sir or Madam:

We are please to advice you that the following mentioned goods has been shipped out. Full details were shown as follows:

____

Invoice Number: ____________

Bill of lading Number: ____________

Ocean Vessel: ____________

Port of Loading: ____________

Date of Shipment: ____________

Port of Destination: ____________

Estimated Date of Arrival: ____________

Containers/Seals Number: ____________

Description of goods: ____________

Shipping Marks: ____________

Quantity: ____________

Gross Weight: ____________

Net Weight: ____________

Total Value: ____________

Thank you for your patronage. We look forward to receiving your valuable repeat orders.

Sincerely yours,

<table>
<tr><td colspan="8">BILL OF EXCHANGE</td></tr>
<tr><td>Drawn under</td><td colspan="4"></td><td>L/C NO.</td><td colspan="2"></td></tr>
<tr><td>Dated</td><td colspan="2"></td><td colspan="2">Payable with interest@</td><td>*****</td><td>%</td><td></td></tr>
<tr><td>NO.</td><td></td><td>Exchange for</td><td></td><td colspan="2">SHIJIAZHUANG</td><td colspan="2">(Date)</td></tr>
<tr><td>At</td><td colspan="3"></td><td colspan="4">Of this FIRST of Exchange (Second of Exchange being</td></tr>
<tr><td colspan="8">Unpaid) Pay to the order of</td></tr>
<tr><td colspan="8"></td></tr>
<tr><td>Value received</td><td colspan="7"></td></tr>
<tr><td>To:</td><td colspan="4"></td><td colspan="3"></td></tr>
<tr><td colspan="8">SHIJIAZHUANG HUAYAN IMPORT & EXPORT CO., LTD.
×××
(Authorized Signature)</td></tr>
</table>

中国银行 BANK OF CHINA

托收委托书
COLLECTION ORDER

致:中国银行河北省分行____________　　　　日期:____________________

托收行(Remitting Bank): BANK OF CHINA **SHANGHAI BRANCH**	代收行(Collecting Bank): 名称: 地址:
委托人(Principal):	付款人(Drawee): 名称: 地址: 电话:

付款交单 D/P (　)承兑交单 D/A (　) 无偿交单 FREE OF PAYMENT(　)	期限/到期日:
发票号码/票据编号:	国外费用承担人: □ 付款人　□ 委托人
金额:	国内费用承担人: □ 付款人　□ 委托人

单据种类	汇票	发票	提单	空运单	保险单	装箱单	重量单	产地证	FORMA	检验证	公司证明	船证明
份数												

特别指示：

1. 邮寄方式：□ 快邮 □ 普邮
2. 托收如遇拒付，是否须代收行作成拒绝证书(PROTEST)：□ 是 □ 否
3. 货物抵港时是否代办存仓保险：□ 是 □ 否
4. 如付款人拒付费用及/或利息，是否可以放弃：□ 是 □ 否
5. ______________________________
6. ______________________________

付款指示： 核销单编号：______________

请将收汇款原币( )人民币( )划入我司下列账上：

开户行：______________________ 账号：______________________

联系人姓名：______________

电话：______________ 传真：______________ 公司签章

12.3 信用证方式下的单据制作

12.3.1 实训目标

能够灵活运用信用证付款方式；掌握信用证方式下各种出口单据的操作。

12.3.2 工作任务

阅读资料，完成信用证方式下各种单据的制作。

12.3.3 能力实训

根据已知资料缮制商业发票、装箱单、装运通知、受益人证明、报关单、产地证、提单和汇票。

ISSUE OF DOCUMENTARY CREDIT

27: SEQUENCE OF TOATL:1/1

40A: FORM OF DOC. CREDIT: IRREVOCABLE

20: DOC CREDIT NUMBER: LKMU4567

31C: DATE OF ISSUE: 150806

40E: APPLICABLE RULES: UCP LATEST VERSION

31D: DATE AND PLACE OF EXPIRY: DATE 151230 PLACE IN CHINA.

51D: APPLICANT BANK: HSBC BANK ,JAPAN

NO 66FLOWER GRADEN, OSAKA, JAPAN

50: APPLICANT: ADE OSAKA SHOES TRADE CO., LTD

NO 18, KINKI ROAD, OSAK, JAPAN.

59: BENEFICIARY: SHANGHAI FGB IMPORT AND EXPORT TRADING. CO., LTD

NO 16, NANJIN ROAD, SHANGHAI, CHINA.

32B: AMOUNT: CURRENCY USD AMOUNT 249900.00

41A: AVAILABLE WITH…BY ANY BANK IN CHINA BY NEGOTIATION

42C: DRAFTS AT SIGHT FOR FULL INVOICE VALUE

42A: DEAWEE: ISSUING BANK

43P: PARTIAL SHIPMENT: NOT ALLOWED

43T: TRANSSHIPMENT: NOT ALLOWED

44E: PORT OF LOADING: SHANGHAI, CHINA

44F: PORT OF DISCHARGE: OSAKA, JAPAN

44C: LATEST DATE OF SHIPMENT: 151015

45A: DESCRIPTION OF GOODS:

+450SETS OF WOMEN'S 100% LEATHER SHOES &350SETS OF MEN'S 100% LEATHER SHOES;

CFR OSAKA, JAPAN, COUNTRY OF ORIGINAL P.R.CHINA.

46A: DOCUMENTS REQUIRED

1, SIGNED COMMERCIAL INVOICES &PACKING LIST IN 4 ORIGINAL AND 4 COPIES DATED THE SAME DATE AS THAT OF L/C ISSUANCE DATE INDICATING COUNTRY OF ORIGIN OF THE GOODS AND CERTIFIED TO BE TRUE AND CORRECT, INDICATING CONTRACT NO. FBG4669/7 AND L/C NO;

2, NEUTRAL PACKING LIST INDICATING QUANTITY, N.W. AND G.W OF EACH PACKAGE. TTL QUANTITY, N.W AND G.W, AND PACKING CONDITIONS AS REQUIRED BY L/C.

3, ONE ORIGINAL OF BENEFICIARY'S CERTIFIED THAT COPY OF SHIPPING ADVICE TO THE APPLICANT ADVISING MERCHANDISE, SHIPMENT DATE, GROSS INVOICE VALUE, NAME AND VOYAGE OF VESSEL, CARRIIER' S NAME, PORT OF LOADING AND PORT OF DISCHARGE IMMEDIATELY ON THE DATE OF SHIPMENT

4, FULL SET OF CLEAN ON BOARD OCEAN BILLS OF LADING MADE OUT TO THE ORDER OF HSBC BANK, JAPAN. NO 66 FLOWER GRADEN, OSAKA, JAPAN. BLANK ENDORSED, MARKED FREIGHT PREPAID AND NOTIFY THE APPLICANT;

5, ORIGINAL CERTIFICATE FOR 1 ORIGINAL 3 COPYS WITH THE WHOLE SHIPMENT DOCUMENTS.

47A: ADDITIONAL CODITIONS

1, ALL DOCUMENTS MUST INDICATE SHIPPING MARKS. .

2, ALL DOCUMENTS MUST BE MADE OUT IN THE NAME OF THE APPLICAT UNLESS OTHERWISE STIPULICATED BY THE L/C;

3: ALL SHIPMENT DOCUMENTS MUST SHOW L/C NO AND DATE OF ISSUE.

71B: CHARGES: ALL CHARGES ARE TO BE BORN BY BENEFICIARY.

48: PERIOD FOR PRESENTATION : WITHIN 15 DAYS AFTER THE DATE OF SHIPMENT, BUT WITHIN THE VALIDITY OF THIS CREDIT .

49: CONFIRMANTION INSTRUCTION: WITHOUT.

附加资料:

贸易方式为:一般贸易

SHIPPING MARKS: ADE OSAKA SHOES
FBG4669/7
SAID
C/NO 1 - UP

发票号码: TYD151015

装箱单日期:2015.09.15

提单号码:COSCO2664689

受益人授权签字:常杰

WOMEN'S:

N/W:15KGS/CTN

G.W: 20KGS/CTN

MEN'S:

20 KGS/CTN;

24 KGS/CTN

MEAS: WOMEN'S SHOSE CTN: 60 * 55 * 45 CM/CTN

MEN'S SHOSE CTN: 75 * 65 * 50 CM/CTN

船名:COSCO V.520

装船日期:2015.10.08

单价:WOMEN'S LEATHER SHOES: USD 322/SET.

MEN'S LEATHER SHOES: USD 300/ SET.

WOMEN'S LEATHER SHOES: 10 SETS/CARTON. (CTN NO.: 1 - 45 CTNS)

MEN'S LEATHER SHOES: 7 SETS/CARTON. (CTN NO: 46 - 95 CTNS)

柜型以及柜号和封条号:1 * 20GP, TRIU0661600 & COCSO45689

牌子:ADE.

商业发票

COMMERCIAL INVOICE

SHANGHAI FGB IMPORT AND EXPORT TRADING. CO., LTD

NO 16, NANJIN ROAD, SHANGHAI, CHINA.

TO: ________

NO: ________　　INV NO: ________

DATE ________

FROM ____________　VIA ____________　TO ____________　BY ____________

MARKS	DESCRIPTION OF GOODS	QUANTITY (SETS)	UNITE PRICE (USD)	AMOUNT (USD)
TOTAL:				
TOTAL AMOUNT: ____________________				

REMARKS:

1: TERMS OF PAYMENT: ____________________

2: TERMS OF TRADE: ____________________

SHANGHAI FGB IMPORT AND EXPORT TRADING. CO., LTD

CHANGJIE　(STAMP & SIGNATURE)

<table>
<tr><td colspan="2">ISSUER</td><td colspan="6" rowspan="2">装箱单
PACKING LIST</td></tr>
<tr><td colspan="2">TO</td></tr>
<tr><td colspan="2"></td><td colspan="3">INVOICE NO.</td><td colspan="3">DATE</td></tr>
<tr><td>Marks and Numbers</td><td>Number and kind of package Description of goods</td><td>Quantity</td><td>Package</td><td>G. W</td><td>N. W</td><td>Meas.</td><td></td></tr>
<tr><td></td><td></td><td></td><td></td><td></td><td></td><td></td><td></td></tr>
<tr><td colspan="8">SAY TOTAL:

签章</td></tr>
</table>

<table>
<tr><td colspan="2">1. SHIPPER</td><td colspan="3" rowspan="5">B/L NO.

COSCO
中国远洋运输(集团)总公司
CHINA OCEAN SHIPPING (GROUP) CO.
ORIGINAL

ORIGINAL
Combined Transport Bill of Lading</td></tr>
<tr><td colspan="2">2. CONSIGNEE</td></tr>
<tr><td colspan="2">3. NOTIFY PARTY</td></tr>
<tr><td>4. PR-CARRIAGE BY</td><td>5. PLACE OF RECEIPT</td></tr>
<tr><td>6. OCEAN VESSEL VOY. NO.</td><td>7. PORT OF LOADING</td></tr>
<tr><td>8. PORT OF DISCHARGE</td><td>9. PLACE OF DELIVERY</td><td colspan="3">10. FINAL DESTINATION FOR THE MERCHANT'S REFERENCE</td></tr>
</table>

11. MARKS	12. NOS. & KINDS OF PKGS	13. DESCRIPTION OF GOODS	14. G.W. (KG)	15. MEAS(M^3)

<table>
<tr><td colspan="6">16. TOTAL NUMBER OF CONTAINERS OR PACKAGES(IN WORDS)</td></tr>
<tr><td>FREIGHT & CHARGES</td><td>REVENUE TONS</td><td>RATE</td><td>PER</td><td>17. PREPAID</td><td>COLLECT</td></tr>
<tr><td>PREPAID AT</td><td>PAYABLE AT</td><td colspan="4">18. PLACE AND DATE OF ISSUE</td></tr>
<tr><td>TOTAL PREPAID</td><td>19. NUMBER OF ORIGINAL B(S)L</td><td colspan="4" rowspan="2">22. SIGNED FOR THE CARRIER

中国远洋运输(集团)总公司
CHINA OCEAN SHIPPING (GROUP) CO.
×××</td></tr>
<tr><td>20. DATE</td><td>21. LOADING ON BOARD THE VESSEL BY</td></tr>
</table>

ORIGINAL

<table>
<tr><td colspan="3">1. Goods consigned from (Exporter's business name, address, country)</td><td colspan="3" rowspan="2">Reference No:
GENERALIZED SYSTEM OF PREFERENCES
CERTIFICATE OF ORIGIN
(Combined declaration and certificate)
FORM A
Issued in THE PEOPLE'S REPUBLIC OF CHINA
(country)
See Notes, overleaf</td></tr>
<tr><td colspan="3">2. Goods consigned to(Consignee's name, address, country)</td></tr>
<tr><td colspan="3">3. Means of transport and route(as far as known)</td><td colspan="3">4. For official use</td></tr>
<tr><td>7. Item Number</td><td>8. Marks and numbers of packages</td><td>9. Nunber and kind of packages; description of goods</td><td>10. Orign criterion(see Notes verleaf)</td><td>11. Gross weight or other quantity</td><td>12. Number and date of invoices</td></tr>
<tr><td colspan="3">13. Certification
It is hereby certified, on the basis of control carried out, that the declaration by the exporter is correct.

Place and date, signature and stamp of certifying authority</td><td colspan="3">14. Declaration by the exporter
The undersigned hereby declares that the above details and statements are correct; that all the goods were produced in
CHINA
(country)
and that they comply with the origin requirements specified
for those goods in the Generalized System of Preferences
for goods exported to
(importing country)
(15)
Place and date, signature of authorized signatory</td></tr>
</table>

中华人民共和国海关出口货物报关单

预录入编号：　　　　　　　　　　　　　　海关编号：

收发货人	出口口岸	出口日期	申报日期	
生产销售单位	运输方式	运输工具名称	提运单号	
申报单位	监管方式	征免性质	备案号	
贸易国(地区)	运抵国(地区)	指运港	境内货源地	
许可证号	成交方式	运费	保费	杂费
合同协议号	件数	包装种类	毛重(公斤)	净重(公斤)
集装箱号	随附单证			
标记唛码及备注				

项号	商品编号	商品名称、规格型号	数量及单位	最终目的国(地区)	单价	总价	币制	征免
1.								
2.								
3.								
4.								

特殊关系确认：　　　　　　价格影响确认：　　　　　　支付特许权使用费确认：

录入员　　　　录入单位	兹申明对以上内容承担如实申报、依法纳税之法律责任	海关批注及签章
报关人员　　　　　　申报单位(签章)		

SHIPPING ADVICE

<table>
<tr><td rowspan="2">EXPORTER</td><td colspan="2">INV NO:</td></tr>
<tr><td>C/T NO</td><td>L/C NO AND ISSUE DATE:</td></tr>
<tr><td rowspan="2">IMPORTER</td><td colspan="2">BILL OF LADING NO. :</td></tr>
<tr><td colspan="2">INVOICE VALUE:</td></tr>
<tr><td>TRANSPORT DETAILS:</td><td colspan="2">PORT AND DATE OF SHIPMENT</td></tr>
<tr><td>SHIPPING MARKS & CONTAINER NO.</td><td colspan="2">NUMBER AND KIND OF PACKAGES ;COMMODITY NO; .
COMMODITY DESCRIPTION.</td></tr>
<tr><td></td><td colspan="2">EXPORT STAMP AND SIGNATURE.</td></tr>
</table>

BILL OF EXCHANGE

NO. ______________________ Date: ______________________

FOR

At ______________________ Sight of THIS SECOND BILL of EXCHANGE

(First of the tenor and date being unpaid)

Pay to

BANK OF CHINA, or order the

ZHEJIANG BRANCH, sum of

HANGZHOU.

Drawn under ______________________

L/C NO. ______________________ Dated ______________________

TO.

____

____

签章

附录 《跟单信用证统一惯例(UCP600)》

Article 1 Application of UCP

第一条 统一惯例的适用范围

The Uniform Customs and Practice for Documentary Credits, 2007 Revision, ICC Publication no. 600 (“UCP”) are rules that apply to any documentary credit (“credit”) (including, to the extent to which they may be applicable, any standby letter of credit) when the text of the credit expressly indicates that it is subject to these rules. They are binding on all parties thereto unless expressly modified or excluded by the credit.

跟单信用证统一惯例,2007 年修订本,国际商会第 600 号出版物,适用于所有在正文中标明按本惯例办理的跟单信用证(包括本惯例适用范围内的备用信用证)。除非信用证中另有规定,本惯例对一切有关当事人均具有约束力。

Article 2 Definitions

第二条 定义

For the purpose of these rules:

就本惯例而言:

Advising bank means the bank that advises the credit at the request of the issuing bank.

通知行意指应开证行要求通知信用证的银行。

Applicant means the party on whose request the credit is issued.

申请人意指发出开立信用证申请的一方。

Banking day means a day on which a bank is regularly open at the place at which an act subject to these rules is to be performed.

银行日意指银行在其营业地正常营业,按照本惯例行事的行为得以在银行履行的日子。

Beneficiary means the party in whose favors a credit is issued.

受益人意指信用证中受益的一方。

Complying presentation means a presentation that is in accordance with the terms and conditions of the credit, the applicable provisions of these rules and international standard banking practice.

相符提示意指与信用证中的条款及条件、本惯例中所适用的规定及国际标准银行实务相一致的提示。

Confirmation means a definite undertaking of the confirming bank, in addition to that of the issuing bank, to honor or negotiate a complying presentation.

保兑意指保兑行在开证行之外对于相符提示做出兑付或议付的确定承诺。

Confirming bank means the bank that adds its confirmation to a credit upon the issuing bank's authorization or request.

保兑行意指应开证行的授权或请求对信用证加具保兑的银行。

Credit means any arrangement, however named or described, that is irrevocable and thereby constitutes a definite undertaking of the issuing bank to honor a complying presentation.

信用证意指一项约定,无论其如何命名或描述,该约定不可撤销并因此构成开证行对于相符提示予以兑付的确定承诺。

Honor means:

兑付意指:

a. To pay at sight if the credit is available by sight payment.

a. 对于即期付款信用证即期付款。

b. To incur a deferred payment undertaking and pay at maturity if the credit is available by deferred payment.

b. 对于延期付款信用证发出延期付款承诺并到期付款。

c. To accept a bill of exchange ("draft") drawn by the beneficiary and pay at maturity if the credit is available by acceptance.

c. 对于承兑信用证承兑由受益人出具的汇票并到期付款。

Issuing bank means the bank that issues a credit at the request of an applicant or on its own behalf.

开证行意指应申请人要求或代表其自身开立信用证的银行。

Negotiation means the purchase by the nominated bank of drafts (drawn on a bank other than the nominated bank) and/or documents under a complying presentation, by advancing or agreeing to advance funds to the beneficiary on or before the banking day on which reimbursement is due to(to be paid the nominated bank).

议付意指被指定银行在其应获得偿付的银行日或在此之前,通过向受益人预付或者同意向受益人预付款项的方式购买相符提示项下的汇票(汇票付款人为被指定银行以外的银行)及/或单据。

Nominated bank means the bank with which the credit is available or any bank in the case of a credit available with any bank.

被指定银行意指有权使用信用证的银行,对于可供任何银行使用的信用证而言,任何银行均为被指定银行。

Presentation means either the delivery of documents under a credit to the issuing bank or nominated bank or the documents so delivered.

提示意指信用证项下单据被提交至开证行或被指定银行,抑或按此方式提交的单据。

Presenter means a beneficiary, bank or other party that makes a presentation.

提示人意指做出提示的受益人、银行或其他一方。

Article 3 Interpretations

第三条 释义

For the purpose of these rules:

就本惯例而言:

Where applicable, words in the singular include the plural and in the plural include the singular.

在适用的条款中,词汇的单复数同义。

A credit is irrevocable even if there is no indication to that effect.

信用证是不可撤销的,即使信用证中对此未做指示也是如此。

A document may be signed by handwriting, facsimile signature, perforated signature, stamp, symbol or any other mechanical or electronic method of authentication.

单据可以通过手签、签样印制、穿孔签字、盖章、符号表示的方式签署,也可以通过其他任何机械或电子证实的方法签署。

A requirement for a document to be legalized, visaed, certified or similar will be satisfied by any signature, mark, stamp or label on the document which appears to satisfy that requirement.

当信用证含有要求使单据合法、签证、证实或对单据有类似要求的条件时,这些条件可由在单据上签字、标注、盖章或标签来满足,只要单据表面已满足上述条件即可。

Branches of a bank in different countries are considered to be separate banks.

一家银行在不同国家设立的分支机构均视为另一家银行。

Terms such as "first class" "well known" "qualified" "independent" "official" "competent" or "local" used to describe the issuer of a document allow any issuer except the beneficiary to issue that document.

诸如"第一流""著名""合格""独立""正式""有资格""当地"等用语用于描述单据出单人的身份时,单据的出单人可以是除受益人以外的任何人 。

Unless required to be used in a document, words such as "prompt" "immediately" or "as soon as possible" will be disregarded.

除非确需在单据中使用,银行对诸如"迅速""立即""尽快"之类词语将不予置理。

The expression "on or about" or similar will be interpreted as a stipulation that an event is to occur during a period of five calendar days before until five calendar days after the specified date, both start and end dates included.

"于或约于"或类似措辞将被理解为一项约定,按此约定,某项事件将在所述日期前后各 5 天内发生,起讫日均包括在内。

The words "to" "unti" "till" "from" and "between" when used to determine a period of shipment include the date or dates mentioned, and the words "before" and "after" exclude the date mentioned.

词语"×月×日止""至×月×日""直至×月×日""从×月×日"及"在×月×日至×月×日之间"用于确定装运期限时,包括所述日期。词语"×月×日之前"及"×月×日之后"不包括所述日期。

The words "from" and "after" when used to determine a maturity date exclude the date mentioned.

词语"从×月×日"以及"×月×日之后"用于确定到期日时不包括所述日期。

The terms "first half" and "second half" of a month shall be construed respectively as the 1st to the 15th and the 16th to the last day of the month, all dates inclusive.

术语"上半月"和"下半月"应分别理解为自每月"1 日至 15 日"和"16 日至月末最后一天",包括起讫日期。

The terms "beginning" "middle" and "end" of a month shall be construed respectively as the 1st to the 10th, the 11th to the 20th and the 21st to the last day of the month, all dates inclusive.

术语"月初""月中"和"月末"应分别理解为每月 1 日至 10 日、11 日至 20 日和 21 日至月末最后一天,包括起讫日期。

Article 4 Credits v. Contracts

第四条 信用证与合同

a. A credit by its nature is a separate transaction from the sale or other contract on which it may be based. Banks are in no way concerned with or bound by such contract, even if any reference whatsoever to it is included in the credit. Consequently, the undertaking of a bank to honor, to negotiate or to fulfill any other obligation under the credit is not subject to claims or defenses by the applicant resulting from its relationships with the issuing bank or the beneficiary.

a. 就性质而言,信用证与可能作为其依据的销售合同或其他合同,是相互独立的交易。即使信用证中提及该合同,银行亦与该合同完全无关,且不受其约束。因此,一家银行做出兑付、议付或履行信用证项下其他义务的承诺,并不受申请人与开证行之间或与受益人之间在已有关系下产生的索偿或抗辩的制约。

A beneficiary can in no case avail itself of the contractual relationships existing between banks or between the applicant and the issuing bank.

受益人在任何情况下,不得利用银行之间或申请人与开证行之间的契约关系。

b. An issuing bank should discourage any attempt by the applicant to include, as an integral part of the credit, copies of the underlying contract, preformed invoice and the like.

b. 开证行应劝阻申请人将基础合同、形式发票或其他类似文件的副本作为信用证整体组成部分的做法。

Article 5 Documents v. Goods, Services or Performance

第五条 单据与货物/服务/行为

Banks deal with documents and not with goods, services or performance to which the documents may relate.

银行处理的是单据,而不是单据所涉及的货物、服务或其他行为。

Article 6 Availability, Expiry Date and Place for Presentation

第六条 有效性、有效期限及提示地点

a. A credit must state the bank with which it is available or whether it is available with any bank. A credit available with a nominated bank is also available with the issuing bank.

a. 信用证必须规定可以有效使用信用证的银行，或者信用证是否对任何银行均为有效。对被指定银行有效的信用证同样也对开证行有效。

b. A credit must state whether it is available by sight payment, deferred payment, acceptance or negotiation.

b. 信用证必须规定它是否适用于即期付款、延期付款、承兑抑或议付。

c. A credit must not be issued available by a draft drawn on the applicant.

c. 不得开立包含有以申请人为汇票付款人条款的信用证。

d. i. A credit must state an expiry date for presentation. An expiry date stated for honour or negotiation will be deemed to be an expiry date for presentation.

d. i. 信用证必须规定提示单据的有效期限。规定的用于兑付或者议付的有效期限将被认为是提示单据的有效期限。

ii. The place of the bank with which the credit is available is the place for presentation. The place for presentation under a credit available with any bank is that of any bank. A place for presentation other than that of the issuing bank is in addition to the place of the issuing bank.

ii. 可以有效使用信用证的银行所在的地点是提示单据的地点。对任何银行均为有效的信用证项下单据提示的地点是任何银行所在的地点。不同于开证行地点的提示单据的地点是开证行地点之外提交单据的地点。

e. Except as provided in sub-article 29 (a), a presentation by or on behalf of the beneficiary must be made on or before the expiry date.

e. 除非如第二十九条(a)款中规定，由受益人或代表受益人提示的单据必须在到期日当日或在此之前提交。

Article 7　Issuing Bank Undertaking

第七条　开证行的承诺

a. Provided that the stipulated documents are presented to the nominated bank or to the issuing bank and that they constitute a complying presentation, the issuing bank must honor if the credit is available by:

a. 倘若规定的单据被提交至被指定银行或开证行并构成相符提示，开证行必须按下述信用证所适用的情形予以兑付：

i. Sight payment, deferred payment or acceptance with the issuing bank;

i. 由开证行即期付款、延期付款或者承兑；

ii. Sight payment with a nominated bank and that nominated bank does not pay;

ii. 由被指定银行即期付款而该被指定银行未予付款；

iii. Deferred payment with a nominated bank and that nominated bank does not incur its deferred payment undertaking or, having incurred its deferred payment undertaking, does not pay at maturity;

iii. 由被指定银行延期付款而该被指定银行未承担其延期付款承诺，或者虽已承担延期付款承诺但到期未予付款；

iv. acceptance with a nominated bank and that nominated bank does not accept a draft drawn on it or, having accepted a draft drawn on it, does not pay at maturity;

iv. 由被指定银行承兑而该被指定银行未予承兑以其为付款人的汇票,或者虽已承兑以其为付款人的汇票但到期未予付款;

v. negotiation with a nominated bank and that nominated bank does not negotiate.

v. 由被指定银行议付而该被指定银行未予议付。

b. An issuing bank is irrevocably bound to honor as of the time it issues the credit.

b. 自信用证开立之时起,开证行即不可撤销地受到兑付责任的约束。

c. An issuing bank undertakes to reimburse a nominated bank that has honored or negotiated a complying presentation and forwarded the documents to the issuing bank. Reimbursement for the amount of a complying presentation under a credit available by acceptance or deferred payment is due at maturity, whether or not the nominated bank prepaid or purchased before maturity. An issuing bank's undertaking to reimburse a nominated bank is independent of the issuing bank's undertaking to the beneficiary.

c. 开证行保证向对于相符提示已经予以兑付或者议付并将单据寄往开证行的被指定银行进行偿付。无论被指定银行是否于到期日前已经对相符提示予以预付或者购买,对于承兑或延期付款信用证项下相符提示的金额的偿付于到期日进行。开证行偿付被指定银行的承诺独立于开证行对受益人的承诺。

Article 8 Confirming Bank Undertaking

第八条 保兑行的承诺

a. Provided that the stipulated documents are presented to the confirming bank or to any other nominated bank and that they constitute a complying presentation, the confirming bank must:

a. 倘若规定的单据被提交至保兑行或者任何其他被指定银行并构成相符提示,保兑行必须:

i. Honor, if the credit is available by:

i. 兑付,如果信用证适用于:

a) Sight payment, deferred payment or acceptance with the confirming bank;

a) 由保兑行即期付款、延期付款或者承兑;

b) Sight payment with another nominated bank and that nominated bank does not pay;

b) 由另一家被指定银行即期付款而该被指定银行未予付款;

c) Deferred payment with another nominated bank and that nominated bank does not incur its deferred payment undertaking or, having incurred its deferred payment undertaking, does not pay at maturity;

c) 由另一家被指定银行延期付款而该被指定银行未承担其延期付款承诺,或者虽已承担延期付款承诺但到期未予付款;

d) Acceptance with another nominated bank and that nominated bank does not accept a draft drawn on it or, having accepted a draft drawn on it, does not pay at maturity;

d) 由另一家被指定银行承兑而该被指定银行未予承兑以其为付款人的汇票,或者虽已承兑以其为付款人的汇票但到期未予付款；

e) Negotiation with another nominated bank and that nominated bank does not negotiate.

e）由另一家被指定银行议付而该被指定银行未予议付。

ii. Negotiate, without recourse 无追索权, if the credit is available by negotiation with the confirming bank.

ii. 若信用证由保兑行议付,无追索权的议付。

b. A confirming bank is irrevocably bound to honor or negotiate as of the time it adds its confirmation to the credit.

b. 自为信用证加具保兑之时起,保兑行即不可撤销地受到兑付或者议负责任的约束。

c. A confirming bank undertakes to reimburse another nominated bank that has honored or negotiated a complying presentation and forwarded the documents to the confirming bank. Reimbursement for the amount of a complying presentation under a credit available by acceptance or deferred payment is due at maturity, whether or not another nominated bank prepaid or purchased before maturity. A confirming bank's undertaking to reimburse another nominated bank is independent of the confirming bank's undertaking to the beneficiary.

c. 保兑行保证向对于相符提示已经予以兑付或者议付并将单据寄往开证行的另一家被指定银行进行偿付。无论另一家被指定银行是否于到期日前已经对相符提示予以预付或者购买，对于承兑或延期付款信用证项下相符提示的金额的偿付于到期日进行。保兑行偿付另一家被指定银行的承诺独立于保兑行对于受益人的承诺。

d. If a bank is authorized or requested by the issuing bank to confirm a credit but is not prepared to do so, it must inform the issuing bank without delay and may advise the credit without confirmation.

d. 如开证行授权或要求另一家银行对信用证加具保兑,而该银行不准备照办时,它必须不延误地告知开证行并仍可通知此份未经加具保兑的信用证。

Article 9 Advising of Credits and Amendments

第九条 信用证及修改的通知

a. A credit and any amendment may be advised to a beneficiary through an advising bank. An advising bank that is not a confirming bank advises the credit and any amendment without any undertaking tohonor or negotiate.

a. 信用证及其修改可以通过通知行通知受益人。除非已对信用证加具保兑,通知行通知信用证不构成兑付或议付的承诺。

b. By advising the credit or amendment, the advising bank signifies that it has satisfied itself as to the apparent authenticity of the credit or amendment and that the advice accurately reflects the terms and conditions of the credit or amendment received.

b. 通过通知信用证或修改,通知行即表明其认为信用证或修改的表面真实性得到满足,且通知准确地反映了所收到的信用证或修改的条款及条件。

c. An advising bank may utilize the services of another bank ("second advising bank") to advise the credit and any amendment to the beneficiary. By advising the credit or amendment, the second advising bank signifies that it has satisfied itself as to the apparent authenticity of the advice it has received and that the advice accurately reflects the terms and conditions of the credit or amendment received.

c. 通知行可以利用另一家银行的服务("第二通知行")向受益人通知信用证及其修改。通过通知信用证或修改,第二通知行即表明其认为所收到的通知的表面真实性得到满足,且通知准确地反映了所收到的信用证或修改的条款及条件。

d. A bank utilizing the services of an advising bank or second advising bank to advise a credit must use the same bank to advise any amendment thereto.

d. 如一家银行利用另一家通知行或第二通知行的服务将信用证通知给受益人,它也必须利用同一家银行的服务通知修改书。

e. If a bank is requested to advise a credit or amendment but elects not to do so, it must so inform, without delay, the bank from which the credit, amendment or advice has been received.

e. 如果一家银行被要求通知信用证或修改但决定不予通知,它必须不延误通知向其发送信用证、修改或通知的银行。

f. If a bank is requested to advise a credit or amendment but cannot satisfy itself as to the apparent authenticity of the credit, the amendment or the advice, it must so inform, without delay, the bank from which the instructions appear to have been received. If the advising bank or second advising bank elects nonetheless to advise the credit or amendment, it must inform the beneficiary or second advising bank that it has not been able to satisfy itself as to the apparent authenticity of the credit, the amendment or the advice.

f. 如果一家被要求通知信用证或修改,但不能确定信用证、修改或通知的表面真实性,就必须不延误地告知向其发出该指示的银行。如果通知行或第二通知行仍决定通知信用证或修改,则必须告知受益人或第二通知行其未能核实信用证、修改或通知的表面真实性。

Article 10 Amendments

第十条 修改

a. Except as otherwise provided by article 38, a credit can neither be amended nor cancelled without the agreement of the issuing bank, the confirming bank, if any, and the beneficiary.

a. 除本惯例第三十八条另有规定外,凡未经开证行、保兑行(如有)以及受益人同意,信用证既不能修改也不能撤销。

b. An issuing bank is irrevocably bound by an amendment as of the time it issues the amendment. A confirming bank may extend its confirmation to an amendment and will be irrevocably bound as of the time it advises the amendment. A confirming bank may, however, choose to advise an amendment without extending its confirmation and, if so, it must inform the issuing bank without delay and inform the beneficiary in its advice.

b. 自发出信用证修改书之时起,开证行就不可撤销地受其发出修改的约束。保兑行可将其保兑承诺扩展至修改内容，且自其通知该修改之时起，即不可撤销地受到该修改的约束。然而，保兑行可选择仅将修改通知受益人而不对其加具保兑，但必须不延误地将此情况通知开证行和受益人。

c. The terms and conditions of the original credit (or a credit incorporating previously accepted amendments) will remain in force for the beneficiary until the beneficiary communicates its acceptance of the amendment to the bank that advised such amendment. The beneficiary should give notification of acceptance or rejection of an amendment. If the beneficiary fails to give such notification, a presentation that complies with the credit and to any not yet accepted amendment will be deemed to be notification of acceptance by the beneficiary of such amendment. As of that moment the credit will be amended.

c. 在受益人向通知修改的银行表示接受该修改内容之前，原信用证(或包含先前已被接受修改的信用证)的条款和条件对受益人仍然有效。受益人应发出接受或拒绝接受修改的通知。如受益人未提供上述通知，当其提交至被指定银行或开证行的单据与信用证以及尚未表示接受的修改的要求一致时，则该事实即视为受益人已做出接受修改的通知，并从此时起，该信用证已被修改。

d. A bank that advises an amendment should inform the bank from which it received the amendment of any notification of acceptance or rejection.

d. 通知修改的银行应当通知向其发出修改书的银行任何有关接受或拒绝接受修改的通知。

e. Partial acceptance of an amendment is not allowed and will be deemed to be notification of rejection of the amendment.

e. 不允许部分接受修改，部分接受修改将被视为拒绝接受修改的通知。

f. A provision in an amendment to the effect that the amendment shall enter into force unless rejected by the beneficiary within a certain time shall be disregarded.

f. 修改书中做出的除非受益人在某一时间内拒绝接受修改，否则修改将开始生效的条款将被不予置理。

Article 11 Teletransmitted and Pre-Advised Credits and Amendments

第十一条 电讯传递与预先通知的信用证和修改

a. An authenticated teletransmission of a credit or amendment will be deemed to be the operative credit or amendment, and any subsequent mail confirmation shall be disregarded.

a. 经证实的信用证或修改的电讯文件将被视为有效的信用证或修改，任何随后的邮寄证实书将被不予置理。

If a teletransmission states "full details to follow" (or words of similar effect), or states that the mail confirmation is to be the operative credit or amendment, and then the teletransmission will not be deemed to be the operative credit or amendment. The issuing bank must then issue the operative credit or amendment without delay in terms not inconsistent with the teletransmission.

若该电讯文件声明"详情后告"(或类似词语)或声明随后寄出的邮寄证实书将是有效的

信用证或修改,则该电讯文件将被视为无效的信用证或修改。开证行必须随即不延误地开出有效的信用证或修改,且条款不能与电讯文件相矛盾。

b. A preliminary advice of the issuance of a credit or amendment ("pre-advice") shall only be sent if the issuing bank is prepared to issue the operative credit or amendment. An issuing bank that sends a pre-advice is irrevocably committed to issue the operative credit or amendment, without delay, in terms not inconsistent with the pre-advice.

b. 只有准备开立有效信用证或修改的开证行,才可以发出开立信用证或修改预先通知书。发出预先通知的开证行应不可撤销地承诺将不延误地开出有效的信用证或修改,且条款不能与预先通知书相矛盾。

Article 12 Nomination

第十二条 指定

a. Unless a nominated bank is the confirming bank, an authorization to honor or negotiate does not impose any obligation on that nominated bank to honor or negotiate, except when expressly agreed to by that nominated bank and so communicated to the beneficiary.

a. 除非一家被指定银行是保兑行,对被指定银行进行兑付或议付的授权并不构成其必须兑付或议付的义务,被指定银行明确同意并照此通知受益人的情形除外。

b. By nominating a bank to accept a draft or incur a deferred payment undertaking, an issuing bank authorizes that nominated bank to prepay or purchase a draft accepted or a deferred payment undertaking incurred by that nominated bank.

b. 通过指定一家银行承兑汇票或承担延期付款承诺,开证行即授权该被指定银行预付或购买经其承兑的汇票或由其承担延期付款的承诺。

c. Receipt or examination and forwarding of documents by a nominated bank that is not a confirming bank does not make that nominated bank liable to honor or negotiate, nor does it constitute honor or negotiation.

c. 非保兑行身份的被指定银行接受、审核并寄送单据的行为既不使得该被指定银行具有兑付或议付的义务,也不构成兑付或议付。

Article 13 Bank-to-Bank Reimbursement Arrangements

第十三条 银行间偿付约定

a. If a credit states that reimbursement is to be obtained by a nominated bank ("claiming bank") claiming on another party ("reimbursing bank"), the credit must state if the reimbursement is subject to the ICC rules for bank-to-bank reimbursements in effect on the date of issuance of the credit.

a. 如果信用证规定被指定银行("索偿行")须通过向另一方银行("偿付行")索偿获得偿付,则信用证中必须声明是否按照信用证开立日正在生效的国际商会《银行间偿付规则》办理。

b. If a credit does not state that reimbursement is subject to the ICC rules for bank-to-bank reimbursements, the following apply:

b. 如果信用证中未声明是否按照国际商会《银行间偿付规则》办理,则适用于下列条款：

i. An issuing bank must provide a reimbursing bank with a reimbursement authorization that conforms with the availability stated in the credit. The reimbursement authorization should not be subject to an expiry date.

i. 开证行必须向偿付行提供偿付授权书，该授权书须与信用证中声明的有效性一致。偿付授权书不应规定有效日期。

ii. A claiming bank shall not be required to supply a reimbursing bank with a certificate of compliance with the terms and conditions of the credit.

ii. 不应要求索偿行向偿付行提供证实单据与信用证条款及条件相符的证明。

iii. An issuing bank will be responsible for any loss of interest, together with any expenses incurred, if reimbursement is not provided on first demand by a reimbursing bank in accordance with the terms and conditions of the credit.

iii. 如果偿付行未能按照信用证的条款及条件在首次索偿时即行偿付，则开证行应对索偿行的利息损失以及产生的费用负责。

iv. A reimbursing bank's charges are for the account of the issuing bank. However, if the charges are for the account of the beneficiary, it is the responsibility of an issuing bank to so indicate in the credit and in the reimbursement authorization. If a reimbursing bank's charges are for the account of the beneficiary, they shall be deducted from the amount due to a claiming bank when reimbursement is made. If no reimbursement is made, the reimbursing bank's charges remain the obligation of the issuing bank.

iv. 偿付行的费用应由开证行承担。然而，如果费用系由受益人承担，则开证行有责任在信用证和偿付授权书中予以注明。如偿付行的费用系由受益人承担，则该费用应在偿付时从支付索偿行的金额中扣除。如果未发生偿付，开证行仍有义务承担偿付行的费用。

c. An issuing bank is not relieved of any of its obligations to provide reimbursement if reimbursement is not made by a reimbursing bank on first demand.

c. 如果偿付行未能于首次索偿时即行偿付，则开证行不能解除其自身的偿付责任。

Article 14 Standard for Examination of Documents

第十四条 审核单据的标准

a. A nominated bank acting on its nomination, a confirming bank, if any, and the issuing bank must examine a presentation to determine, on the basis of the documents alone, whether or not the documents appear on their face to constitute a complying presentation.

a. 按照指定行事的被指定银行、保兑行(如有)以及开证行必须对提示的单据进行审核，并仅以单据为基础，以决定单据在表面上看来是否构成相符提示。

b. A nominated bank acting on its nomination, a confirming bank, if any, and the issuing bank shall each have a maximum of five banking days following the day of presentation to determine if a presentation is complying. This period is not curtailed or otherwise affected by the occurrence on or after the date of presentation of any expiry date or last day for presentation.

b. 按照指定行事的被指定银行、保兑行(如有)以及开证行,自其收到提示单据的翌日起算,应各自拥有最多不超过五个银行工作日的时间以决定提示是否相符。该期限不因单据提示日适逢信用证有效期或最迟提示期或在其之后而被缩减或受到其他影响。

c. A presentation including one or more original transport documents subject to articles 19, 20, 21, 22, 23, 24 or 25 must be made by or on behalf of the beneficiary not later than 21 calendar days after the date of shipment as described in these rules, but in any event not later than the expiry date of the credit.

c. 提示若包含一份或多份按照本惯例第 19、第 20、第 21、第 22、第 23、第 24 或第 25 条出具的正本运输单据,则必须由受益人或其代表按照相关条款在不迟于装运日后的二十一个公历日内提交,但无论如何不得迟于信用证的到期日。

d. Data in a document, when read in context with the credit, the document itself and international standard banking practice, need not be identical to, but must not conflict with, data in that document, any other stipulated document or the credit.

d. 单据中内容的描述不必与信用证、信用证对该项单据的描述以及国际标准银行实务完全一致,但不得与该项单据中的内容、其他规定的单据或信用证相冲突。

e. In documents other than the commercial invoice, the description of the goods, services or performance, if stated, may be in general terms not conflicting with their description in the credit.

e. 除商业发票外,其他单据中的货物、服务或行为描述若须规定,可使用统称,但不得与信用证规定的描述相矛盾。

f. If a credit requires presentation of a document other than a transport document, insurance document or commercial invoice, without stipulating by whom the document is to be issued or its data content, banks will accept the document as presented if its content appears to fulfil the function of the required document and otherwise complies with sub-article 14 (d).

f. 如果信用证要求提示运输单据、保险单据和商业发票以外的单据,但未规定该单据由何人出具或单据的内容。如信用证对此未做规定,只要所提交单据的内容看来满足其功能需要且其他方面与第十四条(d)款相符,银行将对提示的单据予以接受。

g. A document presented but not required by the credit will be disregarded and may be returned to the presenter.

g. 提示信用证中未要求提交的单据,银行将不予置理。如果收到此类单据,可以退还提示人。

h. If a credit contains a condition without stipulating the document to indicate compliance with the condition, banks will deem such condition as not stated and will disregard it.

h. 如果信用证中包含某项条件而未规定须提交与之相符的单据,银行将认为未列明此条件,并对此不予置理。

i. A document may be dated prior to the issuance date of the credit, but must not be dated later than its date of presentation.

i. 单据的出单日期可以早于信用证开立日期,但不得迟于信用证规定的提示日期。

j. When the addresses of the beneficiary and the applicant appear in any stipulated document, they need not be the same as those stated in the credit or in any other stipulated document, but must be within the same country as the respective addresses mentioned in the credit. Contact details (tealeaf, telephone, email and the like) stated as part of the beneficiary's and the applicant's address will be disregarded. However, when the address and contact details of the applicant appear as part of the consignee or notify party details on a transport document subject to articles 19, 20, 21, 22, 23, 24 or 25, they must be as stated in the credit.

j. 当受益人和申请人的地址显示在任何规定的单据上时,不必与信用证或其他规定单据中显示的地址相同,但必须与信用证中述及的各自地址处于同一国家内。用于联系的资料(电传、电话、电子邮箱及类似方式)如作为受益人和申请人地址的组成部分将被不予置理。然而,当申请人的地址及联系信息作为按照第 19、第 20、第 21、第 22、第 23、第 24 或第 25 条出具的运输单据中收货人或通知方详址的组成部分时,则必须按照信用证规定予以显示。

k. The shipper or consignor of the goods indicated on any document need not be the beneficiary of the credit.

k. 显示在任何单据中的货物的托运人或发货人不必是信用证的受益人。

l. A transport document may be issued by any party other than a carrier, owner, master or chartered provided that the transport document meets the requirements of articles 19, 20, 21, 22, 23 or 24 of these rules.

k. 假如运输单据能够满足本惯例第 19、第 20、第 21、第 22、第 23 或 24 条的要求,则运输单据可以由承运人、船东、船长或租船人以外的任何一方出具。

Article 15 Complying Presentation

第十五条 相符提示

a. When an issuing bank determines that a presentation is complying, it must honor.

a. 当开证行确定提示相符时,就必须予以兑付。

b. When a confirming bank determines that a presentation is complying, it must honor or negotiate and forward the documents to the issuing bank.

b. 当保兑行确定提示相符时,就必须予以兑付或议付并将单据寄往开证行。

c. When a nominated bank determines that a presentation is complying and honors or negotiates, it must forward the documents to the confirming bank or issuing bank.

c. 当被指定银行确定提示相符并予以兑付或议付时,必须将单据寄往保兑行或开证行。

Article 16 Discrepant Documents, Waiver and Notice

第十六条 不符单据及不符点的放弃与通知

a. When a nominated bank acting on its nomination, a confirming bank, if any, or the issuing bank determines that a presentation does not comply, it may refuse to honor or negotiate.

a. 当按照指定行事的被指定银行、保兑行(如有)或开证行确定提示不符时,可以拒绝兑付或议付。

b. When an issuing bank determines that a presentation does not comply, it may in its solejudgment approach the applicant for a waiver of the discrepancies. This does not, however, extend the period mentioned in sub-article 14 (b).

b. 当开证行确定提示不符时,可以依据其独立的判断联系申请人放弃有关不符点。然而,这并不因此延长第十四条(b)款中述及的期限。

c. When nominated bank acting on its nomination, a confirming bank, if any, or the issuing bank decides to refuse to honor or negotiate, it must give a single notice to that effect to the presenter.

c. 当按照指定行事的被指定银行、保兑行(如有)或开证行决定拒绝兑付或议付时,必须一次性通知提示人。

The notice must state:

通知必须声明:

i. That the bank is refusing to honor or negotiate; and

i. 银行拒绝兑付或议付;及

ii. Each discrepancy in respect of which the bank refuses to honor or negotiate; and

ii. 银行凭以拒绝兑付或议付的各个不符点;及

iii. a) That the bank is holding the documents pending further instructions from the presenter; or

iii. a) 银行持有单据等候提示人进一步指示;或

b) That the issuing bank is holding the documents until it receives a waiver from the applicant and agrees to accept it, or receives further instructions from the presenter prior to agreeing to accept a waiver; or

b) 开证行持有单据直至收到申请人通知弃权并同意接受该弃权,或在同意接受弃权前从提示人处收到进一步指示;或

c) That the bank is returning the documents; or

c) 银行退回单据;或

d) That the bank is acting in accordance with instructions previously received from the presenter.

d) 银行按照先前从提示人处收到的指示行事。

d. The notice required in sub-article 16 (c) must be given by telecommunication or, if that is not possible, by other expeditious means no later than the close of the fifth banking day following the day of presentation.

d. 第十六条(c)款中要求的通知必须以电讯方式发出,或者,如果不可能以电讯方式通知时,则以其他快捷方式通知,但不得迟于提示单据日期翌日起第五个银行工作日终了。

e. A nominated bank acting on its nomination, a confirming bank, if any, or the issuing bank may, after providing notice required by sub-article 16 (c) (iii) (a) or (b), return the documents to the presenter at any time.

e. 按照指定行事的被指定银行、保兑行(如有)或开证行可以在提供第十六条(c)款(iii)、(a)款或(b)款要求提供的通知后,于任何时间将单据退还提示人。

f. If an issuing bank or a confirming bank fails to act in accordance with the provisions of this article, it shall be precluded from claiming that the documents do not constitute a complying presentation.

f. 如果开证行或保兑行未能按照本条款的规定行事,将无权宣称单据未能构成相符提示。

g. When an issuing bank refuses tohonor or a confirming bank refuses to honor or negotiate and has given notice to that effect in accordance with this article, it shall then be entitled to claim a refund, with interest, of any reimbursement made.

g. 当开证行拒绝兑付或保兑行拒绝兑付或议付,并已经按照本条款发出通知时,该银行将有权就已经履行的偿付索取退款及其利息。

Article 17　Original Documents and Copies

第十七条　正本单据和副本单据

a. At least one original of each document stipulated in the credit must be presented.

a. 信用证中规定的各种单据必须至少提供一份正本。

b. A bank shall treat as an original any document bearing an apparently original signature, mark, stamp, or label of the issuer of the document; unless the document itself indicates that it is not an original.

b. 除非单据本身表明其不是正本,银行将视任何单据表面上具有单据出具人正本签字、标志、图章或标签的单据为正本单据。

c. Unless a document indicates otherwise 另外的, a bank will also accept a document as original if it:

c. 除非单据另有显示,银行将接受单据作为正本单据如果该单据:

i. Appears to be written, typed, perforated or stamped by the document issuer's hand; or

i. 表面看来由单据出具人手工书写、打字、穿孔签字或盖章;或

ii. Appears to be on the document issuer's original stationery; or

ii. 表面看来使用单据出具人的正本信笺;或

iii. States that it is original, unless the statement appears not to apply to the document presented.

iii. 声明单据为正本,除非该项声明表面看来与所提示的单据不符。

d. If a credit requires presentation of copies of documents, presentation of either originals or copies is permitted.

d. 如果信用证要求提交副本单据,则提交正本单据或副本单据均可。

e. If a credit requires presentation of multiple documents by using terms such as "in duplicate", "in two fold" or "in two copies", this will be satisfied by the presentation of at least one original and the remaining number in copies, exceptwhen the document itself indicates otherwise.

e. 如果信用证使用诸如"一式两份""两张""两份"等术语要求提交多份单据,则可以提交至少一份正本,其余份数以副本来满足。但单据本身另有相反指示者除外。

Article 18 Commercial Invoice

第十八条 商业发票

a. A commercial invoice:

a. 商业发票:

i. Must appear to have been issued by the beneficiary (except as provided in article 38);

i. 必须在表面上看来系由受益人出具(第三十八条另有规定者除外);

ii. Must be made out in the name of the applicant (except as provided in sub-article 38 (g));

ii. 必须做成以申请人的名称为抬头(第三十八条(g)款另有规定者除外);

iii. Must be made out in the same currency as the credit; and

iii. 必须将发票币别做成与信用证相同币种;及

iv. Need not be signed.

iv. 无须签字。

b. A nominated bank acting on its nomination, a confirming bank, if any, or the issuing bank may accept a commercial invoice issued for an amount in excess of the amount permitted by the credit, and its decision will be binding upon all parties, provided the bank in question has not honored or negotiated for an amount in excess of that permitted by the credit.

b. 按照指定行事的被指定银行、保兑行(如有)或开证行可以接受金额超过信用证所允许金额的商业发票,倘若有关银行已兑付或已议付的金额没有超过信用证所允许的金额,则该银行的决定对各有关方均具有约束力。

c. The description of the goods, services or performance in a commercial invoice must correspond with that appearing in the credit.

c. 商业发票中货物、服务或行为的描述必须与信用证中显示的内容相符。

Article 19 Transport Document Covering at Least Two Different Modes of Transport

第十九条 至少包括两种不同运输方式的运输单据

a. A transport document covering at least two different modes of transport (multimodal or combined transport document), however named, must appear to:

a. 至少包括两种不同运输方式的运输单据(即多式运输单据或联合运输单据),不论其称谓如何,必须在表明上看来:

i. Indicates the name of the carrier and is signed by:

i. 显示承运人名称并由下列人员签署:

a) The carrier or a named agent for or on behalf of the carrier, or

a) 承运人或承运人的具名代理或代表,或

b) The master or a named agent for or on behalf of the master.

b) 船长或船长的具名代理或代表。

Any signature by the carrier, master or agent must be identified as that of the carrier, master or agent.

承运人、船长或代理的任何签字必须分别表明承运人、船长或代理的身份。

Any signature by an agent must indicate whether the agent has signed for or on behalf of the carrier or for or on behalf of the master.

代理的签字必须显示其是否作为承运人或船长的代理或代表签署提单。

ii. Indicate that the goods have been dispatched, taken in charge or shipped on board at the place stated in the credit, by:

ii. 通过下述方式表明货物已在信用证规定的地点发运、接受监管或装载：

a) Pre-printed wording, or

a) 预先印就的措辞，或

b) A stamp or notation indicating the date on which the goods have been dispatched, taken in charge or shipped on board.

b) 注明货物已发运、接受监管或装载日期的图章或批注。

The date of issuance of the transport document will be deemed to be the date of dispatch, taking in charge or shipped on board, and the date of shipment. However, if the transport document indicates, by stamp or notation, a date of dispatch, taking in charge or shipped on board, this date will be deemed to be the date of shipment.

运输单据的出具日期将被视为发运、接受监管或装载以及装运日期。然而，如果运输单据以盖章或批注方式标明发运、接受监管或装载日期，则此日期将被视为装运日期。

iii. Indicate the place of dispatch, taking in charge or shipment and the place of final destination stated in the credit, even if:

iii. 显示信用证中规定的发运、接受监管或装载地点以及最终目的地的地点，即使：

a) The transport document states, in addition, a different place of dispatch, taking in charge or shipment or place of final destination, or

a) 运输单据另外显示了不同的发运、接受监管或装载地点或最终目的地的地点，或

b) The transport document contains the indication "intended" or similar qualification in relation to the vessel, port of loading or port of discharge.

b) 运输单据包含"预期"或类似限定有关船只、装货港或卸货港的指示。

iv. Be the sole original transport document or, if issued in more than one original, be the full set as indicated on the transport document.

iv. 系仅有的一份正本运输单据，或者，如果出具了多份正本运输单据，应是运输单据中显示的全套正本份数。

v. Contain terms and conditions of carriage or make reference to another source containing the terms and conditions of carriage (short form or blank back transport document). Contents of terms and conditions of carriage will not be examined.

v. 包含承运条件须参阅包含承运条件条款及条件的某一出处(简式或背面空白的运输单据)者，银行对此类承运条件的条款及条件内容不予审核。

vi. Contain no indication that it is subject to a charter party.

vi. 未注明运输单据受租船合约约束。

b. For the purpose of this article, transshipment means unloading from one means of conveyance and reloading to another means of conveyance (whether or not in different modes of transport) during the carriage from the place of dispatch, taking in charge or shipment to the place of final destination stated in the credit.

b. 就本条款而言，转运意指货物在信用证中规定的发运、接受监管或装载地点到最终目的地的运输过程中，从一个运输工具卸下并重新装载到另一个运输工具上(无论是否为不同运输方式)的运输。

c. i. A transport document may indicate that the goods will or may be transshipped provided that the entire carriage is covered by one and the same transport document.

c. i. 只要同一运输单据包括运输全程，则运输单据可以注明货物将被转运或可被转运。

ii. A transport document indicating that transshipment will or may take place is acceptable, even if the credit prohibits transshipment.

ii. 即使信用证禁止转运，银行也将接受注明转运将发生或可能发生的运输单据。

Article 20 Bill of Lading

第二十条 提单

a. A bill of lading, however named, must appear to:

a. 无论其称谓如何，提单必须表面上看来：

i. Indicates the name of the carrier and is signed by:

i. 显示承运人名称并由下列人员签署：

a) The carrier or a named agent for or on behalf of the carrier, or

a) 承运人或承运人的具名代理或代表，或

b) The master or a named agent for or on behalf of the master.

b) 船长或船长的具名代理或代表。

Any signature by the carrier, master or agent must be identified as that of the carrier, master or agent.

承运人、船长或代理的任何签字必须分别表明其承运人、船长或代理的身份。

Any signature by an agent must indicate whether the agent has signed for or on behalf of the carrier or for or on behalf of the master.

代理的签字必须显示其是否作为承运人或船长的代理或代表签署提单。

ii. Indicate that the goods have been shipped on board a named vessel at the port of loading stated in the credit by:

ii. 通过下述方式表明货物已在信用证规定的装运港装载上具名船只：

a) Pre-printed wording, or

a) 预先印就的措辞，或

b) An on board notation indicating the date on which the goods have been shipped on board.

b) 注明货物已装船日期的装船批注。

The date of issuance of the bill of lading will be deemed to be the date of shipment unless the bill of lading contains an on board notation indicating the date of shipment, in which case the date stated in the on board notation will be deemed to be the date of shipment.

提单的出具日期将被视为装运日期,除非提单包含注明装运日期的装船批注,在此情况下,装船批注中显示的日期将被视为装运日期。

If the bill of lading contains the indication "intended vessel" or similar qualification in relation to the name of the vessel, an on board notation indicating the date of shipment and the name of the actual vessel is required.

如果提单包含"预期船"字样或类似有关限定船只的词语时,装上具名船只必须由注明装运日期以及实际装运船只名称的装船批注来证实。

iii. Indicate shipment from the port of loading to the port of discharge stated in the credit.

iii. 注明装运从信用证中规定的装货港至卸货港。

If the bill of lading does not indicate the port of loading stated in the credit as the port of loading, or if it contains the indication "intended" or similar qualification in relation to the port of loading, an on board notation indicating the port of loading as stated in the credit, the date of shipment and the name of the vessel is required. This provision applies even when loading on board or shipment on a named vessel is indicated by pre-printed wording on the bill of lading.

如果提单未注明以信用证中规定的装货港作为装货港,或包含"预期"或类似有关限定装货港的标注者,则需要提供注明信用证中规定的装货港、装运日期以及船名的装船批注。即使提单上已注明印就的"已装船"或"已装具名船只"措辞,本规定仍然适用。

iv. Be the sole original bill of lading or, if issued in more than one original, be the full set as indicated on the bill of lading.

iv. 系仅有的一份正本提单,或者,如果出具了多份正本,应是提单中显示的全套正本份数。

v. Contain terms and conditions of carriage or make reference to another source containing the terms and conditions of carriage (short form or blank back bill of lading). Contents of terms and conditions of carriage will not be examined.

v. 包含承运条件须参阅包含承运条件条款及条件的某一出处(简式或背面空白的提单)者,银行对此类承运条件的条款及条件内容不予审核。

vi. Contain no indication that it is subject to a charter party.

vi. 未注明运输单据受租船合约约束。

b. For the purpose of this article, transshipment means unloading from one vessel and reloading to another vessel during the carriage from the port of loading to the port of discharge stated in the credit.

b. 就本条款而言,转运意指在信用证规定的装货港到卸货港之间的海运过程中,将货物由一艘船卸下再装上另一艘船的运输。

c. i. A bill of lading may indicate that the goods will or may be transshipped provided that the entire carriage is covered by one and the same bill of lading.

c. i. 只要同一提单包括运输全程,则提单可以注明货物将被转运或可被转运。

ii. A bill of lading indicating thattransshipment will or may take place is acceptable, even if the credit prohibits transshipment, if the goods have been shipped in a container, trailer or LASH barge as evidenced by the bill of lading.

ii. 银行可以接受注明将要发生或可能发生转运的提单。即使信用证禁止转运,只要提单上证实有关货物已由集装箱、拖车或子母船运输,银行仍可接受注明将要发生或可能发生转运的提单。

d. Clauses in a bill of lading stating that the carrier reserves the right to transship will be disregarded.

d. 对于提单中包含的声明承运人保留转运权利的条款,银行将不予置理。

Article 21 Non-Negotiable Sea Waybill

第二十一条 非转让海运单

a. A non-negotiable sea waybill, however named, must appear to:

a. 无论其称谓如何,非转让海运单必须表面上看来:

i. Indicate the name of the carrier and be signed by:

i. 显示承运人名称并由下列人员签署:

a) The carrier or a named agent for or on behalf of the carrier, or

a) 承运人或承运人的具名代理或代表,或

b) The master or a named agent for or on behalf of the master.

b) 船长或船长的具名代理或代表。

Any signature by the carrier, master or agent must be identified as that of the carrier, master or agent.

承运人、船长或代理的任何签字必须分别表明其承运人、船长或代理的身份。

Any signature by an agent must indicate whether the agent has signed for or on behalf of the carrier or for or on behalf of the master.

代理的签字必须显示其是否作为承运人或船长的代理或代表签署提单。

ii. Indicate that the goods have been shipped on board a named vessel at the port of loading stated in the credit by:

ii. 通过下述方式表明货物已在信用证规定的装运港装载上具名船只:

a) Pre-printed wording, or

a) 预先印就的措辞,或

b) An on board notation indicating the date on which the goods have been shipped on board.

b) 注明货物已装船日期的装船批注。

The date of issuance of the non-negotiable sea waybill will be deemed to be the date of shipment unless the non-negotiable sea waybill contains an on board notation indicating the date of shipment, in which case the date stated in the on board notation will be deemed to be the date of shipment.

非转让海运单的出具日期将被视为装运日期，除非非转让海运单包含注明装运日期的装船批注，在此情况下，装船批注中显示的日期将被视为装运日期。

If the non-negotiable sea waybill contains the indication "intended vessel" or similar qualification in relation to the name of the vessel, an on board notation indicating the date of shipment and the name of the actual vessel is required.

如果非转让海运单包含"预期船"字样或类似有关限定船只的词语时，装上具名船只必须由注明装运日期以及实际装运船只名称的装船批注来证实。

iii. Indicate shipment from the port of loading to the port of discharge stated in the credit.

iii. 注明装运从信用证中规定的装货港至卸货港。

If the non-negotiable sea waybill does not indicate the port of loading stated in the credit as the port of loading, or if it contains the indication "intended" or similar qualification in relation to the port of loading, an on board notation indicating the port of loading as stated in the credit, the date of shipment and the name of the vessel is required. This provision applies even when loading on board or shipment on a named vessel is indicated by pre-printed wording on the non-negotiable sea waybill.

如果非转让海运单未注明以信用证中规定的装货港作为装货港，或包含"预期"或类似有关限定装货港的标注者，则需要提供注明信用证中规定的装货港、装运日期以及船名的装船批注。即使非转让海运单上已注明印就的"已装船"或"已装具名船只"措辞，本规定仍然适用。

iv. Be the sole original non-negotiable sea waybill or, if issued in more than one original, be the full set as indicated on the non-negotiable sea waybill.

iv. 系仅有的一份正本非转让海运单，或者，如果出具了多份正本，应是非转让海运单中显示的全套正本份数。

v. Contain terms and conditions of carriage or make reference to another source containing the terms and conditions of carriage (short form or blank back non-negotiable sea waybill). Contents of terms and conditions of carriage will not be examined.

v. 包含承运条件须参阅包含承运条件条款及条件的某一出处(简式或背面空白的提单)者，银行对此类承运条件的条款及条件内容不予审核。

vi. Contain no indication that it is subject to a charter party.

vi. 未注明运输单据受租船合约约束。

b. For the purpose of this article, transshipment means unloading from one vessel and reloading to another vessel during the carriage from the port of loading to the port of discharge stated in the credit.

b. 就本条款而言，转运意指在信用证规定的装货港到卸货港之间的海运过程中，将货物由一艘船卸下再装上另一艘船的运输。

c. i. A non-negotiable sea waybill may indicate that the goods will or may be transshipped provided that the entire carriage is covered by one and the same non-negotiable sea waybill.

c. i. 只要同一非转让海运单包括运输全程，则非转让海运单可以注明货物将被转运或可被转运。

ii. A non-negotiable sea waybill indicating thattransshipment will or may take place is acceptable, even if the credit prohibits transshipment, if the goods have been shipped in a container, trailer or LASH barge 子母船 as evidenced by the non-negotiable sea waybill.

ii. 银行可以接受注明将要发生或可能发生转运的非转让海运单。即使信用证禁止转运，只要非转让海运单上证实有关货物已由集装箱、拖车或子母船运输，银行仍可接受注明将要发生或可能发生转运的非转让海运单。

d. Clauses in a non-negotiable sea waybill stating that the carrier reserves the right to transship will be disregarded.

d. 对于非转让海运单中包含的声明承运人保留转运权利的条款，银行将不予置理。

Article 22 Charter Party Bill of Lading

第二十二条 租船合约提单

a. A bill of lading, however named, containing an indication that it is subject to a charter party (charter party bill of lading), must appear to:

a. 无论其称谓如何，倘若提单包含有提单受租船合约约束的指示(即租船合约提单)，则必须在表面上看来：

i. Be signed by:

i. 由下列当事方签署：

a) The master or a named agent for or on behalf of the master, or

a) 船长或船长的具名代理或代表，或

b) The owner or a named agent for or on behalf of the owner, or

b) 船东或船东的具名代理或代表，或

c) Thechartered or a named agent for or on behalf of the chartered.

c) 租船主或租船主的具名代理或代表。

Any signature by the master, owner, chatterer or agent must be identified as that of the master, owner, chatterer or agent.

船长、船东、租船主或代理的任何签字必须分别表明其船长、船东、租船主或代理的身份。

Any signature by an agent must indicate whether the agent has signed for or on behalf of the master, owner or charterer.

代理的签字必须显示其是否作为船长、船东或租船主的代理或代表签署提单。

An agent signing for or on behalf of the owner or chatterer must indicate the name of the owner or chatterer.

代理人代理或代表船东或租船主签署提单时必须注明船东或租船主的名称。

ii. Indicate that the goods have been shipped on board a named vessel at the port of loading stated in the credit by:

ii. 通过下述方式表明货物已在信用证规定的装运港装载上具名船只：

a) Pre-printed wording, or

a）预先印就的措词，或

b) An on board notation indicating the date on which the goods have been shipped on board.

b）注明货物已装船日期的装船批注。

The date of issuance of the charter party bill of lading will be deemed to be the date of shipment unless the charter party bill of lading contains an on board notation indicating the date of shipment, in which case the date stated in the on board notation will be deemed to be the date of shipment.

租船合约提单的出具日期将被视为装运日期，除非租船合约提单包含注明装运日期的装船批注，在此情况下，装船批注中显示的日期将被视为装运日期。

iii. Indicate shipment from the port of loading to the port of discharge stated in the credit. The port of discharge may also be shown as a range of ports or a geographical area, as stated in the credit.

iii. 注明货物由信用证中规定的装货港运输至卸货港。卸货港可以按信用证中的规定显示为一组港口或某个地理区域。

iv. Be the sole original charter party bill of lading or, if issued in more than one original, be the full set as indicated on the charter party bill of lading.

iv. 系仅有的一份正本租船合约提单，或者，如果出具了多份正本，应是租船合约提单中显示的全套正本份数。

b. A bank will not examine charter party contracts, even if they are required to be presented by the terms of the credit.

b. 即使信用证中的条款要求提交租船合约，银行也将对该租船合约不予审核。

Article 23　Air Transport Document

第二十三条　空运单据

a. An air transport document, however named, must appear to:

a. 无论其称谓如何，空运单据必须在表面上看来：

i. Indicate the name of the carrier and be signed by:

i. 注明承运人名称并由下列当事方签署：

a) The carrier, or

a）承运人，或

b) A named agent for or on behalf of the carrier.

b）承运人的具名代理或代表。

Any signature by the carrier or agent must be identified as that of the carrier or agent.

承运人或代理的任何签字必须分别表明其承运人或代理的身份。

Any signature by an agent must indicate that the agent has signed for or on behalf of the carrier.

代理的签字必须显示其是否作为承运人的代理或代表签署空运单据。

ii. Indicate that the goods have been accepted for carriage.

ii. 注明货物已收妥待运。

iii. Indicate the date of issuance. This date will be deemed to be the date of shipment unless the air transport document contains a specific notation of the actual date of shipment, in which case the date stated in the notation will be deemed to be the date of shipment.

iii. 注明出具日期。这一日期将被视为装运日期,除非空运单据包含注有实际装运日期的专项批注,在此种情况下,批注中显示的日期将被视为装运日期。

Any other information appearing on the air transport document relative to the flight number and date will not be considered in determining the date of shipment.

空运单据显示的其他任何与航班号和起飞日期有关的信息不能被视为装运日期。

iv. Indicate the airport of departure and the airport of destination stated in the credit.

iv. 表明信用证规定的起飞机场和目的地机场。

v. Be the original for consignor or shipper, even if the credit stipulates a full set of originals.

v. 为开给发货人或拖运人的正本,即使信用证规定提交全套正本。

vi. Contain terms and conditions of carriage or make reference to another source containing the terms and conditions of carriage. Contents of terms and conditions of carriage will not be examined.

vi. 载有承运条款和条件,或提示条款和条件参见别处。银行将不审核承运条款和条件的内容。

b. For the purpose of this article, transshipment means unloading from one aircraft and reloading to another aircraft during the carriage from the airport of departure to the airport of destination stated in the credit.

b. 就本条而言,转运是指在信用证规定的起飞机场到目的地机场的运输过程中,将货物从一飞机卸下再装上另一飞机的行为。

c. i. An air transport document may indicate that the goods will or may be transshipped, provided that the entire carriage is covered by one and the same air transport document.

c. i. 空运单据可以注明货物将要或可能转运,只要全程运输由同一空运单据涵盖。

ii. An air transport document indicating that transshipment will or may take place is acceptable, even if the credit prohibits transshipment.

ii. 即使信用证禁止转运,注明将要或可能发生转运的空运单据仍可接受。

Article 24 Road, Rail or Inland Waterway Transport Documents

第二十四条 公路、铁路或内陆水运单据

a. A road, rail or inland waterway transport document, however named, must appear to:

a. 公路、铁路或内陆水运单据,无论名称如何,必须看似:

i. Indicate the name of the carrier and:

i. 表明承运人名称,并且:

a) Be signed by the carrier or a named agent for or on behalf of the carrier, or

a) 由承运人或其具名代理人签署,或者

b) Indicate receipt of the goods by signature, stamp or notation by the carrier or a named agent for or on behalf of the carrier.

b) 由承运人或其具名代理人以签字、印戳或批注表明货物收讫。

Any signature, stamp or notation of receipt of the goods by the carrier or agent must be identified as that of the carrier or agent.

承运人或其具名代理人的售货签字、印戳或批注必须标明其承运人或代理人的身份。

Any signature, stamp or notation of receipt of the goods by the agent must indicate that the agent has signed or acted for or on behalf of the carrier.

代理人的收获签字、印戳或批注必须标明代理人系代表承运人签字或行事。

If a rail transport document does not identify the carrier, any signature or stamp of the railway company will be accepted as evidence of the document being signed by the carrier.

如果铁路运输单据没有指明承运人,可以接受铁路运输公司的任何签字或印戳作为承运人签署单据的证据。

ii. Indicate the date of shipment or the date the goods have been received for shipment, dispatch or carriage at the place stated in the credit. Unless the transport document contains a dated reception、stamp, an indication of the date of receipt or a date of shipment, the date of issuance of the transport document will be deemed to be the date of shipment.

ii. 表明货物在信用证规定地点的发运日期,或者收讫代运或代发送的日期。运输单据的出具日期将被视为发运日期,除非运输单据上盖有带日期的收货印戳,或注明了收货日期或发运日期。

iii. Indicate the place of shipment and the place of destination stated in the credit.

iii. 表明信用证规定的发运地及目的地。

b. i. A road transport document must appear to be the original for consignor or shipper or bear no marking indicating for whom the document has been prepared.

b. i. 公路运输单据必须看似为开给发货人或托运人的正本,或没有认可标记表明单据开给何人。

ii. A rail transport document marked "duplicate" will be accepted as an original.

ii. 注明"第二联"的铁路运输单据将被作为正本接受。

iii. A rail or inland waterway transport document will be accepted as an original whether marked as "an original" or not.

iii. 无论是否注明"正本"字样,铁路或内陆水运单据都被作为正本接受。

c. In the absence of an indication on the transport document as to the number of originals issued, the number presented will be deemed to constitute a full set.

c. 如运输单据上未注明出具的正本数量,提交的分数即视为全套正本。

d. For the purpose of this article, transshipment means unloading from one means of conveyance and reloading to another means of conveyance, within the same mode of transport, during the carriage from the place of shipment, dispatch or carriage to the place of destination stated in the credit.

d. 就本条而言,转运是指在信用证规定的发运、发送或运送的地点到目的地之间的运输过程中,在同一运输方式中从一运输工具卸下再装上另一运输工具的行为。

e. i. A road, rail or inland waterway transport document may indicate that the goods will or may be transshipped provided that the entire carriage is covered by one and the same transport document.

e. i. 只要全程运输由同一运输单据涵盖,公路、铁路或内陆水运单据可以注明货物将要或可能被转运。

ii. A road, rail or inland waterway transport document indicating that transshipment will or may take place is acceptable, even if the credit prohibits transshipment.

ii. 即使信用证禁止转运,注明将要或可能发生转运的公路、铁路或内陆水运单据仍可接受。

Article 25 Courier Receipt, Post Receipt or Certificate of Posting

第二十五条 快递收据、邮政收据或投邮证明

a. A courier receipt, however named, evidencing receipt of goods for transport, must appear to:

a. 证明货物收讫待运的快递收据,无论名称如何,必须看似:

i. Indicate the name of the courier service and be stamped or signed by the named courier service at the place from which the credit states the goods are to be shipped; and

i. 表明快递机构的名称,并在信用证规定的货物发运地点由该具名快递机构盖章或签字;并且

ii. Indicate a date of pick-up or of receipt or wording to this effect. This date will be deemed to be the date of shipment.

ii. 表明取件或收件的日期或类似词语。该日期将被视为发运日期。

b. A requirement that courier charges are to be paid or prepaid may be satisfied by a transport document issued by a courier service evidencing that courier charges are for the account of a party other than the consignee.

b. 如果要求显示快递费用付讫或预付,快递机构出具的表明快递费由收货人以外的一方支付的运输单据可以满足该项要求。

c. A post receipt or certificate of posting, however named, evidencing receipt of goods for transport, must appear to be stamped or signed and dated at the place from which the credit states the goods are to be shipped. This date will be deemed to be the date of shipment.

c. 证明货物收讫待运的邮政收据或投邮证明,无论名称如何,必须看似在信用证规定的货物发运地点盖章或签署并注明日期。该日期将被视为发运日期。

Article 26 "On Deck", "Shipper's Load and Count", "Said by Shipper to Contain" and Charges Additional to Freight

第二十六条 "货装舱面""托运人装载和计数""内容据托运人报称"及运费之外的费用

a. A transport document must not indicate that the goods are or will be loaded on deck. A clause on a transport document stating that the goods may be loaded on deck is acceptable.

a. 运输单据不得表明货物装于或者将装于舱面。声明货物可能被装于舱面的运输单据条款可以接受。

b. A transport document bearing a clause such as "shipper's load and count" and "said by shipper to contain" is acceptable.

b. 载有诸如"托运人装载和计数"或"内容据托运人报称"条款的运输单据可以接受。

c. A transport document may bear a reference, by stamp or otherwise, to charges additional to the freight.

c. 运输单据上可以以印戳或其他方式提及运费之外的费用。

Article 27 Clean Transport Document

第二十七条 清洁运输单据

A bank will only accept a clean transport document. A clean transport document is one bearing no clause or notation expressly declaring a defective condition of the goods or their packaging. The word "clean" need not appear on a transport document, even if a credit has a requirement for that transport document to be "clean on board".

银行只接受清洁运输单据。清洁运输单据指未载有明确宣称货物或包装有缺陷的条款或批注的运输单据。"清洁"一词并不需要在运输单据上出现,即使信用证要求运输单据为"清洁已装船"的。

Article 28 Insurance Document and Coverage

第二十八条 保险单据及保险范围

a. An insurance document, such as an insurance policy, an insurance certificate or a declaration under an open cover, must appear to be issued and signed by an insurance company, an underwriter or their agents or their proxies.

a. 保险单据,例如,保险单或预约保险项下的保险证明书或者声明书,必须看似由保险公司或承保人或其代理人或代表出具并签署。

Any signature by an agent or proxy must indicate whether the agent or proxy has signed for or on behalf of the insurance company or underwriter.

代理人或代表的签字必须标明其系代表保险公司或承保人签字。

b. When the insurance document indicates that it has been issued in more than one original, all originals must be presented.

b. 如果保险单据表明其以多份正本出具,所有正本均须提交。

c. Cover notes will not be accepted.

c. 暂保单将不被接受。

d. An insurance policy is acceptable in lieu of an insurance certificate or a declaration under an open cover.

d. 可以接受保险单代替预约保险项下的保险证明书或声明书。

e. The date of the insurance document must be no later than the date of shipment, unless it appears from the insurance document that the cover is effective from a date not later than the date of shipment.

e. 保险单据日期不得晚于发运日期,除非保险单据表明保险责任不迟于发运日生效。

f. i. The insurance document must indicate the amount of insurance coverage and be in the same currency as the credit.

f. i. 保险单据必须表明投保金额并以与信用证相同的货币表示。

ii. A requirement in the credit for insurance coverage to be for a percentage of the value of the goods, of the invoice value or similar is deemed to be the minimum amount of coverage required.

ii. 信用证对于投保金额为货物价值、发票金额或类似金额的某一比例的要求,将被视为对最低保额的要求。

If there is no indication in the credit of the insurance coverage required, the amount of insurance coverage must be at least 110% of the CIF or CIP value of the goods.

如果信用证对投保金额未作规定,投保金额须至少为货物的 CIF 或 CIP 价格的 110%。

When the CIF or CIP value cannot be determined from the documents, the amount of insurance coverage must be calculated on the basis of the amount for which honor or negotiation is requested or the gross value of the goods as shown on the invoice, whichever is greater.

如果从单据中不能确定 CIF 或者 CIP 价格,投保金额必须基于要求承付或议付的金额,或者基于发票上显示的货物总值来计算,两者之中取金额较高者。

iii. The insurance document must indicate that risks are covered at least between the place of taking in charge or shipment and the place of discharge or final destination as stated in the credit.

iii. 保险单据须标明承包的风险区间至少涵盖从信用证规定的货物监管地或发运地开始到卸货地或最终目的地为止。

g. A credit should state the type of insurance required and, if any, the additional risks to be covered. An insurance document will be accepted without regard to any risks that are not covered if the credit uses imprecise terms such as "usual risks" or "customary risks".

g. 信用证应规定所需投保的险别及附加险(如有的话)。如果信用证使用诸如"通常风险"或"惯常风险"等含义不确切的用语,则无论是否有漏保之风险,保险单据将被照样接受。

h. When a credit requires insurance against "all risks" and an insurance document is presented containing any "all risks" notation or clause, whether or not bearing the heading "all risks", the insurance document will be accepted without regard to any risks stated to be excluded.

h. 当信用证规定投保"一切险"时,如保险单据载有任何"一切险"批注或条款,无论是否有"一切险"标题,均将被接受,即使其声明任何风险除外。

i. An insurance document may contain reference to any exclusion clause.

i. 保险单据可以援引任何除外责任条款。

j. An insurance document may indicate that the cover is subject to a franchise or excess (deductible).

j. 保险单据可以注明受免赔率或免赔额(减除额)约束。

Article 29 Extension of Expiry Date or Last Day for Presentation

第二十九条 截止日或最迟交单日的顺延

a. If the expiry date of a credit or the last day for presentation falls on a day when the bank to which presentation is to be made is closed for reasons other than those referred to in article 36, the expiry date or the last day for presentation, as the case may be, will be extended to the first following banking day.

a. 如果信用证的截止日或最迟交单日适逢接受交单的银行非因第三十六条所述原因而歇业,则截止日或最迟交单日,视何者适用,将顺延至其重新开业的第一个银行工作日。

b. If presentation is made on the first following banking day, a nominated bank must provide the issuing bank or confirming bank with a statement on its covering schedule that the presentation was made within the time limits extended in accordance with sub-article 29 (a).

b. 如果在顺延后的第一个银行工作日交单,指定银行必须在其致开证行或保兑行的面涵中声明交单是在根据第二十九条(a)款顺延的期限内提交的。

c. The latest date for shipment will not be extended as a result of sub-article 29 (a).

c. 最迟发运日不因第二十九条(a)款规定的原因而顺延。

Article 30 Tolerance in Credit Amount, Quantity and Unit Prices

第三十条 信用证金额、数量与单价的增减幅度

a. The words "about" or "approximately" used in connection with the amount of the credit or the quantity or the unit price stated in the credit are to be construed as allowing a tolerance not to exceed 10% more or 10% less than the amount, the quantity or the unit price to which they refer.

a. "约"或"大约"用语信用证金额或信用证规定的数量或单价时,应解释为允许有关金额或数量或单价有不超过10%的增减幅度。

b. A tolerance not to exceed 5% more or 5% less than the quantity of the goods is allowed, provided the credit does not state the quantity in terms of a stipulated number of packing units or individual items and the total amount of the drawings does not exceed the amount of the credit.

b. 在信用证未以包装单位件数或货物自身件数的方式规定货物数量时,货物数量允许有5%的增减幅度,只要总支取金额不超过信用证金额。

c. Even when partial shipments are not allowed, a tolerance not to exceed 5% less than the amount of the credit is allowed, provided that the quantity of the goods, if stated in the credit, is shipped in full and a unit price, if stated in the credit, is not reduced or that sub-article 30 (b) is not applicable. This tolerance does not apply when the credit stipulates a specific tolerance or uses the expressions referred to in sub-article 30 (a).

c. 如果信用证规定了货物数量,而该数量已全部发运,及如果信用证规定了单价,而该单价又未降低,或当第三十条(b)款不适用时,则即使不允许部分装运,也允许支取的金额有5%的减幅。若信用证规定有特定的增减幅度或使用第三十条(a)款提到的用语限定数量,则该减幅不适用。

Article 31 Partial Drawings or Shipments

第三十一条 分批支款或分批装运

a. Partial drawings or shipments are allowed.

a. 允许分批支款或分批装运。

b. A presentation consisting of more than one set of transport documents evidencing shipment commencing on the same means of conveyance and for the same journey, provided they indicate the same destination, will not be regarded as covering a partial shipment, even if they indicate different dates of shipment or different ports of loading, places of taking in charge or dispatch. If the presentation consists of more than one set of transport documents, the latest date of shipment as evidenced on any of the sets of transport documents will be regarded as the date of shipment.

b. 表明使用同一运输工具并经由同次航程运输的数套运输单据在同一次提交时,只要显示相同目的地,将不视为部分发运,即使运输单据上标明的发运日期不通或装卸港、接管地或发送地点不同。如果交单由数套运输单据构成,其中最晚的一个发运日将被视为发运日。

A presentation consisting of one or more sets of transport documents evidencing shipment on more than one means of conveyance within the same mode of transport will be regarded as covering a partial shipment, even if the means of conveyance leave on the same day for the same destination.

含有一套或数套运输单据的交单,如果表明在同一种运输方式下经由数件运输工具运输,即使运输工具在同一天出发运往同一目的地,仍将被视为部分发运。

c. A presentation consisting of more than one courier receipt, post receipt or certificate of posting will not be regarded as a partial shipment if the courier receipts, post receipts or certificates of posting appear to have been stamped or signed by the same courier or postal service at the same place and date and for the same destination.

c. 含有一份以上快递收据、邮政收据或投邮证明的交单,如果单据看似由同一块地或邮政机构在同一地点和日期加盖印戳或签字并且表明同一目的地,将不视为部分发运。

Article 32 Instalment Drawings or Shipments

第三十二条 分期支款或分期装运

If a drawing or shipment byinstallments within given periods is stipulated in the credit and any installment is not drawn or shipped within the period allowed for that installment, the credit ceases to be available for that and any subsequent installment.

如信用证规定在指定的时间段内分期支款或分期发运,任何一期未按信用证规定期限支取或发运时,信用证对该期及以后各期均告失效。

Article 33 Hours of Presentation

第三十三条　交单时间

A bank has no obligation to accept a presentation outside of its banking hours.

银行在其营业时间外无接受交单的义务。

Article 34　Disclaimer on Effectiveness of Documents

第三十四条　关于单据有效性的免责

A bank assumes no liability or responsibility for the form, sufficiency, accuracy, genuineness, falsification or legal effect of any document, or for the general or particular conditions stipulated in a document or superimposed thereon; nor does it assume any liability or responsibility for the description, quantity, weight, quality, condition, packing, delivery, value or existence of the goods, services or other performance represented by any document, or for the good faith or acts or omissions, solvency, performance or standing of the consignor, the carrier, the forwarder, the consignee or the insurer of the goods or any other person.

银行对任何单据的形式、充分性、准确性、内容真实性、虚假性或法律效力，或对单据中规定或添加的一般或特殊条件，概不负责；银行对任何单据所代表的货物、服务或其他履约行为的描述、数量、重量、品质、状况、包装、交付、价值或其存在与否，或对发货人、承运人、货运代理人、收货人、货物的保险人或其他任何人的诚信与否，作为或不作为、清偿能力、履约或资信状况，也概不负责。

Article 35　Disclaimer on Transmission and Translation

第三十五条　关于信息传递和翻译的免责

A bank assumes no liability or responsibility for the consequences arising out of delay, loss in transit, mutilation or other errors arising in the transmission of any messages or delivery of letters or documents, when such messages, letters or documents are transmitted or sent according to the requirements stated in the credit, or when the bank may have taken the initiative in the choice of the delivery service in the absence of such instructions in the credit.

当报文、信件或单据按照信用证的要求传输或发送时，或当信用证未做指示，银行自行选择传送服务时，银行对报文传输或信件或单据的递送过程中发生的延误、中途遗失、残缺或其他错误产生的后果，概不负责。

If a nominated bank determines that a presentation is complying and forwards the documents to the issuing bank or confirming bank, whether or not the nominated bank has honoured or negotiated, an issuing bank or confirming bank must honour or negotiate, or reimburse that nominated bank, even when the documents have been lost in transit between the nominated bank and the issuing bank or confirming bank, or between the confirming bank and the issuing bank.

如果指定银行确定交单相符并将单据发往开证行或保兑行。无论指定的银行是否已经承付或议付，开证行或保兑行必须承付或议付，或偿付指定银行，即使单据在指定银行送往开证行或保兑行的途中，或保兑行送往开证行的途中丢失。

A bank assumes no liability or responsibility for errors in translation or interpretation of technical terms and may transmit credit terms without translating them.

银行对技术术语的翻译或解释上的错误,不负责任,并可不加翻译地传送信用证条款。

Article 36 Force Majuro

第三十六条 不可抗力

A bank assumes no liability or responsibility for the consequences arising out of the interruption of its business by Acts of God, riots, civil commotions, insurrections, wars, acts of terrorism, or by any strikes or lockouts or any other causes beyond its control.

银行对由于天灾、暴动、骚乱、叛乱、战争、恐怖主义行为或任何罢工、停工或其无法控制的任何其他原因导致的营业中断的后果,概不负责。

A bank will not, upon resumption of its business, honor or negotiates under a credit that expired during such interruption of its business.

银行恢复营业时,对于在营业中断期间已逾期的信用证,不再进行承付或议付。

Article 37 Disclaimer for Acts of an Instructed Party

第三十七条 关于被指示方行为的免责

a. A bank utilizing the services of another bank for the purpose of giving effect to the instructions of the applicant does so for the account and at the risk of the applicant.

a. 为了执行申请人的指示,银行利用其他银行的服务,其费用和风险由申请人承担。

b. An issuing bank or advising bank assumes no liability or responsibility should the instructions it transmits to another bank not be carried out, even if it has taken the initiative in the choice of that other bank.

b. 即使银行自行选择了其他银行,如果发出指示未被执行,开证行或通知行对此亦不负责。

c. A bank instructing another bank to perform services is liable for any commissions, fees, costs or expenses ("charges") incurred by that bank in connection with its instructions.

c. 指示另一银行提供服务的银行有责任负担被执释放因执行指示而发生的任何佣金、手续费、成本或开支("费用")。

If a credit states that charges are for the account of the beneficiary and charges cannot be collected or deducted from proceeds, the issuing bank remains liable for payment of charges.

如果信用证规定费用由受益人负担,而该费用未能收取或从信用证款项中扣除,开证行依然承担支付此费用的责任。

A credit or amendment should not stipulate that the advising to a beneficiary is conditional upon the receipt by the advising bank or second advising bank of its charges.

信用证或其修改不应规定向受益人的通知以通知行或第二通知行收到其费用为条件。

d. The applicant shall be bound by and liable to indemnify a bank against all obligations and responsibilities imposed by foreign laws and usages.

d. 外国法律和惯例加诸银行的一切义务和责任,申请人应受其约束,并就此对银行负补偿之责。

Article 38 Transferable Credits

第三十八条 可转让信用证

a. A bank is under no obligation to transfer a credit except to the extent and in the manner expressly consented to by that bank.

a. 银行无办理转让信用证的义务，除非该银行明确同意其转让范围和转让方式。

b. For the purpose of this article:

b. 就本条款而言：

Transferable credit means a credit that specifically states it is "transferable". A transferable credit may be made available in whole or in part to another beneficiary ("second beneficiary") at the request of the beneficiary ("first beneficiary").

转让信用证意指明确表明其"可以转让"的信用证。根据受益人("第一受益人")的请求，转让信用证可以被全部或部分地转让给其他受益人("第二受益人")。

Transferring bank means a nominated bank that transfers the credit or, in a credit available with any bank, a bank that is specifically authorized by the issuing bank to transfer and that transfers the credit. An issuing bank may be a transferring bank.

转让银行意指办理信用证转让的被指定银行，或者，在适用于任何银行的信用证中，转让银行是由开证行特别授权并办理转让信用证的银行。开证行也可担任转让银行。

Transferred credit means a credit that has been made available by the transferring bank to a second beneficiary.

转让信用证意指经转让银行办理转让后可供第二受益人使用的信用证。

c. Unless otherwise agreed at the time of transfer, all charges (such as commissions, fees, costs or expenses) incurred in respect of a transfer must be paid by the first beneficiary.

c. 除非转让时另有约定，所有因办理转让而产生的费用(诸如佣金、手续费、成本或开支)必须由第一受益人支付。

d. A credit may be transferred in part to more than one second beneficiary provided partial drawing or shipments are allowed.

d. 倘若信用证允许分批支款或分批装运，信用证可以被部分地转让给一个以上的第二受益人。

A transferred credit cannot be transferred at the request of a second beneficiary to any subsequent beneficiary. The first beneficiary is not considered to be a subsequent beneficiary.

第二受益人不得要求将信用证转让给任何次序位居其后的其他受益人。第一受益人不属于此类其他受益人之列。

e. Any request for transfer must indicate if and under what conditions amendments may be advised to the second beneficiary. The transferred credit must clearly indicate those conditions.

e. 任何有关转让的申请必须指明是否以及在何种条件下可以将修改通知第二受益人。转让信用证必须明确指明这些条件。

f. If a credit is transferred to more than one second beneficiary, rejection of an amendment by one or more second beneficiary does not invalidate the acceptance by any other second beneficiary, with respect to which the transferred credit will be amended accordingly. For any second beneficiary that rejected the amendment, the transferred credit will remain unlamented.

f. 如果信用证被转让给一个以上的第二受益人,其中一个或多个第二受益人拒绝接受某个信用证修改并不影响其他第二受益人接受修改。对于接受修改的第二受益人而言,信用证已做相应的修改;对于拒绝接受修改的第二受益人而言,该转让信用证仍未被修改。

g. The transferred credit must accurately reflect the terms and conditions of the credit, including confirmation, if any, with the exception of:

g. 转让信用证必须准确转载原证的条款及条件,包括保兑(如有),但下列项目除外:

i. The amount of the credit,

i. 信用证金额,

ii. Any unit price stated therein,

ii. 信用证规定的任何单价,

iii. The expiry date,

iii. 到期日,

iv. The period for presentation, or

iv. 单据提示期限,或者

v. The latest shipment date or given period for shipment,

v. 最迟装运日期或规定的装运期间。

Any or all of which may be reduced or curtailed.

以上任何一项或全部均可减少或缩短。

The percentage for which insurance cover must be effected may be increased to provide the amount of cover stipulated in the credit or these articles.

必须投保的保险金额的投保比例可以增加,以满足原信用证或本惯例规定的投保金额。

The name of the first beneficiary may be substituted for that of the applicant in the credit.

可以用第一受益人的名称替换原信用证中申请人的名称。

If the name of the applicant is specifically required by the credit to appear in any document other than the invoice, such requirement must be reflected in the transferred credit.

如果原信用证特别要求开证申请人名称应在除发票以外的任何单据中出现时,则转让信用证必须反映出该项要求。

h. The first beneficiary has the right to substitute its own invoice and draft, if any, for those of a second beneficiary for an amount not in excess of that stipulated in the credit, and upon such substitution the first beneficiary can draw under the credit for the difference, if any, between its invoice and the invoice of a second beneficiary.

h. 第一受益人有权以自己的发票和汇票(如有),替换第二受益人的发票和汇票(如有），其金额不得超过原信用证的金额。在如此办理单据替换时，第一受益人可在原信用证项下支取自己发票与第二受益人发票之间产生的差额（如有）。

i. If the first beneficiary is to present its own invoice and draft, if any, but fails to do so on first demand, or if the invoices presented by the first beneficiary create discrepancies that did not exist in the presentation made by the second beneficiary and the first beneficiary fails to correct them on first demand, the transferring bank has the right to present the documents as received from the second beneficiary to the issuing bank, without further responsibility to the first beneficiary.

i. 如果第一受益人应当提交其自己的发票和汇票（如有），但却未能在收到第一次要求时照办；或第一受益人提交的发票导致了第二受益人提示的单据中本不存在的不符点，而其未能在收到第一次要求时予以修正，则转让银行有权将其从第二受益人处收到的单据向开证行提示，并不再对第一受益人负责。

j. The first beneficiary may, in its request for transfer, indicate that honor or negotiation is to be effected to a second beneficiary at the place to which the credit has been transferred, up to and including the expiry date of the credit. This is without prejudice to the right of the first beneficiary in accordance with sub-article 38 (h).

j. 第一受益人可以在其提出转让申请时，表明可在信用证被转让的地点，在原信用证的到期日之前（包括到期日）向第二受益人予以兑付或议付。本条款并不损害第一受益人在第三十八条(h)款下的权利。

k. Presentation of documents by or on behalf of a second beneficiary must be made to the transferring bank.

k. 由第二受益人或代表第二受益人提交的单据必须向转让银行提示。

Article 39　Assignment of Proceeds

第三十九条　款项让渡

The fact that a credit is not stated to be transferable shall not affect the right of the beneficiary to assign any proceeds to which it may be or may become entitled under the credit, in accordance with the provisions of applicable law. This article relates only to the assignment of proceeds and not to the assignment of the right to perform under the credit.

信用证未表明可转让，并不影响受益人根据所适用的法律规定，将其在该信用证项下有权获得的款项让渡与他人的权利。本条款所涉及的仅是款项的让渡，而不是信用证项下执行权力的让渡。

参考文献

[1] 王楠.外贸单证实务[M].北京:对外经贸出版社,2015.
[2] 杨金玲.张建华[M].北京:首都经济贸易大学出版社,2009.
[3] 缪东玲[M].北京:电子工业出版社,2011.
[4] 芮宝娟.进出口单证实务[M].北京:中国人民大学出版社,2010.
[5] 章安平.外贸单证操作[M].北京:高等教育出版社,2008.
[6] 董宏祥.外贸单证操作实务[M].北京:上海财经大学出版社,2016.
[7] 张颖.外贸单证实务[M].北京:电子工业出版社,2016.
[8] 江波.外贸单证实务[M].北京:中国人民大学出版社,2013.
[9] 王桂姣.物流单证实务[M].北京:中国财政经济出版社,2015.
[10] 戴正翔.国际物流单证实务[M].北京:北京交通大学出版社,2014.
[11] 戴正翔.国际物流单证实务[M].北京:北京交通大学出版社,2014.
[12] 戴正翔.国际物流单证实务[M].北京:北京交通大学出版社,2014.
[13] 凌海生.物流单证制作实务[M].武汉:武汉大学出版社,2014.
[14] 孙新成.物流单证实务[M].北京:高等教育大学出版社,2015.
[15] 罗艳.国际物流单证实务[M].北京:中国商务出版社,2014.

图书在版编目(CIP)数据

国际物流单证实务 / 许妍，李富主编. -- 南京 ：南京大学出版社，2018.7

ISBN 978-7-305-20513-2

Ⅰ. ①国… Ⅱ. ①许… ②李… Ⅲ. ①国际物流—原始凭证 Ⅳ. ①F259.1

中国版本图书馆CIP数据核字(2018)第153266号

出版发行　南京大学出版社
社　　址　南京市汉口路22号　　　　邮　编　210093
出 版 人　金鑫荣

书　　名　国际物流单证实务
主　　编　许　妍　李　富
责任编辑　陈家霞　蔡文彬　　　　编辑热线　025-83592123

照　　排　南京南琳图文制作有限公司
印　　刷　盐城市华光印刷厂
开　　本　787×1092　1/16　印张 17.75　字数 432 千
版　　次　2018年7月第1版　2018年7月第1次印刷
ISBN 978-7-305-20513-2
定　　价　45.00元

网址：http://www.njupco.com
官方微博：http://weibo.com/njupco
官方微信号：njupress
销售咨询热线：(025) 83594756
